Identity/Difference Politics

Identity/Difference Politics

How Difference Is Produced,
and Why It Matters

Rita Dhamoon

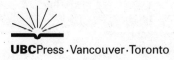

UBCPress · Vancouver · Toronto

20 19 18 17 16 15 14 13 12 11 10 09   5 4 3 2 1

Printed in Canada with vegetable-based inks on FSC-certified ancient-forest-free paper (100% post-consumer recycled) that is processed chlorine- and acid-free.

Library and Archives Canada Cataloguing in Publication

Dhamoon, Rita, 1970-
    Identity/difference politics : how difference is produced, and why it matters / Rita Dhamoon.

Includes bibliographical references and index.
ISBN 978-0-7748-1590-1 (bound)
ISBN 978-0-7748-1591-8 (pbk.)
ISBN 978-0-7748-1592-5 (e-book)

    1. Minorities – Canada – Political activity. 2. Ethnic relations – Political aspects – Canada. 3. Canada – Politics and government – 1867-. I. Title.

FC105.P6D48 2009   323.171   C2008-906207-8

Canadä

UBC Press gratefully acknowledges the financial support for our publishing program of the Government of Canada through the Book Publishing Industry Development Program (BPIDP), and of the Canada Council for the Arts, and the British Columbia Arts Council.

This book has been published with the help of a grant from the Canadian Federation for the Humanities and Social Sciences, through the Aid to Scholarly Publications Programme, using funds provided by the Social Sciences and Humanities Research Council of Canada, and with the help of the K.D. Srivastava Fund.

UBC Press
The University of British Columbia
2029 West Mall
Vancouver, BC V6T 1Z2
604-822-5959 / Fax: 604-822-6083
www.ubcpress.ca

To my nieces and nephews

Contents

Preface

I came to theory because I was hurting – the pain within me
was so intense that I could not go on living. I came to theory
desperate, wanting to comprehend – to grasp what was happening
around and within me. Most importantly, I wanted to make the
hurt go away. I saw in theory then a location for healing.

> – bell hooks, *Teaching to Transgress: Education*
> *as the Practice of Freedom*

The subject of this book is identity/difference politics, both in terms of how it is studied and how it shapes actual socio-political relations. I offer a theory and practice that is based on analyzing and critiquing how and with what effects power shapes difference. Theoretically and politically, I take as my point of departure the liberal multicultural approach. My journey with liberal multiculturalism began when my family and I emigrated from London, UK, to Canada. We did not come to Canada until the early 1990s, but the idea of doing so was planted much earlier. It had its roots in the capillaries of colonialism that had first led my parents to move from Punjab, India, to the UK, and then again, farther west to Canada. This colonial imaginary was and continues to be steeped in a legacy of British colonialism in India, as well as in acts of resistance practised by my great-grandparents and grandparents against British rule in India.

More directly, the prospects of immigrating to Canada were motivated by the overt racism we experienced in London. Several members of my immediate and extended family had been physically attacked there on racial grounds, some of them more than once; at university I watched white professors regularly give preference to white students; as Asians, my sisters and I were very aware of where we were safer and where we were not, and of the differences between our neighbourhood in East London and wealthier neighbourhoods; and despite the hard work he did, my father was routinely treated as a second-class citizen. At every turn I saw my family fight back, but the colonial motherland did not (or would not) deliver.

Canada pledged more – more jobs, liberal education, and multicultural tolerance. But my mother couldn't go to a swimming pool without being told to go back to her own country; my brother couldn't get a job in a bar because they didn't hire Indians (later, he understood that this referred to indigenous people, not just to those who were brown); during my PhD a white senior professor told me that I was naive and stupid for not realizing that the British needed to go to India to civilize the Indians; my family and I regularly experienced racial profiling at the border, both before and after 9/11; while working for a major Canadian airline so as to support myself and my family, I was physically threatened, verbally abused, and deliberately isolated by work colleagues after speaking up against racist practices that discriminated against flight attendants who spoke Hindi, Punjabi, Cantonese, and Mandarin, most of whom were people of colour; and as I sat on the front steps of my home, a white teenage boy and his family walked by me and called me Osama, as if this name alone were a threat to them and an insult to me.

In among the racism has been Canadian liberal multiculturalism, the celebration of diverse cultures and their festivals, clothes, food, and music. The symbol of multiculturalism serves to distinguish Canadians from Americans. As a marker of tolerance and accommodation, it has many appeals: good multicultural television programs exist, and diverse knowledge, art forms, and different foods are exchanged; in the name of cultural diversity, state institutions (such as the police) make a point of hiring more ethnic 'minorities'; and there is a growing dialogue about institutionalizing the cultural and religious practices of marginalized peoples. And yet the histories of oppression experienced by people of colour and indigenous peoples are virtually absent in celebrations of multiculturalism: there is little talk of colonialism, racism, white privilege, sexism, patriarchy, heteronormativity, or capitalism, as if multiculturalism now makes up for the past and can correct present social inequities. It is all about accommodation and diversity, not anti-racism, decolonization, white supremacy, or power. It does not name the oppressors or require that the land of multicultural Canada be given back to indigenous people; nor does it directly attend to the problems of violence, unemployment, and poverty within my community. And it does not acknowledge the ways in which people of colour and indigenous people resist white patriarchal capitalist hegemony. Instead, it focuses on softening the edges that mark 'the Other' and 'Otherness,' namely those socially constructed lines of difference that determine who and what is normal and dominant, and conversely who and what is abnormal and consequently deemed to be inferior.[1]

In Canada my subjective experiences have not been as physically violent as they were in the UK. This is not to negate the ways in which Canadian history and experience have been and continue to be violent; we simply need to recall the internment of Japanese people during the Second World War, the overt Islamophobia against Muslims and Arabs (before and after 9/11), and the attempted eradication of indigenous knowledge and bodies. At the same time, for me, the violence is somehow more dangerous in Canada than in the UK. In the UK I lived with overt racism, with white people calling me a Paki to my face and directly threatening my existence. In Canada, while the number of reported hate-motivated crimes directed toward racial, ethnic, and religious minorities (as well as sexual minorities) remains in the hundreds every year (Dauvergne, Scrim, and Brennan, 2006), multicultural discourse often masks the violence, such that it is sometimes (although not always) more subtle, more insidious, and therefore more difficult to name and resist.

All of this has characterized my journey with Canadian liberal multiculturalism, leaving me with a number of questions. In principle, do I really want to be tolerated and accommodated, especially without questioning the character of tolerance and intolerance within Canadian society? Why is there a growing global defence of multiculturalism at this particular time of political history? Why do non-white people support multiculturalism, even though it can serve as a way to regulate us? Is the state effective in dismantling oppressive relations of power? In a post-9/11 world, is it dangerous to challenge the discourse of multiculturalism, which seems to be the only way to get racial issues on the political agenda? How can alliances be built between people of colour, and between them and indigenous people, while also recognizing the ways in which we become implicated in each other's social location? What should I make of the privilege I experience as a consequence of my upbringing in the West, my education, my English accent, and my able-bodiedness, in relation to the racism and patriarchy I encounter? How do I best enact my responsibilities to other marginalized people, including those with no legal status in Canada or those whose status is illegitimately determined by the state (such as indigenous peoples)? Why is culture-talk the basis of framing the concerns of 'multicultural groups,' and how does this affect an understanding of other aspects of my identity, such as my gender? Do all women, sexual minorities, the disabled, and the poor benefit from multiculturalism? Does change lie within the system or in disrupting the very system itself? What theoretical, conceptual, and political tools would bring to light my own lived experiences as well as those of Others?

This book represents some of my thinking about these questions. When I returned to the academy after several years away, I hoped that theory would help me heal and comprehend what was happening around me. And it has, to some extent at least. But mainstream discourses on liberalism, multi-culturalism, and diversity have not provided me with complete or satisfactory answers. On the contrary, they have closed doors for me. Despite the burgeon-ing literature on radicalizing inclusion, individual and collective identities, and the accommodative role of the state, the focus in mainstream contempor-ary political theory is almost exclusively on culture, ethnicity, and language, not on racism, colonialism, patriarchy, class difference, or privilege. To my mind, this diminishes an analysis of power, for power has been significant in determining my social and political relations, contexts, and positions, as well as those of others.

Other theories, particularly those developed in the fields of feminist and gender theory, cultural studies, and post-colonial, anti-colonial, anti-racist, and critical race studies, are better equipped to answer many of my questions. These fields encompass self-reflexive writings from many people marked as Other and, on a practical and discursive level, tend to directly problematize the existing social order. By drawing on theories and concepts within and beyond political theory, this book represents some of my interventions in the very discourses that frame an understanding of my social identity and social location, as well as that of others – namely, the politics of identity/ difference.

Acknowledgments

Many people supported and helped me through the journey of writing this book. My deepest thanks go to William Dyck for constant support, intellectual curiosity, laughter, and love. Thanks to my family, especially my mother, my *Bhanji* (older sister) Rupa, and Marie Dyck, all of whom made my choices possible.

My heartfelt gratitude to Barbara Arneil, in the Department of Political Science at the University of British Columbia, for opening up spaces for me in the academy, for being available to talk whenever I read something that excited me, and for outstanding mentorship and support during my time as a doctoral student and since. You encouraged me to find my own intellectual voice in ways that will always stay with me. Barbara and others read several versions of earlier draft chapters and provided finely honed comments. Special thanks to Leonora Angeles, Stella Gaon, Olena Hankivsky, Laura Janara, Charles/Carlos Martell, and Emily Moore for countless discussions about identity/difference politics, for pushing my thinking in profound and new ways, and for care. Emily read most of the manuscript in its latest form with unwavering enthusiasm, which was truly wonderful for my spirits. Thanks to Duncan Ivison for questions and comments that got me thinking differently about ideas I thought I had settled on. For her wisdom and courage, and for sharing with me the joys of old Bollywood, I thank Amal Rana, my sister and resister in the struggle for justice.

My appreciation also goes to the reviewers for thoughtful and challenging comments. These not only helped me to develop the theoretical linkages between concepts and chapters in this book, but they also inspired energy. Emily Andrew at UBC Press also deserves particular mention for her guidance throughout the process of publishing this book, and for clarifying and productive feedback. The efficient and helpful assistance of Ann Macklem aided the completion of this book, as did the thoughtful copy-editing done by

Deborah Kerr. UBC Press is truly a model academic press. Thanks goes to David Drummond for designing the vibrant book cover!

This work has been enriched by the support, insights, and conversations generously offered by several other friends and colleagues, including Audrey Ackah, Taiaiake Alfred, Chris Andersen, Bruce Baum, Mridula Nath Chakraborty, Glen Coulthard, Lois Harder, Fairn Herising, Carey Hill, James Ingram, Matt James, Catherine Kellogg, Kiera Ladner, María Pía Lara, Robert Lee-Nichols, Scott Matthews, Munir Meghji, Mrinalini Menon, Sarah Pemberton, Vanita Sabharwal, Roshni Sakhi, Ian Saunders, Jakeet Singh, Cheryl Suzack, Itrath Syed, James Tully, Mark Warren, members of the Anti-racism and Decolonization Network (Alberta), especially Evelyn Hamdon and Aliya Jamal, and participants in the 2007 "Democracy in Crisis" workshop organized by Stella Gaon at Saint Mary's University in Halifax, Nova Scotia.

Many thanks also to the administrative staff in the Departments of Political Science at the University of British Columbia, the University of Alberta, and the University of Victoria for making the bureaucracy easier to navigate, and to Josephine Calazan, Donna Coombes-Montrose, and Dory Urbano for giving personal support.

This book was written with financial and institutional support provided by the Grant Notley Memorial Postdoctoral Fellowship Foundation, which funded my work in the Department of Political Science at the University of Alberta, and by the Social Sciences and Humanities Research Council of Canada Postdoctoral Fellowship Program, which enabled me to spend a productive year in the Department of Political Science at the University of Victoria. My time at these two departments was directly supported by two scholars whose work continues to inform my thinking: Yasmeen Abu-Laban (University of Alberta) and Avigail Eisenberg (University of Victoria). My gratitude to them both. Thanks also to the Research and Graduate Studies Office at the University of Fraser Valley, Abbotsford, British Columbia, for providing funds to complete the book.

Parts of Chapter 1 are based on my article "Shifting from Culture to Cultural: Critical Theorizing of Identity/Difference Politics," which was published in *Constellations: An International Journal of Critical and Democratic Theory* (2006), and my chapter "The Politics of Cultural Contestation," in *Sexual Justice/Cultural Justice: Critical Perspectives in Political Theory and Practice* (Routledge, 2007). I thank the publishers for granting permission to use this material.

Identity/Difference Politics

Introduction

Over recent decades, contemporary Western political theory has consistently framed a wide range of events and struggles as issues of identity/difference politics. Some typical Canadian examples include the 2007 controversy that arose in Quebec when five young girls were told they could not compete in a local tae kwon do match unless they removed their Islamic head scarves; the decision of the Tsawwassen First Nation in British Columbia to vote in favour of a modern-day urban treaty with the provincial government, amidst concerns of some indigenous people that the vote effectively signed away authority over land and resources; and the mobilization of Sikh communities and supporters across Canada to fight Ottawa's 2007 decision to deport a paralyzed Sikh refugee, Mr. Laibar Singh. Meanwhile, in the UK, debates rage about the legal recognition of Islamic-based councils, South Asian arranged marriages, and 'homegrown terrorists' (especially following the July 2005 bombings of London's public transport and the death of Jean Charles de Menezes, a Brazilian man shot by police, who wrongly presumed he was an extremist from Central Asia). In late 2005 in France, months of civil unrest, mostly among disaffected youth of Muslim and African descent, and the death of two teens of Mauritian and Tunisian origin (accidentally electrocuted as they hid from police in a power substation) raised issues of identity/difference politics. In the US, policy and legislative changes continue to increase the policing of American borders along identity lines. Borders are policed not only on the basis of a 'war against terrorism' but also on nationalist, racial, and economic terms; simultaneously borders are challenged along identity lines, as was the case in Los Angeles, 2006, when Latinos mobilized so as to legally gain and maintain rights to work in the US.

More often than not, these kinds of issues are analyzed through the lens of liberal multiculturalism, such that the theoretical framework for examining issues of identity/difference has assumed a specific shape. In particular, through the lens of liberal multiculturalism, culture has become the central category of analysis. Although these kinds of issues do have cultural dimensions, two questions arise concerning the liberal multicultural approach and the study of identity/difference politics in contemporary Western political thought. First, is the study of identity/difference politics best framed through culture as a mode of social identity or, alternatively, are the issues described above better analyzed in terms of gendered Islamophobia, ongoing colonialism, refugee rights, racialized securitization and discrimination, and poverty and unemployment – namely, as struggles of power? Second, what specific and general theoretical insights can be brought to bear regarding such events when the study of identity/difference politics is examined through an analysis of power rather than through liberal multicultural interpretations of culture?

In this book I argue that, rather than developing and/or revising liberal multiculturalism or even reinvigorating its theories and concepts, an alternative path is needed for the study of identity/difference politics, one that directs the analysis to power rather than culture. Although studies of identity/difference politics have been criticized because they sometimes treat identities as if they were ascribed rather than contested, fixed rather than fluid and continuously changing, singular and reified rather than diversely constructed, and narrowly defined by the state rather than self-directed, this does not inevitably require that the study of identity/difference politics should be abandoned. Certainly, the analytic work of the 'identity' concept needs continuous re-evaluation and clarification because it has come to mean either too much or too little (Brubaker and Cooper 2000). But as *a field of study*, the politics of identity/difference has enormous and yet unfulfilled potential to address issues of power.

My core claim is that, in the field of identity/difference politics, it is necessary to make an analytic shift away from the current preoccupation with culture as an explanatory framework through which to grasp conflicts of difference to a critical examination of how meanings of difference are produced, organized, and regulated through power, and the effects of these meanings on socio-political arrangements. This analytic shift can be characterized as one that moves away from the liberal multicultural politics of culture in favour of a critical politics of meaning-making. Although culture is not irrelevant to the politics of meaning-making, it is not the central category of analysis, for this obscures an understanding of the variation between and within cultural groups, privileges one aspect of difference, over others, and separates culture from other dimensions of political difference, such as racialized or gendered difference. Although all concepts are contested, 'culture' is a particularly troubled one in the study of identity/difference politics because it is given primacy over modes of difference, and it continues to be conceptualized in overdetermined ways.

Yet, because culture is the central category of analysis in liberal multicultural theories, and these theories dominate the field of identity/difference politics, the liberal multicultural approach cannot simply be dismissed.[1] Rather, it is important to examine how and why this approach has gained its pre-eminent status and what it obscures with regard to power.

Liberal Multicultural Approaches in the Study of Identity/Difference Politics

Though varied in their normative positions and in terms of the practices they advocate, liberal multicultural theorists broadly claim that the equal treatment of 'minorities' requires public institutions to acknowledge, rather than ignore or downplay, cultural particularities. This contrasts with theories developed from more classical or neutral liberal perspectives, such as those offered by Brian Barry (2001) and Chandran Kukathas (1988, 1992, 2003). These neutralist liberals position universalism, social cohesion, and the authority of a (supposedly) neutral state as values that transcend those of cultural pluralism; accordingly, a neutral liberal perspective sees no difference. By contrast, liberal multicultural theories seek to accommodate specific forms of cultural diversity. Three specific ideas typify this approach: first, because the state does not respond impartially to all individuals and groups, people are not and must not be treated identically; second, liberal views of the self and freedom must be broadened so as to acknowledge the importance of social recognition because individuals are not constituted transculturally or ahistorically; and third, the fabric of social and/or national unity must be maintained while diversity is accommodated – this imperative is often termed unity-within-diversity.

Two major architects of this liberal multicultural approach are Canadian philosophers: Will Kymlicka (1995a, 1995b, 1996, 1998, 2001, 2003, 2005a, 2005b) and Charles Taylor (1993, 1994a, 1994b, 1998).[2] Kymlicka (2007a, 7) understands himself to be a "foot soldier" of the global diffusion of liberal multiculturalism; as such, he has engaged widely with international organizations in the academy, civil society, and state bureaucracies in order to develop models and best practices of liberal multiculturalism. Taylor has also played a significant role in various aspects of political life, especially in Quebec, where, for example, he recently served as a commissioner for the Consultation

Commission on Accommodation Practices Related to Cultural Differences (Bouchard and Taylor 2008), more commonly known as the Bouchard-Taylor commission.

Disagreement certainly exists between these two thinkers in that Kymlicka follows a framework of liberal individualism and Taylor one of liberal-communitarianism (Kymlicka 1989, 1994; Taylor 1994a, 1996). But both also reformulate liberal views of justice so as to accommodate minorities in a manner consistent with fundamental liberal commitments, to accept that goods and resources should be distributed according to some culture-based differences, and to reject monocultural approaches that explicitly defend principles of assimilation and conformity. On these bases, Kymlicka (2001, 22) offers a theory of multicultural citizenship, or what he calls a "liberal culturalist" view, which is based on conceptualizing culture as a context of choice and a site for developing individual self-capacity. And Taylor (1994b, 26) offers a theory of recognition, in which recognition is understood as a vital human need, not merely something that is delivered out of courtesy. These theories of multicultural citizenship and recognition have sparked a burgeoning literature on the study of identity/difference politics within political theory.

The idea that the state should accommodate some cultural particularities has also been prevalent in practice, and not just in political theory. Canada, it is often argued, leads this pluralist response to diversity in that it developed a multicultural policy as early as 1971, its multicultural heritage is constitutionally protected in section 27 of its Charter of Rights and Freedoms, and it was the first country to pass national legislation on multiculturalism, namely, the 1988 Multiculturalism Act. Canada is considered ideal not only because it consists of a secular constitutional liberal-democracy, a market-based economy, and a welfare state, but also because it symbolically and constitutionally accommodates diversity. Kymlicka (2003, 361), for instance, states that the fact that "this model of economics and politics should be adopted is completely undisputed in Canada. Few Canadians doubt that this model is the recipe for a successful country, and most would applaud the adoption of this model elsewhere."

Even while public support for immigrant multiculturalism has retreated in places such as the Netherlands and Australia, in Canada, it is argued, support remains high, in part because levels of illegal migration are low, the cultural practices accommodated are consistent with values associated with liberal-democracy and human rights, and because immigrants are seen as net-contributors to the economy (Kymlicka 2005b, 2007b). Although liberal multiculturalists acknowledge that the Canadian model of multiculturalism has not been fully realized, it is nonetheless presented as being ideally suited to respond to diversity. Even while some Canadians blame liberal multicultural values for creating homegrown terrorists, others see these values as lending themselves to the image that Canadian society is democratic and good because it is tolerant of cultural Others. And though it is in fact highly contested that Canada is an ideal model of multiculturalism, it is represented as such, within both Canada and other geopolitical contexts, including South Africa (Adhikari 2004; Kros 2005; Torr 2004), India (Deb 2002; Upadhya 2002), Asia (Kymlicka and He 2005), and countries of Eastern Europe (Kuzio 2005; Kymlicka and Opalski 2001).[3] In the end, while the implementation of liberal multicultural ideas has been uneven and even a tough sell in some parts of the world (Kymlicka 2007a, 11-19, 315-16), these ideas have also been popularized in both Western political theory and Western liberal-democracies.

The appeal of liberal multiculturalism can be explained in the following ways. Liberal multicultural thinkers are attentive to a wide range of issues, including the historic claims of self-determination made by national minorities and indigenous peoples, language as a cultural marker of distinctiveness, and actual political challenges to the state, especially those regarding legal and constitutional matters. As well, liberal multiculturalism has provided the momentum for some projects that address difficulties faced by marginalized communities (Srivastava 2007, 307). Indeed, in the face of the backlash against immigrants (whether legal or illegal) and in the current heightened climate of Islamophobia and securitization, some versions of multiculturalism provide a recourse to diversity that may be otherwise difficult to negotiate and express. Liberal multiculturalism has, in this sense, mainstreamed issues of diversity and culture.

Overall then, this approach has become popularized because it promises to break from a past that demanded assimilation and to celebrate instead diversity and unity simultaneously. Kymlicka and Taylor both express a desire to renounce historical practices of discrimination, exclusion, and misrecognition in the name of liberal justice, and to demonstrate that strands of liberalism are not intrinsically plagued by inegalitarian impulses. Kymlicka specifically extends the limits of liberal tolerance so as to accommodate national minorities and immigrant groups, while also arguing that such accommodation should not hamper the economic or political success of the nation. Meanwhile, Taylor (1993, 183-89) calls for "deep diversity," which, he says, requires that everyone should be heard and have an equal voice in decision making. This demands not a strong but minimally a weak national identity. Other liberal multiculturalists add to these variations on diversity-within-unity. Tariq Modood (2007, see especially Chapters 2 and 4), for example, argues for a more robust and reconfigured conception of civic multiculturalism than that offered by thinkers such as Kymlicka, specifically in order to include Islam as an organized religion and Muslim identity as a public identity.

Despite the appeal of various brands of liberal multiculturalism, it is my position that, on the whole, this normative-theoretical approach does not and cannot provide a robust analytic framework for addressing issues of power that are central to the study of identity/difference or to the lived experiences of this politics.[4] Certainly liberal multiculturalism is a site of struggle for non-white subjects in that institutionalized multicultural discourses and practices shape socio-political and economic arrangements. But whether intentional or not, liberal multicultural theory obscures issues of power in three key ways. First, it reinvents the nation by forgetting the past and imagining the nation anew over the bodies of those who are marked as multicultural subjects. As Himani Bannerji (2000, 92-93) notes, images of a multicultural mosaic tend to mask over histories of white privilege and engravings of conquest, wars, and exclusions; in Canada's case, she continues, these histories display the "dark side of the nation." Indeed, though some liberal theorists do reflect on the importance of race-thinking in relation to multiculturalism (Mills 2007; Modood 2007), on the whole, liberal multicultural theories do not directly confront the histories and ongoing problems of white supremacy, colonization, slavery, discriminatory immigration legislation, or the practices of resistance undertaken by those marked as multicultural subjects, even when the claims of immigrants and indigenous people are included within the rubric of cultural diversity. On the contrary, the very histories of anti-racist and anti-colonial struggle that shape multicultural policies and practices are often pushed into the background.

The evasion of an analysis of white supremacy, colonialism, and racism is specifically masked by the language of diversity. "Diversity" may appear to be a neutral term that merely describes a multiplicity of identities, and it may also signal a well-intentioned stance against prejudice. Yet, as Sara Ahmed (2007, 235) states, the idea of diversity has also become a way to reify "difference as something that exists 'in' the bodies or cultures of others, such that difference becomes a national property: if difference is something 'they are,' then it is something we 'can have.'" In particular, liberal multiculturalists seem to claim cultural difference as a constitutive feature of liberal-democracies and national identity, and do so by covering over histories of racial domination. The consequence is that historical and continuing problems of discrimination, oppression, marginalization, violence, and domination that arise from forms of racism, patriarchy, capitalism, ableism, and homophobia are whitewashed by the more sanguine language of diversity.

Second, liberal multiculturalism expands the bounds of toleration but continues to assume the superiority of particular liberal values. Bhikhu Parekh (1997, 56) observes, for instance, that "although Kymlicka does not explicitly say so, he implies that, other things being equal, a culture that encourages autonomy and choice [which are core liberal values] is better and richer, and in that sense superior to, one that does not." By privileging liberal values, these theories continue to suggest that 'different' cultural groups should adopt the values of an already existing dominant culture. Not only is there an underlying demand for conformity, but the dominant culture is represented as if it were not fraught with social inequities. Moreover, liberal political theory claims its superiority by downplaying its historical relationship to imperial and colonial ideas. Indeed, as Taiaiake Alfred (2005, 110) asserts, liberalism claims a triumph over socialism, and takes on a cultural particularity that privileges specific versions of individualism, competition, progress, order, and Euro-American culture over non-Western conceptions of sharing, truth, and justice.

The expectation of conformity is not a new feature of liberalism, for, though liberals such as John Stuart Mill and John Locke advanced theories regarding rights and freedom, they also argued that some colonial subjects should be culturally assimilated (Arneil 1996; Parekh 1995). Today, liberal multiculturalists claim that they have no wish to explicitly impose their particular set of values (Kymlicka 1995a, 94, 171); instead, these values are promoted through incentives (Kymlicka 1995a, 168) and dialogical exchange (Taylor 1985, 125) so as to draw multicultural Others into the norms of society. Richard Day (2000, 9) refers to this process as "seductive integration," whereby those who assume/claim authority and confer status to others (dominant groups) create a society in which minorities want to integrate into the dominant norm because doing so improves their chances of political, economic, and social success. In other words, underlying liberal multicultural discourses of diversity is an expectation that multicultural subjects will conform to a set of ostensibly superior liberal values.

Third, because liberal multiculturalism is concerned with why and how the state can legitimately 'manage' culturally different subjects, it not only reduces power to state authority and the liberties of specified cultural groups, it also accords legitimacy to state practices of governance that privilege some kinds of difference over others. Although state agencies and practices are not simply regulatory (they also protect individuals and groups), the modern state has been a key actor in managing diversity. In his study of Canada, Day (2000, 5) notes that diversity "has always involved state-sponsored attempts to define, know and structure the actions of problematic Others (Savages, Québécois, Half-Breeds, Immigrants) who have been distinguished from unproblematic selves (French, British, British-Canadian, European)." Liberal multicultural discourses continue to legitimize this regulatory function of the state by assigning it the role of deciding which specific groups deserve differentiated rights and recognition, and by providing further grounds to gaze upon those deemed most threatening to the state (such as national minorities or Muslims).

Ultimately, liberal multicultural theories mask various issues of power, including (but not limited to) how histories of racial domination continue to shape difference today, why, how, and by whom liberal values are determined to be superior and how these are resisted, and how the state regulates various modalities of difference. This masking occurs because of the narrow conception and overdetermined role of culture in liberal multicultural theories. Indeed, the dominance of liberal multicultural approaches in contemporary political theory has framed the study of identity/difference politics as the politics of culture.

Although culture is an important aspect of identification and thus cannot be ignored, liberal multicultural theories cast a disparate range of social, economic, material, and political issues as considerations of culture, with the effect of eclipsing the multiplicity of ways in which difference performs. Furthermore, claims of culture are often separated from and/or prioritized over such issues as poverty, racial discrimination, homophobia, and heterosexism, effectively erasing some aspects of difference altogether. As well, specified cultures (rather than specified cultural practices) are subject to intense public scrutiny in ways that further legitimize state regulation of those marked as being too different. Overall, in liberal multicultural theories, (specific) identities themselves are the prevailing focus, and the broad political contexts in which various modes and degrees of difference are generated remain underanalyzed. The emphasis, in other words, is on the 'identity' side of identity politics rather than on politics (Josephson 2008).

Certainly, liberal multiculturalism does not claim to offer comprehensive and all-encompassing theories of identity/difference politics. But its dominance has also limited the conversations to certain categories of community and identity, and to certain kinds of concerns (Srivastava 2007, 307). The consequence of this is that problems arising from structural and material differences tend to be deferred. By this I mean that, although practices that enable inclusion or tolerance or recognition may democratize how we engage in political life, they do not fundamentally change the terms on which differences are organized; the problem of these terms is suspended until after rights and recognition have been allocated.

In sum, my critique of liberal multiculturalism is not that it has gone too far – an argument that has gained momentum since fears of homegrown terrorists have been transported into the public consciousness – but that it cannot go as far as is needed to address social, economic, material, and political inequities. Whereas liberal multiculturalism paradoxically imagines the polity as heterogeneous so that differences do not have to be seen (an argument I develop in Chapter 1), I seek to analyze how differences are produced and operationalized through power.

Some concepts that have been developed outside the scope of liberal multiculturalism serve this proposed revision to the study of identity/difference politics in Western political theory. In particular, lessons can be learned from critical theorists who assess the contexts in which differences are produced by linking together history, culture, and power. For instance, well before the recent liberal turn to identity/difference politics, Aimé Césaire, Frantz Fanon, Edward Said, and Gayatri Chakravorty Spivak, among other anti-colonial and post-colonial thinkers, explicitly addressed the violence of naming, misnaming, and not naming different racialized peoples and structures (Bannerji 1995, 23). The lessons from anti-colonial and post-colonial theory, as well as from post-structuralism, feminist and gender theory, queer theory, sociology, cultural studies, and critical anthropology – all of which deploy concepts of power, difference, identity, subject formation subjectivity, subjection, and justice – are crucial to political theory's study of identity/difference politics and help to push against the boundaries of liberal multicultural thought.

Shifting from Culture to Power

In Chapter 1, I elaborate on the work and limitations of liberal multicultural conceptualizations of culture. Subsequently, to counter the dominant liberal multicultural approach to the study of identity/difference politics, I reframe this field of study so that the focus is not on culture but on how difference is constituted by, and generative of, vehicles of power. Power is the organizing force of difference and also the subject of social struggle/transformation. My concern in this book lies not in the fact that power exists, but in how it functions. I approach power in Foucauldian terms as a relation and as a capacity that is spread throughout the socio-political body, rather than as something that is possessed or held by a sovereign subject or the state. Although agents and institutions of the state are instrumental in constructing and regulating difference, questions about the politics of identity/difference are not concerned solely with the state; nor is the state the singular site of social change. As Michel Foucault (1980, 158) argues, "One impoverishes the question of power if one poses it solely in terms of legislation and constitution, in terms solely of the state and the state apparatus. Power is quite different from and more complicated, dense and pervasive than a set of laws or a state apparatus." Accordingly, though I consider how aspects of the state, such as the law, generate meanings (in positive and negative ways), I also assess how power functions through other structures of society to generate meanings of difference. I pay particular attention to the differences within and between social groups. This contrasts with liberal multicultural theories, which tend to be preoccupied with why and how the state should accommodate specified cultural groups.

Furthermore, in my approach, power is not conceived solely as coercive in nature – it is also conceptualized as a productive force. As Foucault (1995, 194) suggests, "we must cease once and for all to describe the effects of power in negative terms: it 'excludes,' it 'represses,' it 'censors,' it 'abstracts,' it 'masks,' it 'conceals.' In fact, power produces: it produces reality, it produces domains of objects and rituals of truth." I seek to examine precisely these domains and rituals, and the specific rationalities behind them. My analysis therefore explores how power produces subjects and how subjects are vehicles of power; people, in other words, exercise power and are not simply possessed by it. From this understanding of power, I show not only that meanings of difference are historically generated, but that they are also subject to change.

My work in part thus generates a critique of reductive conceptions of power in which power is defined solely in terms of domination. The role of dominating power is without doubt central to an understanding of identity/difference politics in that meanings of difference that are closed off, blocked, invariable, and/or appear fixed (dominant ones) are distinguishable from those that are open, variable, reversible, and fluid. But the concept of power is not synonymous with that of domination, and thus issues regarding power expand beyond its contractual reorganization, or the need to move power to more legitimate hands (i.e., the sovereign subject or sovereign state), or the desire to overcome or minimize its illegitimate or excessive use. Instead, I theorize domination as an instrument and effect of power as opposed to the constitutive feature of power. In short, power is not in general the opposite of freedom. In the words of Foucault scholar David Couzens Hoy (2005, 82), "Conceptually, all domination is power, but not all power is domination. Domination is exclusively power over, whereas power in a broader sense can be positive and productive."

In the chapters to follow, I specifically examine how power produces forms of subjectivity and subjection, how it invites occasions for resistance to domination, and how subjects are "put into action" through power (Cruik-shank 1999, 41) whereby they become subjects and perform as subjects in and through power. Thus, rather than arguing for a form of politics that seeks to eradicate power, I opt for one that disrupts the vehicles of power that generate penalizing and privileging meanings of difference, namely, those that give rise to social hierarchies.

Analyzing Power and Difference: Taking an Account of Meaning-Making

To make the shift from an analysis of culture to one of power, I develop an approach in which the analyst contextualizes how difference is produced, organized, and regulated, and what effects these meanings of difference have on social hierarchies. This approach is constituted of accounts of meaning-making, namely, interpretative explanations of the processes that generate and organize meanings of difference. An account of meaning-making is driven by an analysis of power so as to deconstruct the processes that make and mark subjects differently and differentially. I develop this analytic approach not to empty, minimize, or manage difference, but to expose and disrupt the naturalized, calcified, and relational conditions under which privileging and penalizing meanings of difference emerge in the first place. In doing so, I rearticulate the study of identity/difference politics as the very process of *becoming* a subject through meanings of difference.

In my approach, identity is not the base of a subject but an effect of being produced as a subject through meanings of difference. An identity is thereby a symbol of difference rather than a synonym for a person. To put it simply, *identity is difference.* This is why I use the term "identity/difference politics" rather than "identity politics" or "difference politics," for it signals a relationship between these two concepts. Difference cannot be reduced to culture, and difference always implicates power. It is an instrument and an effect of power rather than an essential or passive entity. It is specifically that which contingently and relationally distinguishes variedly positioned subjects in and through power. It is both desired and disavowed; it can be given positive and/or negative meanings; it is contestable but not always a source of contention; and it can never be erased. Representations of difference are created and modified over time and space, shaping well-worn markers of social division as well as new ones. Social divisions, as Nira Yuval-Davis (2006, 198) puts it, take on organizational, intersubjective, experiential, and representational forms. Accordingly, difference performs in and through institutions (state agencies, trade unions, and the family), and it exists in the relationships between people at the level of representation and in the ways they experience subjectivity and subjection. In each of these social divisions, meanings of difference are not constituted unidimensionally (that is, primarily through culture) but through multiple interactions between distinct but mutually constituted modalities of difference.

Not all representations of difference are equally salient in determining privilege and penalty, for some are voluntarily and others coercively adopted, some shape social relations without the effect of creating subjugation, and some are systemic and institutional, whereas others are not; in other words, not all differences carry the same essential characteristics or effects. The torturing of suspected Muslim and/or Arab terrorists, for instance, is not the same as differentiating Muslims and Arabs from Christians 'merely' on the basis of religion. Yet, all forms of difference are circumscribed by social norms, such that in this instance the suspected terrorist is subject to physical and psychological violence, and the practice of making religious distinctions provides a basis for the war on terror and the American-led attacks on Iraq and Afghanistan. In this sense, even interpretations of 'mere difference' can consolidate structures of Western imperialism.

As I elaborate in Chapter 2, accounts of meaning-making attempt not to discover differences, but to deconstruct how and why differences are created and sustained, and with what effects. My aim is to describe, explain, and critique the processes by which subjects are differently and differentially constituted in ways that create and recreate relations of penalty and privilege. Such an analysis provides an understanding of how interpretations of difference constitute material and structural inequities, and how the material and structural transform discourses of difference. For example, as I argue in Chapter 3, Immigration Regulations are premised on racialized, gendered, class-based, heteronormative, and ablest meanings concerning the ideal potential immigrant, whereby some kinds of subjects are preferred over others. These meanings affect legal status, job opportunities, family relationships, and where one lives. Simultaneously, these institutionalized regulations also constitute and alter meanings about the ideal immigrant, such that differences between the model minority immigrant and the undesirable immigrant determine social and economic opportunities. Discourse, in other words, shapes the actual lived experiences of people, and social structures shape discourse. Given this, radical social change on the level of discourse effects social change on the material level, and vice versa.

My intent in critically analyzing meaning-making is not simply to identify who dominates or is dominated (or oppressed or marginalized or excluded or exploited), but, as noted above, to examine how power works to make difference in the first place. In this regard, an account of meaning-making driven by a focus on analytics of power is a *mode of analysis.* As a deconstructive method of analysis, this device does not simply reveal that differences are contingently produced and that an infinite number of meanings is possible: it also radically contextualizes interpretations of difference to show that and how these meanings are circumscribed by power. To put it another way, an account of meaning-making does not aim to smooth out differences but provides a mechanism to interpret how differences are produced and rationalized in and through power. This analytical approach thereby enables an understanding of the contingency of difference – how it is made, how it changes, and how it is operationalized in various penalizing and privileging ways.

Further, in as much as this analysis demystifies processes of subject formation, and thereby disrupts existing fields of meaning, it also serves as a politics seeking alternative representations of difference; it is, in this sense, a *mode of critique* that illuminates possibilities for political change. By rendering visible the mechanisms that produce difference rather than simply the agents who are marked as different, an account of meaning-making simultaneously interrupts the specific meaning that is produced and the norms and values in which that meaning is operationalized.

As a mode of analysis and of critique, an account of meaning-making is therefore simultaneously critical (deconstructive) and positive (prescriptive) in that it *disrupts* the prevailing processes of subject formation and, in doing so, points toward the possibility of constituting difference in new and alternative ways. As I discuss in more detail in Chapter 6, disruption is important because, when the processes of meaning-making that produce privileging and penalizing meanings are put into question, this opens up a space to refuse a characterization of difference that depends on the subordination of others and to also interpret difference in ways that are self-reflexive about power (on an individual and group level).

Accounts of meaning-making are directed toward ethics of accountability and responsibility. Accountability, states Sherene Razack (1998, 10), is "a process that begins with a recognition that we [as individuals and collectivities] are implicated in systems of oppression that profoundly structure our understanding of one another." The ethics of accountability specifically direct analysts to "invest our energies in exploring the histories, social relations, and conditions that structure groups unequally in relation to one another and *that shape what can be known, thought, and said*" (Razack 1998, 10, emphasis in original). Accountability is distinguishable from responsibility in that it concerns the intentionality of agents, the rectification of past moral and legal crimes/failings, and "keeping the actions of the powerful within the law and minimally honest" (I.M. Young 2000, 175). Responsibility, by contrast, is an infinite obligation that goes beyond one's intentions and private obligations (Bernasconi 2008). An account of meaning-making has the potential to lead to both kinds of ethical practices.

Mobilizing Accounts of Meaning-Making

As a way to deconstruct the operations and effects of meaning-making, I mobilize accounts of it in three ways. First, I examine simultaneously the processes of meaning-making that differentiate meanings of the Norm/Other and those that produce various meanings of Otherness. In other words, I take accounts of the processes that produce general categories of Otherness and varied meanings of Otherness, both of which are implicated in the production of privilege and penalty. Second, at individual, inter- and intragroup, and institutional levels, I study how self-directed and externally imposed meanings are produced through one another and in reaction to one another. I examine how these differences are regulated through dominant norms as well as through those adopted by groups marked as Other. Rather than valorizing or dismissing the latter, I subject all meanings to scrutiny because those developed by subjects marked as Other are not extractable from power. Third, I take accounts of relational processes of meaning-making so as to attend to degrees and forms of penalty and privilege. These relational differences are described and explained in the context of "a matrix of meaning-making." This matrix idea describes and explains the interactive relationships between multiple processes. In sum, I seek to illuminate the import of taking an account of, first, various processes of differentiation rather than singular objects of difference, second, processes of meaning-making operationalized by the state and other members of society, and, third, diverse interrelated processes of meaning-making that constitute differences between and among social groups.

Accounts of meaning-making enrich and advance the study of identity/difference politics in three significant theoretical-conceptual ways. First, they provide a way to *rethink* key social categories of difference by analyzing how these are constituted beyond the scope of culture. Second, accounts of meaning-making *expand* the analysis by going beyond the ontological and substantive logic of the form of identity/difference politics that conjures identities as fixed categories and as either singularly dominant or subordinate. This expansion occurs by examining how structures of difference are produced, de-formed, and re-formed in relational and historical ways with the effect of producing totalizing and also variable categories of Otherness and normality. Third, accounts of meaning-making *complicate* the field of identity/difference politics in that they deconstruct the relationship between multiple processes of meaning-making rather than analyzing one dimension of difference alone. Such an analysis enables an understanding of how modes of difference function through one another, how differences vary in content and form, and why one meaning of difference is not reducible to another (cultural difference, for example, is not reducible to gender, class, or sexual difference).

To make these claims, I draw on a number of examples related to the production and operationalization of whiteness, ableism, and heteronormativity (Chapter 3), Deaf identity and trans-sexuality (Chapter 4), and various modes of racialized gendering (Chapter 5). These illustrate the concrete value of shifting from the politics of culture to the politics of meaning-making. Each exemplifies how a critical political analysis of meaning-making widens and deepens the study of identity/difference politics by engaging an analysis of power. The examples also bring into view modes of differentiation that are largely ignored or undertheorized in liberal multiculturalism. Following Joseph Carens (2000, 5-6), I hold the view that "there is a lot to be gained by multiplying unfamiliar narratives if we can draw out the implications of these narratives for familiar theoretical positions." For instance, representations of whiteness, disability, Deafness, and trans-sexuality are not conventionally examined in the liberal multicultural study of identity/difference politics, but valuably illustrate broader ways in which differences are produced, governed, and resisted within a matrix of meaning-making. Conversely, examples related to immigrants or indigeneity are not as unfamiliar in mainstream discourses. However, I consider the production of these differences through lenses beyond the unidimensional scope of culture so as to illuminate the complex relationships between processes of gendering, culturalization, racialization, and capitalism, all of which are pertinent to the historical experiences of identity/ difference politics. Overall, these various examples provide a way to illustrate the theoretical-conceptual benefits of taking accounts of meaning-making, and they also help to navigate the terrain of identity/difference theorizing.

As I discuss these diverse examples, I am mindful that I speak not for Others but to the construction and effects of Othering. Conscious of the risk in drawing on instances related to differences that I myself do not experience – a risk in which the analyst gazes upon the Othered – I see it as my responsibility to address the ways in which various differences are constituted and managed through dominant historical norms. To do this, I focus on the processes of Othering rather than focusing on the subjects marked as Other. As well, because meanings of the Norm and of Otherness are relationally constituted through a complex matrix of meaning-making, and because we are never outside of these meanings (even though they may not affect us directly or consistently or heavily), I am implicated in the webs of power that produce difference. Therefore, regardless of whether I embody a particular mode of difference, because my own penalizing and privileging differences are constituted in relation to those of others, I carry responsibilities to disrupt broader social hierarchies.

Most of the examples I deploy come from the context of contemporary Canada. Although I extend the analysis of the politics of identity/difference beyond an inquiry into culture, I am mindful that culture is individually, collectively, and legally important to the lives of people in Canada. This may be especially the case for those groups facing systemic hostility and who understand culture as an important site of belonging and social change. Given this, while I critique liberal multicultural interpretations of culture and the primacy assigned to this concept, I also argue that culture cannot be ignored. This is especially the case because claims of culture are often tied up with claims of nationhood, community, and home. In Canada, culture is relevant, for example, to many indigenous peoples whose nationhood status and practices of reindigenization are, in part at least, predicated on meanings of culture.

At the same time, precisely because Canada is a settler society, what Taiaiake Alfred (2005, 207) calls "an artifice of Euroamerican rationality"

based on colonial territorial consolidation, culture needs to be analyzed in
the historical context of nation and nation-building, colonialism, white
supremacy, patriarchy, capitalism, and heteronormativity, as well as anti-
colonialism and decolonization. The national identity of Canada is premised
on the attempted eradication, assimilation, and suppression of indigenous
knowledge and bodies, the appropriation of indigenous land and resources,
practices of slavery as well as conquest and genocide, a historical tension
between two colonial powers (British and French), and racialized and racist
policies of immigration. Since the Canadian nation has been and continues
to be imagined through colonial ideas that function through norms of gendering, capitalism, ableism, oralism, and heteronormativity, and indeed the
very legitimacy of the nation-state is challenged by some indigenous peoples
(G.R. Alfred 1995; T. Alfred 1999, 2005, 2007), difference needs to be interpreted through a lens that can recognize the continuation of the past into
the present. To put it simply, history and context matters to an understanding
of culture and difference.

I conclude this introduction with two final notes: first, given my focus
on how processes of meaning-making constitute subjects to the effect of
producing social hierarchies, domination, and marginalizations, this analysis
foregrounds issues related to privilege and penalty rather than other areas of
study; many aspects of identity/difference are not examined in any detail
here. Second, even though I work to extend and deepen an understanding of
the inner dynamics of identity/difference politics beyond what liberal multiculturalism can illuminate, this book necessarily does not offer a complete
or conclusive analysis. I am still *interpreting* meanings through particular
lenses, and what I see as salient may differ from what others consider important. Moreover, the very nature of deconstructive work is that it enables speci-
ficity and contextualization rather than universal or complete knowledge;
indeed, since contexts of meaning-making are in a constant state of motion,
something is always eclipsed. This inevitable partiality of analysis should not
disappoint or disturb students of identity/difference politics, for it merely
invites complementary projects and confirms that critical analysis is needed
on a broad and continuous basis.

1
The Problem with 'Culture'

In the fall of 2006, two stories related to Sikhs living in Canada circulated in the news. The first centred on the violent attacks against three South Asian women by their male South Asian husbands: Manjit Panghali and Navreet Kaur Waraich were allegedly killed by their husbands; Gurjeet Kaur Ghuman was shot in the face by her husband and, although she survived, she is now blind due to the shooting (Bolan 2006a, 2006b, 2006c). The second story concerned the deliberate and violent beatings of two Sikh seniors, Mewa Singh Bains, aged eighty-four, and Shingara Thandhi, aged seventy-six, which concluded with manslaughter rather than hate-crime sentences of the attackers, two white boys aged thirteen and fifteen when they committed the crimes (CBC 2006). The mainstream media articulated the first story, of domestic and sexual violence, as a problem with and within Sikh culture; in the second story, however, the media erased the cultural (as well as religious and racialized) differences of the attacked men and the white male attackers, and framed the assaults as problems of individual behaviour rather than of systemic racism. In the first instance, culture was hyper-visible, in the second, invisible. Thus, *the* Sikh culture was blamed as the source of patriarchal and sexist violence against Sikh women (even though such gendered violence is exercised in many, if not all, cultural contexts), and the hate crimes against two Sikh men were deemed to be free of any culture-based (let alone racialized) discourse. Both cases shook the families and communities affected.

On a theoretical level, what is significant in these stories is the manner in which culture is taken up: depending on the context, it is either present or absent; it refers to those who are viewed as incompatible with liberal values of tolerance and equity; it is treated as the explanation of societal relations in some cases and depoliticized in others; and it comes to be understood as a fully coherent entity, as a way to differentiate 'them' from 'us.' It is precisely these differing representations of culture that I consider in this chapter.

The concept of culture has, of course, been subject to hundreds of definitions (Vallance 2006, 97). As Barbara Arneil (2007, 51-58) notes, culture has been interpreted as "civilization" (and thus the antonym of nature), as "constructed and relative," as a "contested terrain," as an object made up of "incommensurable entities" (as in current discourses of cultural wars of religion versus secularism, Christianity versus Islam, traditional versus modern, modern versus postmodern), and as a "fluid category" that goes beyond ethnic and national difference to include categories of colour, sexual orientation, and disability. And yet, in liberal multicultural theory, a somewhat different definition of culture is adopted, one that seemingly rejects all of the above but is still shaped by ideas of civilization, some limited forms of contestation, and incommensurability. This concept of culture is specifically given meaning in terms of particular ethnic, national, and linguistic groups as discrete and bounded entities. Will Kymlicka (1995a, 19; 1998, 103) offers two reasons for limiting the scope of culture in this way: first, culture is commonly defined in reference to ethno-cultural minorities; and second, certain distinctions are necessary so as to avoid misunderstandings and false analogies. These are important explanations, and they reflect a certain awareness of some pressing social issues. Yet such reasons are also troubling, for they fail to interrogate who and what is being studied, and who and what is masked when culture is articulated as the primary category of analysis. Given this, a goal of this chapter is to elucidate what culture represents in liberal multicultural interpretations and what is at stake in them.

In particular, I consider how Kymlicka and Charles Taylor conceptualize and operationalize culture, why this should be the case, and what effects these conceptions have for the study of identity/difference politics. Neither Kymlicka nor Taylor claim to offer theories that address or resolve all issues of culture and diversity, and indeed this is not possible. But, as I suggested earlier, their respective theories of multicultural citizenship and recognition have taken on enormous significance and are thus useful points of entry for examining the work of culture as a diagnostic and organizing concept in liberal multicultural thought. After analyzing how and to what end the culture concept is deployed in the work of Kymlicka and Taylor, this chapter also briefly evaluates the ways in which culture has been reconceptualized by some critics of liberal multiculturalism. I conclude that, ultimately, these reconceptualizations also tend to narrow the terrain of identity/difference politics.

The Concept of Culture in Liberal Multicultural Thought

CULTURE AS ETHNIC/ETHNO-RELIGIOUS, NATIONAL, AND LINGUISTIC DIFFERENCE

In liberal multicultural discourses (and even in some critical discourses), "culture" is an umbrella term used to describe *specified* ethnic groups, historical nations, and linguistic minorities rather than all cultural groups. The specific cultural groups most commonly addressed are national minorities who are territorially concentrated and who share a common language (such as indigenous people, and French Canadians living in Quebec), as well as immigrant/ polyethnic minorities whose members are assumed to share language, history, and a broad belief system (Kymlicka 1995a, 18; Taylor 1994b, 52-55). With regard to immigrants, due to the politicization of religion in recent years, liberal multicultural theorists have increasingly paid attention to the cultures of specific ethno-*religious* collectivities (Modood 2007). This is most evident in discussions regarding Muslims, whose identities may be simultaneously ethnic (Muslim), national (British Pakistani), linguistic (Urdu), and religious (Islamic).

This conception of culture as ethnic/ethno-religious, nationality, and linguistic difference gives rise to two serious methodological flaws in the study of identity/difference politics: first, it privileges one family of differences over other kinds of difference, and second, it overdetermines the bounds of social group identity. In particular, culture is pinpointed as the site of trouble that must be remedied and as an identity that should be subject to limited forms of regulated accommodation. In what follows, I examine how and why this takes place, and the theoretical and normative consequences of such an understanding of culture.

CULTURE AS A BOUNDED ENTITY

In situating culture as the primary lens through which to examine specific ethnic, ethno-religious, national, and linguistic groups, Kymlicka and Taylor tend to treat it rather nominally, in which it becomes an object. This essentialist view of culture risks "reifying cultures as separate entities by over-emphasizing their boundedness and mutual distinctness; it risks over-emphasizing the internal homogeneity of culture in terms that potentially legitimize repressive demands for communal conformity" (Turner 1994, 407). These essentializing tendencies have been much critiqued by such scholars as Seyla Benhabib (2002, 4, 60), who argues that liberal multiculturalists ground culture on faulty epistemological premises, delineate cultures as whole, assume that they are congruent with population groups, and dismiss similarities between cultures as well as differences within them.

Even though Kymlicka (1995a, 17-18) states that he uses "culture" broadly in a non-ethnic sense so as to refer to customs or civilization, he also asserts that culture is "synonymous with 'a nation' or 'a people' – that is, as an intergenerational community, more or less institutionally complete, occupying a given territory, or homeland, sharing a distinct language and history." Kymlicka (1995a, 75) specifies societal culture – the culture of national minorities – as "a set of institutions, covering both public and private life, with a common language, which has historically developed over time on a given territory, which provides people with a wide range of choices about how to lead their lives." Culture, in this sense, becomes characterized in terms of stability, formal structures, longevity, and the choices it provides. In defending his two poles of national and polyethnic minorities, Kymlicka (2001, 59) asserts that there are legitimate reasons "to show that ethnocultural groups do not form a fluid continuum, in which each group has infinitely flexible needs and aspirations"; this is because "there are deep and relatively stable differences between various kinds of ethnocultural groups." In order to legitimize the boundaries of his identity categories, Kymlicka (1995a, 85) adds that each of us belongs to one culture and that generally people do not move between societal cultures, although they can enjoy other cultures.

This characterization of culture is a form of cultural essentialism, which arises as a consequence of the liberal need to categorize the subject as a coherent identity. Such an understanding of culture obscures similarities between groups and also conflates ethnic, national, and linguistic differences within groups. Although Kymlicka (1995a, 100, 104) is cognizant of variation within cultures such that he understands that cultures are dynamic and not static, he underestimates, for instance, the hybridity between modes of *racialized* and ethnic, national, and linguistic difference. He (Kymlicka 1998, 96) overdetermines Québécois culture by including "anyone who participates in the French-language society in Quebec, regardless of ethnic descent," and, in doing so, underrates the importance of ethnic and religious differences among French speakers. Indeed, even in Quebec, the importance of the French language varies, and not all francophones have the same options or possibilities because of gendered, classed, and racial differences. Kymlicka also ignores the differences between those racialized as white and non-white, including those from Africa, the Caribbean, and the Middle East, whose first language may well be French. Although these 'cultural Others' may share sentiments of Quebec nationalism with other francophones, this should not be assumed. Moreover, the racialization of francophones as white and non-white has important consequences for how claims of culture are framed, particularly if they challenge claims of Quebec nationalism. Accordingly, although Kymlicka is right to suggest that societal cultures involve a shared vocabulary of tradition and convention, he freezes specific configurations of culture and overestimates the boundedness of groups.

Although Taylor takes the position that identities are dialogically constituted, he too tends to assume the uniformity and boundedness of a culture. Thus, on the one hand, he provides a more nuanced view of identity production than does Kymlicka in that he understands that recognition takes place within shared meanings, where 'we' define who we are. In the process of recognition, Taylor suggests, it is required that we investigate other cultures, while always leaving open the possibility that the standards we employ will also be transformed. On the other hand, despite Taylor's turn to broaden our horizons so as to understand 'them,' he tends to adopt an essentialist approach to evaluating Other cultures. Specifically, in arguing that judgments about worth are possible and necessary, he evokes the idea that cultures must be unified and homogeneous in such a way as to make assessments about them as whole entities. Since, for Taylor (1994b, 67), it is necessary to avoid what he sees as the dangers of relativism, he offers a criterion to judge the worth of cultures: the "validity of the claim has to be demonstrated concretely, in the actual study of the culture."

These judgments, however, are possible only if a culture is assumed to be unified and homogeneous such that judgments concerning it as a whole entity can be made (Benhabib 2002, 58). Generalizations about entire cultures tend to assume that dominant norms within a culture are central to everyone who belongs to that group, such that particular harmful practices of a minority culture become the responsibility of an already essentialized group. A harmful sexist practice, for example, tacitly becomes a feature of an entire community rather than the result of the particular meaning given to that practice by some members of a culture. This form of cultural essentialism often leads to false or skewed conclusions regarding oppression within a culture and can further impede resistance against oppressive practices within particular communities by constructing those who engage in resistance as traitors (Narayan 2000).

Taylor is clearly aware that cultures are more than bounded entities, for he draws on Hans-Georg Gadamer's notion of the fusion of horizons and webs of significance. However, even when Taylor asserts that members of a culture share modes of intelligibility, he undercuts the idea that cultures are changeable through dialogical exchange when he suggests that cultures worthy of recognition should contain some key characteristics, such as temporal longevity. Therefore, a tension exists in Taylor's theory of recognition in that he argues that cross-cultural evaluation is aimed at avoiding Eurocentric assumptions about culture, and yet he underestimates the ways in which cultures are also sites of internal contestation. He (Taylor 1994b, 66-67) states, "But merely on the human level, one could argue that it is reasonable to suppose that cultures that have provided the horizon of meaning for large numbers of human beings, of diverse character and temperaments, over a long period of time – that have, in other words, articulated their sense of the good, the holy, the admirable – are almost certain to have something that deserves our admiration and respect, even if it is accompanied by much that we have to abhor and reject." Here, Taylor is suggesting that cultures need to be stable, time-endured, mature, and encompassing of many people in order for them to be worthy of recognition. Accordingly, he (Taylor 1994b, 66) dismisses "partial cultural milieux within a society as well as short phases of major culture."

But, in conceptualizing cultures in this way, Taylor's theory immediately excludes many cultures, cultures that may be shifting, transforming, in-between, partial, or only more recently organized. Spatial and temporal dimensions have enormous implications for Deaf, disabled, and queer cultures, which may not be recognized as having the historically documented longevity of some cultural groups (as a result of the historical forces of power) but that have more recently made claims for recognition. These cultural groups would be largely discounted because, according to Taylor (1994b, 66), they have "not animated whole societies over some considerable stretch of time." What is more, to the extent that queer politics is directed at shifting modes of identification, partial meanings, and unbounded fluid definitions, queer cultures are marginalized in a theory of bounded and mature culture.

This is not to suggest that Taylor would dismiss recognition claims made by those signified as disabled or sexual minorities. However, his theory of recognition is very much centred on his concern for Québécois demands in Canada rather than on claims of injustice more broadly defined. Thus, Taylor wrongly treats claims of recognition as if they were generalizable across social groups and contexts (Nicholson 1996). His preoccupation with Quebec obscures important differences across groups, especially because he assumes that the modern need for recognition of difference is commonly shared across different kinds of cultural contexts.

In the end, though some scholars such as anthropologist Christoph Brumann (1999, S9, S11) argue that there is communicative expediency when speaking of a cluster of elements, features, parts, or traits of a culture, I hold that such shorthand tends to represent some sort of megaculture without adequate qualification or interrogation. This uncritical essentialist tendency ultimately presents cultures as if they can be studied, known, and managed according to the standards set by dominant cultures.

Culture as a Pre-social Identity

Liberal multiculturalists also tend to treat culture as if it were a given fact of identity or a pre-existing entity with identifiable characteristics. Cultures specifically become identifiable not through a careful and situated analysis of practices, histories, and relations, but through assumptions regarding natural affinity with culture. Although we are born into particular cultural contexts and, as a consequence, do have attachments to them, this does not mean that our cultural identities are prior to the political production of difference.

Kymlicka is aware of the dangers of naturalizing identity, but despite this, he eventually collapses into precisely this understanding of culture. Although he concedes that the societal culture in which one makes choices need not be that into which one was born, he argues that adaptation to a new societal culture is extremely difficult and demanding. On this basis, he concludes that it is reasonable for people to want to access their native culture (Carens 2000, 55), namely, their natural culture. Further, though Kymlicka (1998, 97) states that ethno-cultures are not united by shared blood, he also suggests that culture-as-nationality is more significant than other aspects of identification; this is because socialization of nationality takes place early in life. He (Kymlicka 1998, 98) goes on to claim that we learn about our sexual identity after we are socialized into national communities. Such a position suggests that culture-as-nationality is primary because one is born, or at least socialized at an early age, into certain nationalities. This is telling, not only because national identity outweighs sexual identity for Kymlicka, but also because lifespan rather than historical context determines which identities are most important.

This argument regarding homosexual identity is troubling for three other reasons: first, it assumes that national identities are pre-given; second, it neg-lects the ways that even culture-as-nationality is changeable as a consequence of shifts in government, emigration, or loyalty; and third, it assumes that sexuality is necessarily gleaned later in life, whereas in fact much debate exists concerning the origins of sexual orientation and gender identification. Accordingly, it is impossible to make generalizations about the intensity or saliency of one form of identification over another.

Even if one accepted that cultural identities were to some extent natural rather than socially constructed, this would not justify focusing, as Kymlicka does, on a specific set of ethnic, national, and linguistic social groups, thereby narrowing the scope of culture. He certainly explores the broader application of multiculturalism. In determining whether multiculturalism should be extended to non-ethnic groups, Kymlicka (1998, 90-103) considers whether gays, lesbians, and the Deaf fit into his model of multicultural citizenship. Deaf cultures, he notes, bear a particular resemblance to other cultural groups. He (Kymlicka 1998, 102) states that they are akin to national minorities because "Deaf people were raised in a Deaf culture, and indeed this is the only culture they are effectively able to participate in." He (Kymlicka 1998, 95) also recognizes that, like other minority language groups, the Deaf have suffered persecution because Sign languages have been suppressed. Gay and lesbian groups, he continues, are more like immigrant groups than are the Deaf in that they wish to integrate into mainstream society.

Yet, because the Deaf do not meet his criterion of having a full societal culture, Kymlicka concludes that they are entitled only to special representation rights. He acknowledges that the Deaf have a commitment to their own language (Sign) in the same way as do national minorities, and he maintains that the Deaf have developed substantial institutional completeness (unlike gays and lesbians). But, because the Deaf are too few in number, territorially dispersed, and unable to guarantee the *reproduction* of Deaf children, Kymlicka (1998, 102) declares that they "can never become a genuinely 'national' minority. They will always remain at best a quasi-national group, and will have a difficult time developing and maintaining a complete societal culture."

This naturalized relationship between identity and culture seems entirely at odds with Kymlicka's (1998, 102, emphasis added) statement that, because "the obstacles to integration in the mainstream are enormous – *much greater than for immigrant groups, or even more traditional 'national' minorities*," the cultural nationalist aspirations of the Deaf must be respected and accommodated. It is also at odds with Kymlicka's (1998, 96) position that ethnocultural groups deserve recognition not because of ethnic descent, but because they share a culture that provides them with shared meaningful options and a sense of belonging and identity. Thus, even though Kymlicka insists on a justice-driven framework and on using culture in an ethnic sense, he does not fully disentangle culture from the idea that we are born into particular ways of being.

In the end, this means that Kymlicka's (1992, 141) criterion to "match the rights to the kinds of disadvantage being compensated for" is both arbitrary and skewed. With regard to Deaf culture, the linguistic distinctiveness of Deaf immigrants should concern Kymlicka, even by his own definition. A Deaf person from a non-English-speaking background, for example, may well have to operate within a Deaf culture and language, a dominant English culture and language, and a third culture and language in which she is immersed at home because her family is neither Deaf nor English-speaking (Christensen and Delgado 1993, 1). Deaf ethno-cultural minority immigrants could there- fore be multicultural in the strictest sense of multiculturalism.

Taylor is less overt in naturalizing culture, but this trend in his theory resembles that of Kymlicka in two key ways. First, in articulating and redis- covering authenticity, Taylor (1994b, 31) argues that we should be true to our "own culture." The bond between the self and culture suggests that, for Taylor, markers of culture are naturally part of identity. Second, in discussing the Québécois (as a distinct nation or society), he does not specify features of their culture because he assumes that language inherently connects mem- bers of a culture. For Taylor, language is not solely an instrument of com- munication: it also represents the essence of the human subject. As Andres Lecours (2000, 504-5) argues, Taylor thinks that, above all, man is a "language animal" and that the crucial role of language in the constitution of the self makes it an inevitable and pre-political aspect of culture. Lecours (2000, 505) contends that Taylor has a primordial view of culture in which "the bond between individuals and culture is so fundamental that individual dignity and self-respect are directly connected to group status." The preserva- tion of culture protects language and, by extension, a way of life; given this, culture becomes a natural part of identity. Such an understanding precludes investigation of "the mechanics of identity formation, transformation, pol- iticization and mobilization that are central to the politics of cultural identity" (Lecours 2000, 504).

The naturalizing of culture thus seems to serve two purposes in liberal multicultural thought: first, it gives legitimacy to a defence of why culture is a valuable good (I return to this in the next section); and second, it serves to bolster the idea that cultures are bounded entities that can be pinpointed and judged.

CULTURE AS A RESOURCE

The concept of culture is also put to work in liberal multiculturalism by making it a valuable resource. Two problems arise from this. The first is that the value of culture tends to be justified in universal terms. For Kymlicka (1995a, 83), culture is instrumentally valuable in the Rawlsian sense, whereby it is a primary good for all individuals. Access to culture provides individuals with contexts of choice that enable personal agency and development, as well as equality (Kymlicka 1989, 208). The significance of choice is particularly necessary because "it's only through having a rich and secure cultural structure that people can become aware, in a vivid way, of the options available to them, and intelligently examine their value" (Kymlicka 1989, 155). Culture is hence both the object (that is, what individuals have) and background of choice (a way of life) (Markell 2003, 156-61). To be denied access to one's culture or to be prohibited from acting in accordance with it is, for Kymlicka, a form of injustice (Markell 2003, 171).

Whereas, for Kymlicka, the moral and epistemological imperative for respecting culture is instrumental, for Taylor (1994b, 34), culture is intrinsically valuable; it is an essential part of the communal good, and it helps us to discover our own identities. Taylor (1985, 136) states that culture "is not a mere instrument of the individual goods. It can't be distinguished from them as their merely contingent condition, something they could in principle exist without. That makes no sense. It is essentially linked to what we have identified as good. Consequently, it is hard to see how we could deny it the title of good, not just in some weakened, instrumental sense, like the dam, but as intrinsically good." Culture is thus a necessary social good to him, and not just of instrumental value. However, though culture holds intrinsic value in his theory (which is consistent with his communitarianism), I would argue that, for Taylor, culture also holds instrumental value. This is because it is valuable to groups (not solely to individuals) as a way to be self-reflective about group authenticity and because it provides a multi-generational collective resource for identity formation.[1]

Kymlicka, then, conceives of culture as a primary good for the individual, and Taylor perceives it as a social good. In both instances, culture is a resource, a thing that can be drawn on for instrumental and/or seemingly naturally important reasons. Recognition of culture-based difference is something we are subsequently owed because it enables self-realization. But, in approaching culture as a resource, liberal multiculturalists are forced to justify why culture should be respected. This necessity traps them into providing universalizing philosophical and moral justifications for tolerating and accommodating Othered cultures. Although theories should be explained, the defence of culture is particularly fraught. This is because interpretations about the meaning of culture are so varied, contested, and constantly shifting; as a result, deriving definitive and universal reasons as to why cultures should be generally valued is nearly impossible. In other words, though Kymlicka and Taylor present general theories about why (and which) diverse cultures should be respected, no such generalizations can hold, precisely because cultural differences vary as a result of the wide-ranging transmission of meanings to people. This is especially the case because cultures do not possess people, but people actually create, enact, and iterate cultural practices, symbols, and differences.

The second and more pressing political problem is that culture becomes treated as a resource that can be and is owned by individuals, groups, and the state. The point must now be obvious that cultures are not in fact entities that can be owned, but when culture takes on instrumental value for the state, it becomes a guise through which to manage difference according to global economic market demands. This is important in places such as Canada, where 'multicultural subjects' are migrating from diverse countries (Statistics Canada 2001) and where applicants who apply under the business/independent class are preferred to those in the family class (Abu-Laban 1998, 73-78). The point system of immigration specifically works in tandem with the idea that cultural diversity is a core part of Canadian identity, whereby culture is a resource that helps to build the nation on economic as well as social terms. Culture is, in this sense, "a national property" (Ahmed 2007, 235).

Kymlicka and Taylor do not directly conceptualize culture on these in-strumental market terms, for they tend to refer to culture as a resource that aids individual self-realization and identity development. Their conceptions of culture cannot, however, be entirely separated from what George Yúdice (2003) calls "cultural economy" and Yasmeen Abu-Laban and Christina Gabriel (2002) conceptualize as "selling diversity." Market multiculturalism (that is, the commodification of culture) is tied up with the idea that culture has individual and group value, whereby in both instances the identities of subjects within a nation and the identity of the nation itself are (in part at least) predicated on the idea that culture has instrumental value.

CULTURE AS THE OTHERED

Unlike traditional Western anthropologists who study non-Western places, liberal multiculturalists also utilize culture in reference to non-Western people who make claims within the boundaries of the West. Culture specifically translates into what Gayatri Chakravorty Spivak (1999, 355) calls "a nice name for the exoticism of the outsiders" and Uma Narayan (2000, 84) sees as the construction of an identity that systematically ignores the "profound similarities between Western culture and many of its Others, such as hierarchical social systems, huge economic disparities between members, and the mistreatment and inequality of women."

This separation between 'their' cultures and 'ours' underlies the work of both Kymlicka and Taylor, who reference culture directly in relation to groups marked as Other. Although Kymlicka does refer to the problem of Anglo-conformity, he implicitly suggests that the cultures of those who do not conform create difficulty for the state, whereas dominant cultures do not. Indeed, he is concerned not with redistributing rights for all groups – which would shift the balance of power between dominant and subordinated groups rather than simply extend differentiated rights to marginalized cultures – but only with the rights of specific minority cultures. And Taylor assumes that recognition can be assigned to misrecognized Othered cultures without taking into account the ways in which the values of dominant groups become, by default, the standards of recognition. In other words, because neither thinker addresses what changes are required of dominant groups, they render invisible the power and privilege assigned to some cultures. Cultures that are normalized (dominant cultures) form the background of both Kymlicka's and Taylor's theories but ultimately receive little analytical and critical attention. In this, the Anglo cultures (as per Kymlicka) and Canadian culture as North American, modern, and Christian (as per Taylor) become homogenized and inserted as a stable norm.

Despite this underlying support for the status quo, liberal multiculturalism continues to present itself as being a theory and policy of social change, one that is tolerant of Other cultures. This image appears to be necessary not only to free liberalism of the legacy of cultural imperialism, but also to construct a self-image as non-cultural. This, however, is disingenuous precisely because liberal multiculturalists attempt to liberalize culture by linking it to particular brands of liberal tolerance, freedoms, rights, and dignity, thus creating a cultural formation most acceptable to the liberal paradigm. What is especially striking is that the process of shrinking the status of culture by converting its communal dimension to universalistic principles of rights and recognition is, ironically, dependent on revering culture (Brown 2004). In other words, only by claiming the concept of culture (in the form of the Othered who needs liberalizing or recognizing) can liberal multiculturalists transcend it. By claiming culture in this way, liberals seek to maintain the hegemony of liberalism (regardless of the brand of liberalism employed) and to situate it as transcendental to culture. Paradoxically, then, liberal multiculturalists maintain the self-image of being tolerant and accommodating of cultural difference while simultaneously promoting only those versions of tolerance and accommodation that meet liberal standards. The effect is that the centre remains invisibilized, and a regulated boundary remains between the Other and the Norm in which liberal multicultural values occupy the centre, and values that do not correspond are repeatedly positioned on the margins.

CULTURE AS A PROXY FOR RACE

The conceptual parameters around questions of culture in liberal multicultural theory have effectively placed a wide range of differences outside the scope of identity/difference politics. One key example lies in how race-thinking, racialization, racism, and colonialism are undertheorized and/or reframed as issues of culture. References to culture and multiculturalism are, more often than not, used to package those who share some aspects of difference without adequately addressing historical and global racialized relations, colonialism, neo-colonialism, and other forms of domination. Kymlicka and Taylor tend to theorize polyethnic minorities, for example, without any reference to the global racial and colonial histories that have marked their identities within Canada. In fact, it seems that the same kinds of Othered subjects that were historically categorized and subjugated by race-thinking and racism are now being analyzed through meanings about culture. In reflecting on the use of culture in political theory, anthropologist David Scott (2003, 103-4) argues that culture has indeed become the most recent way of conceiving and constructing Otherness. The Renaissance, he states, constructed the non-European Other through Christianity; in the Enlightenment the Other was interpreted through distinctions between European Reason and non-European Ignorance; through the nineteenth century, race organized the paradigms of normalcy and Otherness. In the twentieth century, Scott (2003, 104) continues, culture "becomes the grid and horizon of difference. It becomes, so to speak, the commanding natural language of difference."

One of the effects of privileging culture as *the* grid and horizon of difference is that the operations and effects of race-thinking are virtually erased. Kymlicka (1998, 96) is quite explicit about this move when he remarks that "the shift from racialism to culturalism is an obvious moral improvement." This shift certainly has the potential to characterize the meaning of culture developed by Franz Boas and his followers in which culture was an alternative to racist and racial categories of difference (Upadhya 2002, 184). However, the separation of ideas about race and culture leads Kymlicka to virtually expunge the discursive, material, and ideological relationship between culture, racism, and colonialism. In consequence, sometimes, culture becomes a proxy for race; at other times, the race category is culturalized (Fleras 2004; Mills 2007, 94).[2] Perhaps confusion exists regarding race as a culturally constructed category and racial categories that are (falsely) based on cultural differences (Cowlishaw 1987, 227). But even if Kymlicka is responding to the criticism of race-as-biology, his conception of culture continues to obscure the material and historical construction of cultural groups. Consequently, it veils the impact of processes of racialization and racism, and reinscribes the same essentialism that has characterized the idea of race.

Although some liberal pluralists, such as Tariq Modood (2007) and Charles Mills (2007), approach multiculturalism with questions of race-thinking, Islamophobia, and white supremacy very much in mind, Kymlicka brackets issues of racism and racialization outside the scope of multiculturalism. In these instances, race-thinking appears extraneous, even though it is constitutive of socio-political difference and shapes the very backdrop through which multiculturalism has emerged. This trend extends across other strands of liberal thought, whereby liberal modernity tends to deny its racialized history and hides behind some idealized dismissal of race as a morally relevant category (Goldberg 1993, 7). The swathe over race-thinking is especially troubling because it depoliticizes the ways in which culture is intertwined with systems of racialization; this depoliticization occurs both by making race-thinking seem less significant and by framing difference in terms of tolerance rather than in terms of the impact of white supremacy.

The effect of masking over contexts of white supremacy is that histories of racism and the privilege assigned to groups marked as white remain unexamined. In the Canadian context, this depoliticized (rather than apolitical) character of culture has been especially criticized by indigenous scholars who view indigenous groups as nations, not as multicultural or cultural groups (T. Alfred 1999; Green 2000), and by those who understand the legacies of slavery, segregation, racial violence, and hate in terms of racism rather than culture. Although racism often has cultural dimensions (in that people categorized as members of a race have different cultural values, beliefs, and practices), racial differences are not simply the result of failing to recognize or know a culture. Rather, they are the product of economic, social, and political white domination. As Charles Mills (2007, 97) says in reference to Taylor's theory of recognition, "If cultural distinctiveness were the sole or primary obstacle to white acceptance, then culturally assimilated people of color would not encounter racism."

It is perhaps the case that, since the war on terror has provoked a backlash against multiculturalism, liberal multicultural theorists may be increasingly drawn to anti-racist discourses, either as a way to supplement multiculturalism or to expand its boundaries. Steps toward anti-racism discourses may occur specifically because the previous justifications of multicultural tolerance and accommodation are under attack by those who call for explicit practices of integration and assimilation, and because, as Jakeet Singh (2007) notes, multiculturalism is increasingly being scripted as the *enemy* of integration and therefore the *friend* of terrorism. Liberal multiculturalists will no doubt continue to respond to this charge so as to defend liberalism. The turn toward anti-racism may have less of an impact in places such as the UK where anti-racism and multiculturalism already come together. But in Canada, where the lines between multiculturalism and anti-racism are sometimes blurred and sometimes clearly divergent, such a move could potentially foreground issues of racial discrimination currently ignored and masked in liberal multicultural theory.

Yet, appropriation of critical race and anti-racism discourses by liberal multiculturalists may simply end up being another way to claim the higher moral ground of liberal freedom and tolerance at the neglect of issues of privilege and penalty. Such a position may nonetheless gain legitimacy because multiculturalism has become the most palatable expression of difference allowable in Western mainstream discourse. Although anti-racism and anti-colonialism should be front and centre so that relations of power are foregrounded, if liberal multiculturalists approach race-thinking in terms of liberal tolerance – namely, as individual irrational prejudice – and cross-cultural education and exchange rather than as a problem of historic and systemic white hegemony, they will be no further ahead in addressing racial violence. Indeed, as Sarita Srivastava (2007) argues, anti-racist multicultural practices can shift the focus from grassroots political priorities to state-defined priorities, give legitimacy to uncritical (race-free) narratives of nation-building, and limit radical forms of anti-racism.

CULTURE AS A UNIDIMENSIONAL SIGNIFIER OF DIFFERENCE

The tendencies toward essentialism, a naturalized conception of cultural identity, and a deracialized notion of culture are also reflected in and produced by the privilege assigned to culture over other aspects of difference. More specifically, liberal multicultural theory privileges culture in such a way as to mask cultural differences that are formed through modes of racialization, gendering, ability, class, sexuality, and so on. Indeed, liberal pluralist inter-pretations present multiculturalism as if it were conceived outside the context of gendered, racialized, ablest, and class-based relations. This (mis)representation merely serves to reinscribe dominant forms of nationalism and to mask vari-ous power inequities. Paradoxically, therefore, though liberal multiculturalists wish to recognize a multiplicity of cultural differences, they tend to erase the differences within cultures.

There are some exceptions to the unidimensional focus on culture, where, for example, the rights of women within their cultures are examined. But while such an examination is important, the patriarchal cultural practices of dominant society tend to go unscrutinized, and cultural identity and gender identity tend to be framed as oppositional to one another. Certainly, Kymlicka and Taylor are both right not to treat cultures as amorphous entities, but they also underestimate the ways in which members of a culture are shaped through interactions between multiple modes of identification. The experience of culture, in other words, varies according to modes of identification beyond the scope of ethnicity, nationality, and linguistic difference. Since the position of members of minority cultures is also affected by historical relations of power drawn along *non*-ethno-cultural lines, a theory of social identity and difference should seek to address a complex range of interlocking historical systems of oppression and privilege. But nowhere in their analysis is there an adequate treatment of the interactions between different systems of oppres-sion. Given this, as Richard Day (2004, 37) rightly argues, the discourse of liberal multiculturalism fails to live up to its own standards of justice and equality.

Indeed, the overemphasis on culture promotes a unidimensional analysis of difference, a form of analysis that has been much criticized by feminists of colour and indigenous feminists who stress the simultaneity of oppres-sions. Unidimensional analysis contributes to what American critical race scholar Kimberle Crenshaw (2000) calls "intersectional invisibility," in which the interactions between gender and race discrimination, for example, become hidden and made imperceptible. Crenshaw asserts that the foregoing critique of the single-issue framework renders problematic the claim that the struggle against racism is distinguishable from, much less prioritized over, the struggle against sexism. Mohawk scholar Patricia Monture (Monture-Angus 1995, 136-41) also makes this point in her critique of section 15 of the Canadian Charter of Rights and Freedoms. She suggests that, in part, the enumerated grounds in the Charter are inadequate because they list separated entities (race, sex, religion) that fail to account for the combined impact of multiple grounds of discrimination experienced by indigenous women.

Following feminist approaches that go beyond unidimensional theories of gender, students of identity/difference politics also need to question the primacy accorded to culture in liberal multiculturalism. This primacy obscures an understanding of how meanings about culture perform through other systems of meaning. To be clear, I am not suggesting that other dimensions of identification should take priority over aspects of culture so that gender, or class, or sexuality becomes the central organizing concept. Rather, my point is that systems of identification are integral to one another, and accordingly culture cannot be prioritized as the main axis of difference.

The capacity of liberal multiculturalists to address the interactions between multiple systems is perhaps ultimately limited to an additive response because of the demand for a clearly-defined subject. This additive understanding of identity simply appends one dimension to another and maintains a unidimensional categorization of identity. Such a perspective continues to emphasize some dimensions of identity at the cost of examining the interdependency of multiple dimensions and emphasizes difference without adequately examining *relations* of difference. In consequence, a tension is produced between culture-based forms of identification and other aspects of identification, such that these may appear irreconcilable. This tension has been especially illuminated in debates about whether multiculturalism is bad for women (Okin 1994).

Another approach to examining the relationship between multiple modes of identification is to broaden the meaning of culture. This has been suggested by Barbara Arneil. Arneil (2007, 65) suggests that the definition of culture be expanded to include "all groups who have been treated unjustly within liberal theory." For Arneil, this includes groups marked as sexual minorities and those marked by social disabilities. Arneil (2007, 67) is especially interested in exploring "the processes by which cultural 'others' are defined as deviant" within the context of liberal norms of industry, reason, autonomy, heterosexuality, and the public/private divide. She contends that a broader definition of culture will enable subjects to draw from the tools made available by liberalism (such as liberal rights) and to temper the assimilationist tendencies of liberalism by rejecting constraining expressions of cultural difference.

This conception of social difference is certainly appealing because it recognizes that, in multicultural discourses, some formulations of difference are problematically privileged over others. It also reflects the importance of culture to groups conventionally outside the scope of liberal multiculturalism. But such an expansion of the culture concept may also serve to undermine the vision of agonistic pluralism that Arneil argues is necessary for justice; this is because culture becomes a catch-all monolithic way of characterizing difference. Indeed, as Arneil (2007, 58-60) herself observes, even if the meaning of culture were broadened, it could simply make other subjects susceptible to precisely the liberal modes of cultural assimilation and normalization that reiterate Otherness. Theresa Man Ling Lee (2006) reaches a similar conclusion. In response to arguments that people marked by disabilities are no different from people of colour, Jews, Muslims, or gays and lesbians, and that disabled groups are like any other cultural group, Lee contends that characterizing persons with disabilities as a quasi-ethnic group is unproductive, potentially divisive, and hierarchical. This is because such meanings of culture create two tiers of minority groups: those who are deemed to be 'properly' cultural and therefore deserving of multicultural accommodation, and those who are not.

The narrow scope of culture cannot therefore be countered by an additive approach or by extending the meaning of culture. Both responses simply replicate liberal multicultural trends to overdetermine the separation between aspects of difference and/or to see all differences through the lens of culture.

STATE REGULATION OF DIVERSE CULTURES

The following discussion illuminates how liberal multiculturalism substantiates an understanding of culture as something that is, at best, deserving of regulated accommodation. The culture concept, in other words, appears accommodative of diversity, but underlying this pluralism is a form of state-led governmentality of difference.

In particular, state regulation of cultural Others takes place through the requirement that 'they' be included in dominant society. Although this underlying goal of inclusion is driven by notions of liberty, equality, and recognition, it is also a troubled ideal. First, the language of inclusion de-politicizes the problem of power. This occurs by defining social transformation in terms of the expansion and pluralization of an existing core/centre, rather than in terms of fundamental change of the conditions that give meaning to that core/centre, and by collapsing all kinds of exclusions. On this latter point, Iris Marion Young (2000, 13) remarks that the "concepts of exclusion and inclusion lose meaning if they are used to label all problems of social conflict and injustice." In fact, she continues, "where the problems are racism, cultural intolerance, economic exploitation, or a refusal to help needy people, they should be named so."

Second, the goal of including Others into the mainstream falsely assumes that those who are currently included are equally included and that inclusion brings equity. But inclusion is premised on defining the inside and outside of a delimited core, such that an inclusive sphere exists only in relation to a sphere of exclusion. Inclusion, therefore, paradoxically depends on the con-tinued denial of itself – it can be realized only if some subjects are excluded. These modes of exclusion, or hierarchies of difference, are masked, however, by simply pluralizing the core and leaving the unequal character of that core intact. The following quote from Amarpal Dhaliwal (1994, 43) characterizes this problem very well:

> [The politics of inclusion] does not account for the ways inclusion
> can still oppress or fail to alter structures of domination. The in-
> ability of radical democratic inclusion politics to deal with inclu-
> sion retaining peripheralization is a key limitation, especially given
> that, in many liberal democratic societies, many democratic groups
> have been 'included' by being accorded certain formal rights like
> the right to vote. If inclusionary attempts often reaffirm a hegem-
> onic core to which the margins are added without any significant
> destabilization of that 'core' or continue to valourize [sic] the very
> centre that is problematic to begin with, then it is clear that the
> motivation to include needs questioning.

Indeed, in assuming that there is a primary (if not singular) mainstream culture in which to include Others, the goal of inclusion erases the experience of having many centres of inclusion or sites of belonging. Furthermore, it does not attend to the ways in which the boundaries of inclusion and exclusion are regulated by those with an established reign of authority. In Kymlicka's theory, for example, inclusion is premised on the values of dominant societal cultures, and in Taylor's, inclusion requires those who dominate to bestow recognition. In both instances, there is an assumption that those who do not need differentiated rights and recognition (dominant subjects) are active participants who are fully integrated into Canadian society.

Third, underlying the desire for inclusion are corresponding but subtextual agendas that may emerge from a desire for peace and social harmony but that may also arise in contexts of exploitation and domination. In the latter case, the value of inclusion is advanced not for the sake of equity or justice, but as necessary in order to promote such ideologies as market liberalism, as I suggested above. Abu-Laban and Gabriel (2002, 169) refer to this as multiculturalism selling business, "whereby the skill, talents, and ethnic backgrounds of men and women are commodified, marketed, and billed." In these instances, inclusion is not simply about providing access and opportunity for cultural minorities: it is about the financial prosperity of the state and the implementation of a neo-liberal agenda. Inclusion of diverse cultures can, therefore, mask the desire to use and exploit the intellectual, linguistic, and material capacities of Othered subjects in order to maximize the benefits of a market-driven economy.

Fourth, because the terms of inclusion are set by the state, its regulatory role is further legitimized. The state can certainly bring some benefits to the people of a nation in that it can protect the rights of individuals and groups, enhance the capacity-building potential of subjects, and facilitate active citizenry by engaging subjects in political life. Yet, in order to maintain its own authority, the state necessarily acts as a gatekeeper of social differences. Indeed, as Patchen Markell (2003, see 27-32) notes, though the state is a disproportionately powerful actor, it too depends on subjects and other states to recognize its sovereignty. Liberal multicultural theory expands and justifies state management of those marked as different and threatening, even potentially threatening, to the nation.

One needs simply to recollect that Kymlicka published *Multicultural Citizenship* in 1995, and that Taylor published a collection of essays titled *Reconciling the Solitudes* in 1993, when the legitimacy of the Canadian state was at question and the country was in a state of constitutional crisis. Both thinkers were preoccupied by issues of self-determination for Quebec, especially in light of heated and divisive debates over Canadian unity and constitution-alism. Tensions were particularly high because Quebec never signed on to the Constitution Act of 1982 and because of the failures of the two constitu-tional accords (Meech Lake and Charlottetown) in the 1980s and 1990s. Re-sponding to these political events, Kymlicka and Taylor articulated their theories through discourses that enabled them to pinpoint specific cultures, which in turn allowed them to evaluate those groups that were deemed to pose an actual or potential threat to the state and to national unity. This same sense of crisis continues to shape liberal multicultural theory today with the preoccupation that Muslims can/do threaten the nation's identity, its people, its borders, and its security (Abu-Laban and Gabriel 2002; Arat-Koc 2006; Razack 2007). From a liberal multicultural perspective, if the state can both accommodate and manage diverse cultures, fragmentation can (at least for the moment) be avoided.

The consequence of this crisis-driven approach is that some modes of difference become constructed as more pressing than others. Of course, some issues are more urgent than others in specific contexts, but the dual focus on national minorities and immigrants obscures the context in which other groups are marginalized, including "transported forced labour, political and economic refugees, guest workers," all of whom are colonial and racialized subjects who make up "a large portion of the forebearers of contemporary multicultural minorities" (I.M. Young 1997, 50). Although Kymlicka (1995a, 99; 2002, 357-59; 2005a, 23-28) has over recent years nuanced his concep-tion of immigrant and national minority groups, it is clear that he is not con-cerned about difference per se but with questions of diversity that are most pressing for the state to address.

The authority of the state is without doubt a legitimate concern for those who study the politics of identity/difference. However, when the focus is on how and why the state should manage difference, the perspectives of those who are marginalized due to their perceived difference are taken to be sec-ondary. Moreover, from a state-centred stance, culture emerges as a problem because Othered cultures are making demands that threaten national and political unity. The function of the state is to secure the nation against this disunity. These threats, Arneil (2007, 56, emphasis on original) argues, are especially salient to Kymlicka and Taylor because of their intellectual, ideo-logical, and geographic locations: "As *political theorists*, as opposed to anthropologists or cultural studies' scholars, the central concern is the origin of *political* authority. As *liberals*, they seek to theorize the liberal democratic state in relation to the rights of individuals and communities ... [and] as *Canadians*, the theoretical problem of national unity took on a very concrete and acute form at the close of the twentieth century." Liberal political thought is specifically premised on establishing the limits of justified coercion, or, to put it differently, on justifying state interference to protect individual liberty without undermining individual freedoms and rights. Liberal multiculturalists adjust the goal for liberals because they are driven by a concern to be sensitive to group difference, which they argue is not contrary to the liberal tradition of tolerance and dignity. Hence, they enable specific groups to engage in specific practices that would otherwise be contrary to liberalism. Even though (some) group differences are acknowledged, the liberal multicultural paradigm ultimately requires the establishment of new parameters of justified state coercion. The focus is now not only on the extent of individual liberties but also on group liberties.

Reconceptualizing Culture: Turning to Anthropology

If, then, liberal multiculturalism *analytically* narrows the terrain of identity/difference by focusing almost exclusively on that aspect of identity named "culture," *theoretically* interprets culture in obscuring and depoliticizing ways, and *normatively* masks the ways in which the state regulates Others through the ideal of inclusion, is there analytic worth or possibility of reconceptualizing the concept of culture so as to confront issues of power? My short answer is yes, but culture needs to be extracted from the bounds of liberal multiculturalism, and it cannot be the primary lens through which to examine issues of identity/difference politics. To make this argument, I turn to developments in anthropology as a discipline that has historically and normatively situated culture. Although I am suspicious of what Linda Smith (1999, 11, 42) calls the "imperial eyes" of anthropology, in this discipline culture has also been theorized in the context of political arrangements between groups, and this link to power is central to my own approach.

Political scientists have long relied on specific anthropological notions of culture in indirect and sometimes unacknowledged ways. Over recent years, some political theorists have been explicitly mindful of the lessons to be learned from theoretical developments in anthropology. The turn to anthropology is noteworthy in itself because it indicates that the intellectual tools for studying the politics of identity/difference within political science need to be supplemented and that theories of culture transcend disciplinary boundaries. In this section, I explore how and why political theorists Seyla Benhabib and James Tully turn to postmodern anthropology. Whereas traditional anthropology stressed the organic unity, boundedness, and self-sufficiency of the object of culture, "the critical potential of postmodern anthropology ... lies in the fact that anthropological categories of cultural difference, though articulated from within a Western tradition, nevertheless make available perspectives of otherness" (CCSG 1994, 121). Postmodern anthropology especially emphasizes cultural relativism, the importance of displacing Eurocentrism, and the need to reject essentialist and conflated understandings of culture and race. These ideas inform the work of Benhabib and Tully in ways that counter the narrowing and obscuring effects of liberal multicultural interpretations of culture.

Seyla Benhabib: Culture as Narrative

In her important book *Claims of Culture: Equality and Diversity in the Global Era* (2002), Benhabib develops a social constructivist conception of culture that directly challenges Kymlicka's and Taylor's normatively suspect conception. She utilizes feminist anthropological concepts of culture as a way to differentiate between moral, ethical, and evaluative concerns. Benhabib specifically offers an intersubjective and localized notion of culture-as-narrative, which challenges cultural essentialism. An analysis of culture, she asserts, becomes essentialized from the standpoint of the social observer. By contrast, from the standpoint of the participant, culture is shaped through narratives that arise from traditions, stories, rituals, symbols, and material conditions. For Benhabib, the production of culture is hence embedded in experiential knowledge.

In this narrative view of culture, Benhabib (2002, 6, emphasis in original) states, there is no need for culture to appear as whole: instead, it arises through contested narratives because "we identify *what* we do through an *account* of what we do." Hence, cultures take on meanings through webs of narratives. This resonates with Taylor's notion of webs of interlocution, although Benhabib places more emphasis on questions of power than does Taylor. Benhabib (2002, 33-41, 60, 103, 137) specifically understands cultures as heterogeneous, dynamic, porous, hybrid, and as communities of dialogue fraught with power. Further, culture-as-narrative encompasses what she calls second-order narratives in which we take evaluative stances about what we do. For Benhabib (1995, 240), cultures are not "hermetic and sealed wholes" that represent only some kinds of delimited difference; rather, they are systems of articulating the material and the symbolic. Cultures are likened to associations of people that provide expressions of ways of living. Through this understanding of culture, Benhabib (1995, 240) suggests, it becomes possible to avoid flattening the internal contradictions and debates within cultures.

There are, in sum, several propositions from Benhabib's model of culture: culture is narratively constituted; cultures are communities in conversation; culture is power-laden; cultures are heterogeneous, dynamic, and contested; and cultures tend to be porous and hybrid in that people and the practices/ideas within them move across and between cultures (Peritz 2004, 269-70). This narrative account of culture is conducive to the notion of intersubjectivity and the critique of essentialism that I wish to advance in my approach to the politics of identity/difference. As well, I agree with Benhabib (2002, 8) that "human groups should be defended in the name of justice and freedom and not of an elusive preservation of cultures."

Benhabib's conception of culture-as-narrative could be applied more widely so as to address multiple standpoints, not solely those related to culture. This, however, could collapse into the same problem identified by Arneil, a problem in which culture comes to stand for everything. Moreover, some narratives may emphasize gender, class, or sexual orientation (or interactions between these systems and other systems) in ways that destabilize the primacy of culture. In other words, culture may not be of principal significance for the participant or may take on distinct subjective forms in relation to two or more aspects of identification, which may or may not include culture. Moreover, it is unclear whether Benhabib intends cultures to be defined by cultural narratives alone. If narratives constitute culture, the potential to change cultural meanings would depend heavily on the agency of marginalized individuals and groups. Although a key attraction of Benhabib's notion of culture-as-narrative is the agency of those marked as Other, cultural meanings emerge from sources that extend beyond the agent. Benhabib argues that cultures themselves are torn by conflicts concerning their own boundaries, but it is not simply that cultures continually create, recreate, and renegotiate the imagined boundaries between insiders and outsiders; rather, the boundaries can be imposed by members of other cultures as well as by members of one's own culture. Culture, in this sense, should be examined as both a productive and a constraining site of difference rather than something that is valorized.

Benhabib's theory also has a tendency to universalize the notion that contested and hybrid narratives of culture are an empirical fact, which she later qualifies by acknowledging that a discourse theory of democracy should not definitively exclude claims based in reified understandings of culture but should require instead that such claims respect democratic equality and autonomy (Peritz 2004, 274). The important point is that, though cultures are constantly changing, essentialized conceptions of culture can provide a radical critique of the hegemonic order; as Glen Coulthard (forthcoming) and Nikolas Kompridis (2005, 2006) argue, reified narratives of culture need not be any less meaningful to the participant than fluid, open, hybrid, and contested notions of culture. Indeed, it is critical to ask for whom culture is deemed to be hybrid – the analyst or the person/people whose culture is under analysis.

This tension between non-essentializing and essentialist discourses of culture has preoccupied some theorists, but I will argue in later chapters that this preoccupation is less fruitful than examining why and with what effects these understandings of culture gain meaning. For now, I simply note that only some features of Benhabib's notion of culture-as-narrative are useful when assessing alternative ways to theorize culture. In particular, she carefully shows that holistic conceptions of culture offered by liberal multiculturalists are inadequate for considering issues of democratic public reason. She does not simply object to essentialist notions of culture for the sake of anti-essentialism: rather, she evaluates interpretations of culture from the perspective of how well they respect democratic norms (Peritz 2004, 267, 274). And she also offers a social constructivist perspective in which culture is the effect of continuous contestation and narration. Not only does this understanding contrast with liberal multicultural accounts of culture as a bounded entity, but it also corresponds to how I approach cultural identities as socially produced markers of difference.

JAMES TULLY: CULTURE AS CONTESTED TERRAIN

In *Strange Multiplicity: Constitutionalism in an Age of Diversity* (1995, 10, 14, 46, 65, 101), James Tully also reflectively draws upon anthropological conceptions of culture, specifically to examine whether a modern constitution can recognize and accommodate cultural diversity. He offers a theory of cultural diversity that explicitly rejects ideas of empire that justify European imperialism, imperial rule of former colonies over indigenous peoples, and cultural imperialism. Tully (1995, 5) contends that culture is an "irreducible and constitutive aspect of politics," but in order to fully recognize cultural diversity, the modern concept of culture must be reconsidered. According to Tully, this entails dissociating culture from the modern concept of nation because recognition of a culture need not require the establishment of separate nations or states. Although developments from the seventeenth century to the twentieth century articulate cultures as "separate, bounded and internally uniform" entities, Tully (1995, 10) rejects this "billiard-ball conception of culture, nations and societies."

In order to formulate a concept of culture that is not "separate, closed, internally uniform and relative to a stage of development," Tully (1995, 65, 10-11) argues that "there is no end or exception to this criss-crossing and overlapping," that cultures "overlap geographically and come in a variety of types," and that "cultures are not internally homogeneous." To reflect the idea that the modern age is intercultural, Tully (1995, 11) further states that cultures "are continuously contested, imagined and reimagined, transformed and negotiated both by their members and through interaction with each other. The identity, and so the meaning, of any culture is thus aspectival rather than essential." He emphasizes the dynamic interaction in the formation of cultures, as well as the divergence and parallels between cultures. Overall, Tully (1995, 11, emphasis in original) shows that "cultural diversity is a tangled labyrinth of intertwining cultural differences *and* similarities, not a panopticon of fixed, independent and incommensurable worldviews in which we are either prisoners or cosmopolitan spectators in the central tower." His interpretation of culture therefore importantly moves away from the liberal multicultural notion of a bounded entity in that he treats culture as an identity that is contested and in motion.

At the same time, in *Strange Multiplicity*, Tully tends to depend on a broad cluster of concepts that continue to privilege some ethnic, national, and linguistic modes of difference over other kinds of difference. This is reflected in his concern for nationalist, multicultural, and supranational movements, linguistic and ethnic minorities, and indigenous claims for self-government. The exception is feminism, specifically cultural feminism, which Tully states raises demands within and across national, supranational, minority, and intercultural struggles. Although it is not entirely clear whether Tully intends to locate cultural feminists as members of identifiable cultures or as members who create their own distinct cultural group, and whether women are simply members of a cultural group or in fact also form culture, his conception of culture moves the analysis toward issues of power. In particular, the shift to culture-as-contested-terrain has radical potential for political theory. It is this characterization of culture as an activity – in which culture is relationally given meaning rather than taken as given – that I emphasize in my own thinking on the politics of meaning-making. As Tully (1995, 15) states, "Culture is a way of relating to others in any interaction, a way of following or challenging a social rule, and so a dimension of any social relation, from a cultural slur in the workplace to the relations among nations."

Difference beyond Culture

In light of the more robust conceptions of culture developed by Benhabib and Tully, can culture still be centred in the analysis of identity/difference politics? This depends on the normative project of a political theory. To the extent that the descriptive and diagnostic value of the culture concept in liberal multiculturalism describes specific groups to whom the state must respond and also provides a liberal defence as to why the state should accommodate particular group-based claims, the work of culture serves the purpose of liberal multiculturalists. Yet, as the above analysis demonstrates, liberal multicultural interpretations of culture are narrow in scope and shallow in depth, such that they obscure many key aspects of identity/difference theorizing. An understanding of the politics of identity/difference is constrained because difference is reduced to specific kinds of cultural Otherness and also because of essentializing and naturalizing tendencies, the unidimensional emphasis on one mode of identification, the construction of culture as the problem of the Other, universalizing assumptions about the intrinsic and instrumental value of culture, and the imperative of the state to regulate cultures that deviate from the norm. Overall, though all concepts are generative and all carry their own tensions, this interpretation of culture and the primacy assigned to it obscures more than it reveals. Liberal multicultural interpretations of culture not only frustrate analytic and political clarity, they also legitimize subtle (and not so subtle) forms of governmentality. To put it simply, liberal multicultural interpretations of culture are not sufficient for examining the complexities of identity/difference politics.

This is not to say that liberal multiculturalism has had no positive influence on political life or political theory. It has, in some instances, opened up avenues of social change and minority participation in politics. But the liberal multicultural lens of culture can provide only limited insight into issues of power that are central to identity/difference politics. Indeed, if we return for a moment to the news stories that opened this chapter, liberal multicultural conceptions of culture cannot adequately describe or explain why these instances of violence occurred. These conceptions would end up constructing the problem of violence against Sikh women as one essentially about Sikh religion (that is, Sikh culture is sexist), and they would effectively depoliticize the contexts of white supremacy in which the two senior Sikh men were attacked. In effect, this would conceal the broader sources and consequences of political injury. Given this, one might think of culture as a red herring, a distraction from issues of power.

In a manner quite different from that of Kymlicka and Taylor, Benhabib and Tully revise the concept of culture in order to emphasize the agency of subjects. Benhabib argues for an understanding of culture that emerges most successfully within deliberative democratic contexts; and Tully contends that intercultural dialogue is necessary because culture is a site of contestation. Both attempt to expand the boundaries of the centre to include Others previously excluded (a goal not unlike that of Taylor and Kymlicka) but do so by reconceptualizing culture as a mode of identity and practice that is constantly changing, meaningful for different people in different ways, and situated in relations of power. Culture, in short, is not conceptualized as a passive and deracialized identity but as something that is constituted, experienced, and changed in and through power. It is not an object of difference but an intersubjective and contested site in which differences are constituted and transformed.

Despite these important reconceptions of culture as a dynamic feature of human life, culture continues to be treated as the central site of analysis. Cultural diversity is a problem that needs solving, and a reimagined notion of culture serves as the prescription for the problem. Yet, the primacy assigned to culture, even if it is revised, does not altogether eliminate the slippery slope that produces essentialized depictions of difference. This is because the composition of a culture continues to require definition even when it is narratively (Benhabib) and dialogically (Tully) constituted in non-Eurocentric and self-directed ways. Although the conceptions of culture offered by Benhabib and Tully certainly expand its meaning, these revisions continue to assign primacy to one dimension of difference and to underestimate how discourses of culture sometimes constitute regulatory paradigms and sites of resistance.

The argument that culture is an inadequate starting point of the study of identity/difference is not new. If you recall, neutral liberal scholars such as Chandran Kukathas have voiced this same critique, specifically by claiming that liberalism already entails the capacity and will to address inequities; accordingly, the state need do nothing about cultural claims. Although these are not my grounds for evaluating liberal multiculturalism, my critique does nonetheless overlap with that of some liberal thinkers – notably liberal pluralists rather than neutral liberals. Feminist theorist Anne Phillips (2007), for example, offers a liberal pluralist theory of multiculturalism but does so by critiquing essentialist views of culture. She suggests that culture is treated too much like a solid entity, as the primary source of identity, and as being far more definitive of each individual's horizon than is likely to be the case. The effect of this understanding is to erase differences between members of a culture and to encourage an unhelpful distinction between modern and traditional culture, between 'us' and 'them.'

More specifically, Phillips (2007, 23) continues, culture is much more ordinary than is commonly assumed; its significance is exaggerated such that "there is a tendency to call on culture when faced with something we cannot otherwise understand." For example, culture comes into view in debates regarding forced arranged marriage among South Asians, when in fact these issues may be more concerned with the difficulty of breaking out of a culture, the need to change particular practices, the consequence of political experiences grounded in violence, and the authoritarian response of parents faced with unfamiliar sexual norms. Accordingly, she concludes, it is necessary to dilute the significance of culture. Phillips' (2007, 21, emphasis in original) point "is not that there are *no* cultural differences, or that the differences are sufficiently minor to be ignored in public policy ... [but] that when culture becomes the catch-all explanation for everything that goes awry in non-Western societies or minority cultural groups, while remaining an invisible force elsewhere, something has gone wrong with the use of the term."

Something indeed has gone wrong with the use of this term. Yet, though I am sympathetic to Phillips' critique of culture, I am not of the mind that diluting the notion of culture will in fact fundamentally resolve the problems underlying a liberal approach to the politics of identity/difference. This is because the problem is not simply that culture has become a catch-all category, but that the operations and effects of power are obscured. Diluting the significance of culture may well make sense in some instances, but this cannot be a general rule in principle, for the weight of culture will vary, culture may well be an expression or symptom of a political problem, and it also might be a site of mobilization and resistance. This cannot be pre-determined for all groups and in all contexts. Nor can it be assumed that culture is the primary way of socially identifying difference, or, conversely, that culture is simply part of a long list of discrete objects of difference, for it is given meaning through interactions with other modes of difference. As such, it is not possible to simply shelve the relevance of culture; nor can culture be centred at the cost of neglecting other formations of difference.

My argument, therefore, is not simply that the significance of culture should be weighted differently (Phillips) or revised to become more self-directive, fluid, and heterogeneous (Benhabib, Tully), but that it is necessary to analyze difference from a position that does not assume the primacy of culture or, conversely, the dismissal of culture, and that situates specific cultural practices in their relevant relations of power. This requires more critical reflection about why and how culture gives meaning to, and gains meaning from, many sites of difference. As Lisa Wedeen (2002, 720) notes, since culture is a way of looking at the world rather than an object with essential traits, it is important to take into account "how symbols operate in practice, why meanings generate action, and why actions produce meaning, when they do." In particular, it is necessary to contextualize the historical, legal, political, symbolic, and personal significance of culture, to consider how meanings of culture change even when recognized in positive ways, to approach culture as only one dimension of the politics of identity/difference, and to do so with a critical eye on how and why one mode of difference gains specific meaning in relation to other modes of difference. To do this, I turn my attention to the politics of meaning-making.

2
The Politics of Meaning-Making

An analytic shift from the politics of culture to that of meaning-making changes the kinds of questions asked in the study of identity/difference politics. Broadly, liberal multicultural theories tend to be preoccupied with three general questions: Why should culture be respected by the state? How do 'we' affirm diverse cultures without undermining 'our' social/national unity and the authority of the state? What are the limits to this accommodation? These are important questions from a liberal multicultural perspective in which the goal is to promote inclusion and draw new lines regarding the extent and limits of state and societal tolerance. A critical study of the politics of meaning-making is premised on questions that diverge from those posed by liberal multiculturalists. They are as follows: How are meanings of difference constituted relationally through discourse (historically, institutionally, and practically)? How do the forces of power constitute subjects differently and differentially, why, and with what effects? How are meanings of difference constituted in different historical social contexts, and how do these meanings constitute social-political arrangements? How can penalizing and privileging meanings of difference be disrupted?

The Study of Meaning-Making
Meaning-making is a context-specific socio-historical process that generates and inhibits signs of difference. The study of signs, or semiotics, as developed by anthropologists and cultural studies scholars, examines how a representation comes to stand for something else through modes of knowledge, discourse, and social relations. As anthropologist Clifford Geertz (1973, 91) states, the symbol or sign is "any object, act, event, quality, or relation which serves as a vehicle for a conception – the conception being the symbol's 'meaning.'" Although anything (including behaviour, language, names, and

material objects) can be a sign when it is interpreted to have meaning, not all significations are granted equal force or authority in their meaning.

This idea that some signs have more potency than others – that representation is intimately linked to power – has been richly explored by members of the Centre for Contemporary Cultural Studies (CCCS) at the University of Birmingham under the direction of Stuart Hall (the centre was closed down in 2002). They conceptualized representation not in the institutional sense that is centrally entertained in political science (as the number and type of representatives in legislatures), but in terms of cultural context, agency, identity, and the body. Through the lens of semiotics, the relationship between a wide range of representations was studied, including interwoven social articulations of culture, gender, sexuality, disability/ability, class, racialization, and ethnicity. Scholarship from the CCCS was especially effective in reframing identity beyond ethnicity and geography by exploring ways to destabilize, dereify, and denaturalize a broad range of what proved to be socio-historically produced signs.

Drawing from the field of semiotics, I develop an analytic approach that redirects the study of identity/difference politics to decode, demystify, and explain standing representations of difference. To enact this power-driven approach, I deploy accounts of meaning-making. These accounts deconstruct the processes and conditions in which meanings of difference make and mark subjects in penalizing and privileging ways. Where I use the terminology of "an account" or "an account of meaning-making," I refer directly to this definition. Since signs of difference are not fixed or autonomous but transformable and transformative, this analysis contextualizes how signs of difference are shaped by, and are generative of, vehicles of power. In this chapter, I spell out the analytic work of deconstructing meaning-making to identify what it can illuminate about the production of difference and how it (re)formulates the study of identity/difference politics.

Accounts of Meaning-Making: Deconstructing Differences

An account of meaning-making starts from a social constructivist premise that assertions about differences – which may appear to be apparent, natural, universal, sometimes permanent, and unquestionable – are generated socially and historically through systems of signification. This form of analysis critically examines the social and rhetorical contexts in which a meaning is constructed by author, text, culture, and interpreter. Judith Butler (1995, 49) notes that the purpose of such deconstruction is "not to negate or dismiss, but to call into question and, perhaps most importantly, to open up a term, like the subject, to a reusage of redeployment that previously has not been authorized." "The 'de-' of deconstruction," as Jacques Derrida (1988, 147) remarks, "signifies not the demolition of what is constructing itself, but rather what remains to be thought beyond the constructivist or destructionist scheme."

As a device of deconstruction, an account of meaning-making illuminates the following points about the production and operationalization of difference. First, it reveals the contingency, variability, and contested character of subject formation. It does so by exposing the philosophical and linguistic assumptions made about difference. Even when some modes of representation create profound forms of identification that appear to be ahistorical and unquestionable in that they are experientially real and defining for subjects, an account of meaning-making unveils how interpretations of difference change over time and space, and how these engender positive and/or injurious representations of subjecthood. An account of meaning-making explicitly calls into question the representational processes that construct difference, with the intent of deconstructing the discourses that give authority and legitimacy to that particular mode of difference.

Second, accounts of meaning-making illuminate why and how context matters. Meaning-making is an everyday practice that occurs in every sphere of life; it is both intentionally and unintentionally operationalized; rooted in the past, it is also new and emerging; and it is practised both by subjects signified as dominant and subordinate. It is therefore necessary to contextualize specific meanings of difference so as to assess the scope, force, and efficacy of particular signs of difference and to simultaneously contextualize how the structures amid which these signs emerge function in privileging and penalizing ways. James Johnson (2000, 409) describes the scope of a sign as its range of social contexts, the force of a sign as its centrality or marginality in the lives of relevant actors, and the efficacy of a sign as the scope actors attribute to it. The parameters of a pertinent context can be illuminated by analyzing the scope, force, and efficacy of a sign of difference. I seek to critically analyze power-generated signs of difference in their particular contexts as productions of power, with power conceptualized in Foucauldian terms as a force that entails both self-generated and imposed meanings. To be clear, I do not claim that difference is formed only by imposing meanings or that self-understandings of one's identity are simply about intense struggles concerning power; on the contrary, meaning-making processes do not all have the same intensity, and nor is power always about struggle. Nor am I arguing that representations of difference are void of any real meaning. Instead, I mobilize accounts of meaning-making not to empty meanings, but to situate them in contexts of power.

Third, this deconstructive tool sheds light on the social nature of subject formation with difference as a key dimension through which understandings of self and understandings of others are constituted on an individual, group, and institutional level. Whether an individual or set of individuals takes an account of its own self-directed meanings, these are always socially generated and socially interpreted. Butler understands this process of accounting for oneself as an act that is made possible only in relation to somebody else, such that the 'external' regimes of knowledge are always beyond simply the 'me.' This is why, for Butler (2005, 36), "No account takes place outside the structure of address, even if the addressee remains implicit, unnamed, anonymous, and unspecified." She (Butler 2005, 21) says, "An account of oneself is always given to another, whether conjured or existing, and this establishes the scene of address as a more primary ethical relation than a reflexive effort to give an account of oneself. Moreover, the very terms by which we give an account, by which we make ourselves intelligible to ourselves and to others, are not of our making. They are social in character, and they establish social norms, a domain of unfreedom and substitutability within which our 'singular' stories are told." Moreover, Butler continues, only through contestation can the self possibly appear. In other words, the 'I' becomes an 'I' only so long as there is no singular story of origin or universal regime of truth. Thus, societal norms are created and recreated in relation to the self or individual, and subjects are invested in identifying with a specific set of social norms precisely because they appear through these norms. Subjectivity, therefore, is the product of meaning-making processes and constitutive of power. Accordingly, the conditions under which an account of oneself is possible lie beyond the control of the self and are subject to change, although the self and others shape these conditions. Indeed, there are occasions in which an account feels forced or demanded (Narayan 1997). Given this, because meanings of self-difference arise and are transformed in social contexts, it is important to examine how meanings are produced and are also constitutive of penalty and privilege at the individual, group, and structural level.

Finally, critical accounts of meaning-making show that, because difference is socially interpreted rather than naturally assigned, it is always subject to reinterpretation and alternative *kinds* of interpretations. This critical-hermeneutical dimension of taking accounts of meaning-making is not centrally directed toward self-clarification or the realization of one's own authenticity; nor is it dependent on a fused horizon of meanings. Although self-clarification and self-realization are not irrelevant aspects of an interpretative analysis, my approach draws attention to the relationship between two particular dimensions of difference: how and why a particular meaning is interpreted as it is in a particular socio-historical context (as, for instance, in the meaning of the term "gay") and, simultaneously, how it is operationalized in that context through systems of meaning-making (such as heteronormative and gender systems) and how those systems are shaped by the meanings they produce. An account of meaning-making therefore situates a specified meaning in its context and evaluates how this context generates meanings of difference, and simultaneously, how it is also shaped by the production of this difference.

Importantly, the deconstruction of meaning-making does not ever fully capture circulating meanings of difference, not least because it is possible to decipher only that which is intelligible. Accounts of meaning-making can never *fully* translate all nuances of a historical mode of representation because these can never capture all the social norms that infiltrate meanings, all the circumstances and modes of communication that shape a meaning, and all the ways in which a sign is interpreted and received by variously situated historical interpreters of difference. In this sense, an inherent blindness exists in the study of difference. Accounts of meaning-making are themselves practices of deconstructing and articulating difference that are not outside the social context in which they perform. In this sense, there is no ideal or neutral account of meaning-making. However, this mode of analysis and critique is specific about particular interpretations of difference and situates these interpretations in relational, spatial, historical, and political contexts. It is this radical contextualization that gives political saliency to accounts of meaning-making.

Revising Concepts and Identifying New Avenues of Analysis
The study of how meanings of difference are produced both alters some key concepts in the field of identity/difference politics and opens up avenues of exploration that are largely ignored or undertheorized in liberal multicultural thought. In this section, I identify some of these changes and new avenues, specifically in relation to concepts of authenticity, community, hybridity, essentialism and anti-essentialism, intersectionality, and a matrix of meaning-making.

Authenticity and Meaning-Making

The idea of authenticity has been a feature of some theories of identity/difference politics, so much so that authenticity sometimes seems to be the ideal standard of emancipation. Charles Taylor (1994b, 29-30), for instance, suggests there is an inner moral voice and original way of being, and that recognition of this authenticity is crucial to the politics of difference. Authenticity, Taylor (1991, 66) contends, constitutes how individuals resist the demands of conformity so that they can truly discover and become themselves, define themselves in dialogue, and be open to horizons of significance. For Taylor, recognition and authenticity are entwined sources of identity. The latter is necessary for the self in order to be genuinely recognized; at the same time, recognition must be socially valued so that we can come to know our authentic selves. Taylor (1991, 29, emphasis added) suggests that, by creating a context in which my difference is socially recognized, I can be "true to my own *originality* and that is something only I can articulate and discover. In articulating it, I am also defining myself." Taylor's theory suggests that an ideal process of meaning-making would therefore be one that is self-directed (on an individual and group level) in a free although not asocial way, so as to (re)discover authenticity.

Yet, precisely because self-directed meanings are socially and dialogically constituted, there is no one singular or uniform authentic individual or group identity to be understood. In the act of recognition, the recognizer acknowledges who she is and who the other/Other is *relationally*, and because who she is and who the other/Other is varies according to what specific relations of difference are at play, there is no singular original version of the self or the other/Other. Indeed, pre-political, recoverable, or original – authentic – conceptions of identity are not possible because there is no fixed, universal, or singular meaning of who we already and really are. As such, authenticity cannot serve as a political basis for imagining an ideal process of subject formation or for conceptualizing identity/difference. To construct authenticity as an end goal is to assume that, in some time and space, difference could exist without power. But, precisely because meanings about difference are in a constant state of flux as a consequence of power, meanings of authenticity are also changeable.

Of course, it is possible to mark what was and what is recognizable about an identity before or after a historical moment. Indeed, as Linda Tuhiwai Smith (1999, 73) holds, authenticity is a useful tool to mark the historical difference between pre- and post-colonial contexts: "[Authenticity is an important idea to decolonization] as a form of articulating what it meant to be dehumanized by colonization; and, second, for reorganizing 'national consciousness' in the struggles for decolonization ... It does appeal to an idealized past when there was no colonizer, to our strengths in surviving thus far, to our language as an uninterrupted link to our histories, to the ownership of our lands, to our own life and death, to a sense of balance among ourselves and with the environment, to our authentic selves." Authenticity is, in this sense, a *reminder* of the past and of how the past shapes the present, rather than a stable, fixed, and romanticized original way of being. Authenticity tends to assume that the pre-colonial subject was somehow free of the repressive and productive forces of power, whereas studies show that in some places, pre-colonial modes of patriarchy and class privilege produced and organized subjectivity and subjection (Bannerji, Mojab, and Whitehead 2001; Chakravarti 2001). The idea of recovering an original way of being is especially troubled, continues Smith (1999, 74), because it has come to be used to determine who is purely the Other, who is really worth saving, and who is free of Western contamination.

Identities do not, therefore, come into being by returning to an earlier and more innocent moment in time or space. Rather, accounts of meaning-making show that specific historical semiotic practices and social meanings were altered and/or destroyed, how this history shapes present-day social relations, and how subjects affected by these actions reimagine those practices and structures. The changeability of our sense of self (as an individual or as a member of social groups) does not mean that subjects are not uniquely constituted or that agents do not understand their own identities to be distinct. Nor does it mean that subjects do not experience their social identities and differences as real; there is a real 'me' who exists in *specific* contexts and relations, such that 'I' can appeal to *particular* audiences and locate myself in *particular* arrangements of power. But a deconstructive analysis shows that representations of the self are in a permanent state of becoming and therefore are not frozen in time or space.

THEORIZING COMMUNITIES
Accounts of meaning-making also illuminate that communities are both products and sites of meaning-making. This analytic device specifically opens up ways to question representations of community that arise both inside and outside the bounds of that collectivity. It also describes and explains the shared histories and modes of oppositional consciousness that designate

particular individuals and groups as members of a particular community. For example, it helps to examine how politically shared histories of attempted assimilation, eradication, and exclusion give rise to representations of 'an indigenous community' at the same time that it deconstructs the idea that this 'community' is homogeneous.

Communities are important social points of contact for people and are therefore analytically significant to understanding any social phenomenon related to the politics of identity/difference. As well as being sites of exclusion, discipline, and struggle, as Shane Phelan (1994, 87-88) observes, depending on the specific practices and composition of a community and one's relationship to those practices and people, communities can also insulate subordinated individuals and groups from hostility: they can break and/or ease invisibility by providing a sense of home and belonging; they can help members interpret their lives; and they can serve as a base for political mobilization. Membership in a community can provide a sense of belonging, even when individuals are not fully accepted by all members of that community or when they have membership in more than one community. However, signifiers that define a community shift and have varying intensities. In particular, the values, norms, and beliefs of subjects within a community can and do change according to spatial cohesion, consensus, shared knowledge, levels of familiarity, interest, commitment levels, space and time, ideology, and the function a community plays in one's life. Thus, communities are marked by all sorts of meanings – both internally and externally generated meanings – but these are contingently formed, not permanent or fixed. Indeed, communities become meaningful to us when we are able to negotiate what we will have in common, what we will share, and how we will share it, rather than through fixed notions and criteria of what we have in common (Phelan 1994, 95).

By deconstructing the vehicles of power that give shape to a specific characterization of a community, the analyst can reach a better understanding of how power produces these meanings and with what effect for socio-political relations. More specifically, the analyst can examine why some characterizations of a community are constituted as preferable to others, who makes these meanings authoritative, how and why communities are socially and hierarchically differentiated from one another, and what is at stake for community members when making claims of difference. The study of meaning-making does not take as its subject matter only those communities that are marked by homogeneity and boundedness or, conversely, heterogeneity and fluidity. Rather, accounts of meaning-making are useful in analyzing the significance of particular meanings and how these impact people's lives, regardless of whether a community is deemed to be a fragmented and amorphous hybrid entity, a tightly knit collectivity, or somewhere in between in which there are relatively porous but shared systems of meaning-making.

Hybrid Processes of Meaning-Making

Accounts of meaning-making also open up an analytic space to explore how representations of difference are constituted and reconstituted through modes of hybridity. Homi Bhabha (1994, 4) conceptualizes hybridity in terms of the "liminal space," the sites "in-between the designations of identity," and the "connective tissue that constructs the difference between upper and lower, black and white." He describes this liminal space as the third space, the interstitial passage between fixed identities that "entertains difference without an assumed or imposed hierarchy." This passage is, according to Bhabha (1994, 38), "the cutting edge [site of] translation and negotiation" because it is radically heterogeneous, discontinuous, and in a permanent state of flux. For Bhabha, hybridity is "an active moment of challenge and resistance against a dominant cultural power" (R.J.C. Young 1995, 23), in which colonial authority loses its grip on defining the Othered as contact between native and colonial cultures challenges the dominance of a colonial culture and its very purity.

An analysis of the dynamics between modes of difference reveals that no identity is pure, for all criss-cross *in various degrees*. Given this, a hybrid representation of difference does not stand in contrast to a pure one, for all differences are cross-pollinated to some extent. Some representations of difference may be more stable in that they conform to a particular normalized way of understanding that difference, but these too are constituted by intricate processes of intrusion and fusion. This idea of crossing entrenched boundaries of difference is an important aspect of identity/difference theorizing. Whereas liberal multiculturalists say little of such boundary crossing, it is taken up by other theorists of identity/difference politics, including Chicana lesbian feminist Gloria Anzaldúa. She presents the metaphor of borderlands as a way to address hybridity. The borders, Anzaldúa (1999, 25) states, depict a dividing line, "a narrow strip along a steep edge. A borderland is a vague and undetermined place created by the emotional residue of an unnatural boundary. It is in a constant state of transition." Anzaldúa is not referring solely to the geopolitical borderland of the US and Mexico but also to the linguistic, psychological, sexual, and spiritual borderlands in which the presence of two or more cultures whose edges come together form representations of a *mestiza* or hybrid identity. In the borderland a process of cross-pollination occurs, in which the pillars of mestiza are a historical and dynamic mixing of blood, cultural experiences, sexualities, and languages.

It may seem that, by punctuating mestiza with the mixing of blood, An-zaldúa is conceptualizing identities in terms of pure and impure blood. However, in *Borderlands/La Frontera* (1999), she provides a history of pollina-tion between racialized groups – rather than imagining miscegenation out of biological racial groups – that have come to constitute Hispanic, Chicano, and Mexican American identities. In this regard, she recognizes that identities are historically and culturally constituted and always mixing. Anzaldúa (1999, 103) herself is what she calls the embodiment or cross-breeding of opposite qualities (male and female, homo and hetero, Chicana and American), which come together to produce her mestiza voice. The multiplicity of a mestiza identity may signal a failure to build an integrated identity in the liberal sense, but it reflects actual socio-political realities of many subjects, wherein rep-resentations of difference are neither oppositionally one thing nor the other. Moreover, this 'incompleteness' does not render marginalized identities to inaction, for signifiers of hybridity are not unique in their experiences of ambiguity, complexity, and fluidity; nor should they be understood as such, for this merely reinscribes the idea that a pure identity stands in contrast to a hybrid one.

While there is a danger that hybrid forms of difference themselves become uniformly represented (Beltran 2004), accounts of hybridization do not as-sume that hybridity equals ambiguity; rather, one can ascertain how far a particular hybrid process of meaning-making moves from a particular char-acterization of pure identity and how this distance affects the ways in which difference is understood by the self and others. Katya Gibel Azoulay (1997, 5), for example, argues that hybridity can produce positive feelings of belonging, not simply negative representations of ambiguity. As a subject who self-signifies as a Jewish and black woman, Azoulay is especially interested in representations of interethnic and interracial identity. Within the social context of the US and her family genealogy, Azoulay describes her subjectivity by identifying the ways in which her physical appearance signifies her as black while erasing her Jewishness, and the simultaneous cumulative impact of anti-Semitism among blacks and racism from white Jews. As well, she consid-ers how the markers of difference attached to her sons, one of whom passes as white and one who does not, shape her identity. Azoulay (1997, 1-28) situates these representations of difference in the historical contexts of the Holocaust, the colonization of the West Indies (where her father was born), slavery in the US, and ongoing racism and anti-Semitism in the US. She notes that these fused identities do not constitute her identity as ambivalent. From her self-directed and situated standpoint, Azoulay (1997, 32, emphasis in original) says that her identity "encompasses and incorporates the cognitive and experiential fact of *being and belonging* in various subject positions marked by social boundaries."

In sum, hybridity does not necessarily produce an ambiguous form of identification when two or more inscriptions of identity are grafted together "in a way that makes the same no longer the same, the different no longer simply different" (R.J.C. Young 1995, 26). Accounts of meaning-making processes that produce representations of hybrid difference are important to the study of identity/difference because they disrupt the idea that pure and fixed categories of identity (such as male/female, colonizer/colonized, homo-sexual/heterosexual) actually do exist and because they reveal that, though representations of difference may appear ambiguous, this does not mean that the constituent parts of an identity can be dismissed or that subjects marked by hybridity understand their own identities as ambiguous.

Essentialist, Anti-essentialist, and Strategic Essentialist Meanings

As I remarked earlier, the deconstruction of difference indicates that, because differences both circumscribe various norms and are variedly produced by them, they are infinitely constructed and reconstructed. This position may lead some to conclude that, because the array of differences to be examined is unruly, an essentialist notion of identity is necessary so as to concretize an analysis of complex socio-historical phenomena. Following from this conclu-sion, essentialists argue that constructivist interpretations of identity do not assume enough (because they assume that there is no such thing as a social group); conversely, social constructivists contend that essentialist readings of identity often assume too much (namely that a fixed and permanent social group identity exists). Polarization between essentialist and constructivist approaches to identity/difference suggests an impasse between them.

A benefit of taking an account of meaning-making is that it rejects the terms of this impasse, providing instead a way to critically examine how and why meanings of difference emerge in essentialized, anti-essentialized, or strategically essentialized ways. Rather than simply dismissing essentialist significations as overdetermined or deploying them merely for unqualified political purposes, this tool contextualizes when and why privileging and penalizing signs of difference gain legitimacy. So, for instance, it is not necessary to agree that sexual orientation is natural or socially learned, because the focus is on analyzing the *conditions* in which sexual orientation is given meaning in positive or demeaning ways. Thus, whereas essentialist representations of difference are criticized by those who adopt post-structuralist approaches to identity, and post-structuralism is criticized for denying the existence of almost everything, an account of meaning-making illuminates both essentialized and fluid representations of difference by examining the conditions in which they gain their meaning. This form of analysis leads to a double movement, which Butler (1993, 222) describes as a way to "invoke the category and, hence, provisionally to institute an identity and at the same time to open the category as a site of permanent political contest."

Such a double movement seems to inform Gayatri Chakravorty Spivak's notion of strategic essentialism. This concept has sometimes been misread as licence to essentialize identities for progressive purposes (to make political demands and legal claims regarding inequity and injustice), so much so that Spivak has questioned its phraseology (Danius and Jonsson 1993, 35-36). Yet, in my understanding of strategic essentialism, what is required is a critical account of the socio-historical conditions in which a representation of identity is deployed for a given situation. This contextualization of positionality destabilizes the idea that an identity is ontologically one thing or another, while also situating difference within identifiable social relations to advance what Spivak (1987, 205) calls "a scrupulously visible political interest."

This kind of accounting enables analysts to examine how and when meaning-making processes produce representations of difference that replicate and reinstitute dominant meanings. Uma Narayan (2000), for example, criticizes how Third World cultures become essentialized by seemingly progressive feminists who theorize patriarchy and cultural imperialism from a Western perspective. Lisa Lowe (1996, 71) also shows how "the discourse may remain bound to and overly determined by the logic of the dominant culture" when dominant categories (especially binaries such as white/nonwhite or majority/minority) caricature colonial modes of representation. To counter the logic of dominant overdetermined conceptions of difference, it is therefore necessary to examine the contingency of the foundations of difference. This, as Butler (1995, 47) states, is necessary because the "subject is neither a ground nor a product [of essentialism], but a permanent possibility of a certain resignifying process, one which gets detoured and stalled through mechanisms of power, but which is power's own possibility of being reworked."

One way in which I examine this contingency is to account for the processes that constitute one form of difference *in relation to another*. This form of analysis illuminates that strategic essentialist meanings do not gain relevance by virtue of the necessity to speak about a particular social group; rather, they gain force because specific *relations* of socio-political inequity can be usefully contested by locating one form of difference in relation to another. Accounts of meaning-making deconstruct, for example, why and in what ways the category of woman gains significance in relation to that of man. This analysis would not only show how these two categories are mutually constituted through gendered norms about the body, sexual desire, and the sexual division of labour, but it would demystify the different *kinds* of experiences that arise from these norms (I.M. Young 2005). Woman, in other words, would be socially situated and simultaneously destabilized as a category of difference, revealing the relational differences between women along class, racial, religious, and national vectors, and also the constructed relational nature of the binary-based (man/woman) gender system. Accounts of the processes that produce varied meanings of womanhood would not automatically legitimize or delegitimize essentialist meanings of "woman": rather, they would contextualize these, thereby disrupting the idea that there is a universal, natural, or singular way to characterize "woman" as a social category.

A MATRIX OF MEANING-MAKING

Accounts of meaning-making also provide a way to examine the interactive relationships between systems of meaning-making. This kind of interactive approach has been developed by feminists, often under the rubric of intersectionality. Although there is no single unified feminist method of intersectionality, it can be understood as a research paradigm as well as a theoretical-normative argument (Hancock 2007b, 63). Broadly, intersectionality refers to "the complex, irreducible, varied, and variable effects which ensue when multiple axes of differentiation – economic, political, cultural, psychic, subjective and experiential – intersect in historically specific contexts. The concept emphasizes that different dimensions of social life cannot be separated out into discrete and pure strands" (Brah and Phoenix 2004, 76). Since "intersectionality" is a contested term and other terms are used, I refer to this broad body of work as a form of "intersectional-type" analysis.[1] An intersectional-type approach generates important epistemological insights, methodological developments, and new interpretative frameworks that illuminate social phenomena related to oppression (Collins 2000, 252).

Working from theoretical developments in intersectional-type scholarship, particularly Patricia Hill Collins' notion of the matrix of domination, I develop the idea that meaning-making constitutes and operates in a matrix, in which multifarious manifestations of difference are mutually constituted and organized. Drawing on bell hooks' (1989, 175) notion of a politics of domination, Collins (1990, 222) uses the matrix concept to describe and explain how distinctive systems of oppression are "part of one overarching structure of domination." For Collins (1990, 222), the matrix of domination "expands the focus of analysis from merely describing the similarities and differences" between systems of oppressions and domination by giving "greater attention to how they interconnect."[2] Although Collins (1990, 225-26; 2000, 245) is interested in examining the axes of race, class, gender, and sexuality that are experienced by black women in the US, she also recognizes that other groups may encounter different intersections, such as citizenship status or age. Accordingly, there is "considerable variability ... from one matrix of domination to the next as to how oppression and activism will be organized" (Collins 2000, 228).

Collins (1990, 227) notes that the matrix of domination operates and is resisted on multiple levels, including "the level of personal biography; the group or community level of the cultural context created by race, class, and gender; and the systemic level of social institutions." With respect to the first level, Collins notes that each individual has a unique personal biography and that, as a consequence, no two individuals occupy the same social experiences or consciousness. On the second level, that of cultural context, an individual's biography is rooted in multiple identifiable histories, geographic locations, social institutions, forms of knowledge, and standards used to evaluate thought and behaviour. On the third level, of social institutions, domination also operates and is resisted in schools, churches, the media, and other formal organizations. An analysis of all three levels puts the idea of an authentic identity into question, specifically because meanings of authenticity will vary according to context. As Collins (2000, 274) observes, domination is "an intangible entity that circulates within a particular matrix of domination and to which individuals stand in varying relationships."

Building on Collins' analysis, I develop her concept into a matrix of meaning-making as a way to foreground the productive dimensions of power. Although Collins (2000, 274-88) too draws on a Foucauldian conception of power in that she addresses individual and group agency, resistance, and interpersonal power, and she locates these aspects to dominating power, by foregrounding the productive forces of power, I emphasize the value of analyzing how *processes* of meaning-making generate difference interactively, not solely in dominating ways but in *productive* ways as well. A power-driven analysis of a matrix of meaning-making enriches the study of identity/difference politics in the following ways. First, it attends more accurately to the complexities of difference that structure everyone's lives. It does so by conceptualizing identities (including, but not exclusively, culture) in the context of those markers of difference that are so salient to this strand of feminist theory – namely, race, class, and gender. An intersectional-type approach has provided a deeper and more complicated understanding of the interactions between race, class, and gender, specifically to show that no form of difference stands alone. It could be extended to analyze the interactions between culture, race, class, and gender because everyone's subjectivity is variedly and simultaneously culturalized, racialized, gendered, and located within class structures. As a result, it is important to examine the variations and how these are produced through the interactions between systems of meaning-making.

At the same time, this intersectional-type approach goes beyond what Patricia Monture (2007, 199) calls the race-class-gender trinity, in which some categories of difference are privileged over others. Although much has been learned about difference from the study of race-class-gender, especially in terms of the lived experiences and social locations of marginalized non-white women, intersectionality is not a content-based specialization that simply incorporates previously ignored and excluded populations into pre-existing frameworks. Rather, it is a research approach that can be applied beyond the study of non-white women (Hancock 2007a, 2007b). This is exemplified through the analysis of interactions between systems of race, gender, class, and sexuality (Fogg-Davis 2006), disability, sexuality, and gendering (D'aoust 1999; Garland-Thomson 2002; Shuttleworth 2001), disability, race, culture, and ethnicity (Jakubowicz and Meekosha 2003; Vernon 1999), and racialization, gendering, and sexuality (Harper et al. 1997; Hawley 2001).

The second benefit of undertaking a deconstructive analysis of a matrix of meaning-making is that it focuses on the *processes* of differentiation rather than on categories of difference. Though at times, concepts such as race or gender are used interchangeably with those of racialization and gendering, the study of categories does not perform the same analytic work as that of socio-historical processes of differentiation. Distinguishing categories from processes makes it possible to see that categories of difference are the products of processes of differentiation and that they are also generative of meanings of difference. This distinction between processes and categories is especially important because it helps to avoid the tendency of declaring that an identity is socially constructed but subsequently treating that identity as if it had a biological and/or natural essence.

Third, while an account of a matrix of meaning-making assumes that one mode of difference functions through others, it does not conflate them. To put it differently, plural processes of meaning-making interact with one another, but they are not reducible to one another. Making a claim, for instance, about the oppression of a black woman is not another way of saying that she suffers from a triple oppression because she is a black person, a woman, and a working-class subject, or that to be black or a woman is another way of being working class (Yuval-Davis 2006, 195, 200). To treat all identities alike in content and form is to conflate positions, identities, and values (Anthias 1998, 2001; Anthias and Yuval-Davis 1983, 1992; Yuval-Davis 2006). Accordingly, it is important to examine how the content and form of one kind of meaning-making process interacts with others, and how these also differ from another.

Fourth, and following from the above point, accounts of a matrix of meaning-making attend to the variation among social collectivities that arises in historically constituted processes of meaning-making. Precisely because various representations of difference are produced through diverse interactions, subjects not only experience social categories differently but the shape of those categories is also wide-ranging because vehicles of power operate variously. Accordingly, not all subjects marked as women of colour or as indigenous women, for example, experience processes of gendering and racialization in the same way, and processes of gendering and racialization do not universally perform in the same way for all non-white women. Therefore, though it is important to distinguish how modern industrialized Western discourses consolidate distinctive forms of racial, masculinist, and bourgeois power (Brown 1997, 88), an analysis is also needed of how historically specific formations of racialization, gendering, and class are produced. This is because racialization, gendering, and class differentiation do not operate in the same way across time and space.

Fifth, a critical analysis of a matrix of meaning-making attends to the various levels of social life to which Collins refers, namely, the personal, the group, and the systemic. Other feminists formulate these levels in additional terms. Floya Anthias and Nira Yuval-Davis, for instance, refer to organizational, intersubjective, experiential, and representational social divisions (Anthias 1998; Anthias and Yuval-Davis 1983, 1992; Yuval-Davis 2006). Regardless of how these levels of analysis are conceptualized, the key point is that a matrix of meaning-making is not only constituted by various interactions between systems of meaning-making, but that these interactions function on multiple levels of human experience and that these levels are linked. The level of personal biography is not, for example, isolated from the group or systemic level. A deconstructive analysis of these linkages seeks to describe and explain how self-directed meanings of difference are produced by circulating discourses in tandem with the production of other-directed meanings.

Sixth, since *all* social differences, including those signified as privileged, are constituted through multiple interactive systems of meaning-making, the study of matrices of meaning-making reveals differing forms and degrees of penalty and privilege. Any identity is situated within a historically specific matrix of meaning-making, whereby "each individual derives varying amounts of penalty and privilege from the multiple systems of oppression which frame everyone's lives" (Collins 1990, 229). This variation does not, however, mean that subjects are equally or similarly dominant or Othered; such a claim would be tantamount to arguing that difference does not matter (Razack 1998, 161). The relativity of penalty and privilege does not negate the fact that pronounced inequalities arise from these roles and in specific social sites, for though an individual may be victimizer in one context, this does not cancel out the fact that she is victimized in another, and vice versa. Accordingly, despite the ways in which we may all experience degrees of dominance and subordination, there is political efficacy in examining how power *specifically* operates to structure different socio-political arrangements. Given this, it is necessary to shift from a binary conception of difference to a more complex understanding of it, one recognizing that individuals and groups do not represent either the power to govern or the state of being governed but, rather, that the context determines the degree and form of social difference at play.

Finally, an account of a matrix of meaning-making provides a way to examine how and why one form of difference is implicated in the meanings of other forms of difference. This relation of implication arises because representations of subjectivity and subjection are situated in a myriad of differentiating schemes that variously privilege and penalize people, and because the privilege assigned to them is fundamentally tied to the concomitant disadvantage of others, and vice versa. People are not therefore simply either dominant or subordinate: rather, subjects embody *relative* representations of dominance and subordination. On the basis of this relativity, Sherene Razack (1998, 10) calls for an account of which voices are given legitimacy, how they are heard and re- or misinterpreted, and by whom, and of the interest we protect in the knowledge we have of Others. The purpose, Razack (1998, 8, 10, 170) argues, of directing our efforts to the conditions of communication and knowledge production is to communicate across social hierarchies, disturb relations of domination, and challenge "hegemonic ways of seeing through which subjects make themselves dominant." For Razack (1998, 159, emphasis in original), we must begin to "recognize how we are *implicated* in the subordination of other[s]." Accounts of a matrix of meaning-making can be deployed to elucidate this condition of being implicated in structures of difference and to identify relations of accountability.

Deploying Accounts of Meaning-Making

In the rest of this book, I return to these above concepts and theoretical insights to illuminate how the historical, contingent dimensions of difference can be better grasped when the focus shifts from the liberal multicultural emphasis on culture to the vehicles of power that determine relations of difference. The following three chapters provide accounts of how technologies of power operationalize and produce varied social relations of difference through matrices of meaning-making composed of norms of whiteness, ableism, heterosexuality and desire, gender, oralism, and racialization. I examine state-prescribed discourses of differentiation, such as immigration policy and law, as well as contexts in which subjects marked by marginality make meanings. As well as questioning which immigrants analysts are referring to in the study of identity/difference politics, I investigate aspects of difference typically ignored in liberal multicultural thought, namely, those that signify Deaf identities, trans-sexuality, and the relational differences between subjects marked as non-white women. Each of these chapters seeks to show that accounts of meaning-making complicate knowledge about identity/difference politics by pointing toward research, explanations, and questions that are currently unexplored or ignored when culture is narrowly conceived and prioritized over other sites of difference.

3
Rethinking Accounts of the 'Immigrant'

In September 2005, Bahudur Singh Bhalru, a legal immigrant in Canada, was deported to India, his country of origin. The events leading to his deportation started in 2001, when Bhalru and Sukvir Singh Khosa killed a pedestrian, Irene Thorpe, in Richmond, British Columbia, while street racing. Both men were convicted of criminal negligence causing death, and in February 2003, the BC Supreme Court ruled that the two men should serve two-year conditional sentences, after which time they would have to perform 240 hours of community service with the local police forces, and be on probation for three years and barred from driving for five years. The family of Irene Thorpe and the Attorney General of British Columbia (BC) were dissatisfied with the ruling. Subsequently the case was taken to the BC Court of Appeal, which rejected the Crown's appeal of the Supreme Court decision. In the same year, the Immigration and Refugee Board issued a deportation order, and a two-to-one decision was made to deport both convicted men in April of 2003. The lawyers of the two men appealed to the Federal Court of Appeal on the grounds that returning to India was unsafe for them and that they were Canadians. In September 2005, after his application was dismissed, Bhalru was deported to India. The Federal Court of Appeal made a decision to allow Khosa to remain in Canada, and in October 2007 the Supreme Court of Canada agreed to hear his deportation order appeal. The Supreme Court heard the appeal in February 2007, and a judgment is being awaited.

Importantly, the liberal legal mode of distinguishing between victim (Irene Thorpe and her family) and perpetrator (Bhalru and Khosa) served to protect the rights of those injured and to ensure, on some level at least, responsibility for the injury caused by the latter. At the same time, the initial conviction was controversial on two fronts: first, the family of Irene Thorpe – supported by some public opinion – wanted a stronger sentence (10 years in prison is the maximum), and second, the decision to deport the two criminals, rather than keep them in Canada and have them subject to a Canadian system of justice, was seen as racist. With regard to this latter controversy, the deportation of a Canadian immigrant back to 'his country' raised questions about the ways in which some immigrants are marked as foreigners even when they have legal status in Canada and identify as Canadian. Specifically, Bhalru was constructed as non-Canadian, as someone who did not respect 'our' Canadian laws, as an alien who came from and belonged somewhere else and should therefore be sent back to his own country. His crime, it was argued by the Minister of Citizenship and Immigration Canada at the Supreme Court level, would justify his removal from the Canadian nation and the domain of Canadian citizenship because he violated the rules set for immigrants. Although the legal distinctions between resident and citizen inevitably produce differences in status, deportation affects those subjects who are deemed to be outsiders, from somewhere else. This is because (specific) immigrants are signified as subjects who are never really fully Canadian but foreigners within 'our' midst.

In this chapter, I examine some of the contexts in which meanings about the foreign immigrant are constructed and what is at stake for the state in regulating meanings of the desirable and undesirable immigrant. In the case of Bhalru, what was at stake for the Canadian state was the status and meaning of 'our culture,' namely, Canadian culture, into which immigrants from non-Western countries fail to integrate (if they could, they would not break 'our' laws). The response of the state was especially revealing because it acted to discipline the 'unruliness' of immigrants by deporting Bhalru. He was constructed as a criminal immigrant *who should be deported* (as opposed to a criminal who should be jailed in Canada), revealing that the state regulates and re-entrenches norms of whiteness, nation building, and citizenship through the law. Although the criminality of the actions of Bhalru and Khosa is indeed serious and has been rightly condemned, and the liberal legal model of victim-perpetrator held the perpetrators responsible, the action taken by state agencies to deport Bhalru also served to discipline a non-white immigrant who deviated from the established norms by expelling him from the country and stripping him of immigrant rights. It is precisely this work of established norms that the device of taking accounts of meaning-making deconstructs.

Immigrants and immigration are important to consider in the study of identity/difference not only because they are already centred in theories about social difference, but because state-led immigration practices and policies shape citizenship, belonging, and nation building. My goal in this chapter is not to consider or reconsider ways in which the state should respond to diversity (as neutral or pluralist multiculturalists tend to do). Rather, following Wendy Brown's (1995, 170) argument that the state simultaneously provides some legal protections and engages in the discipline and surveillance of specific subjects, I analyze how immigration policy and law delineate who is deemed a desirable or undesirable potential citizen and why. In particular, I consider how diverse and reductive representations of the immigrant are constituted in privileging and penalizing ways.

My analysis sharply brings into view the complex interactive processes of meaning-making that produce representations of immigrants as strange and strangers, and how these also constitute the 'host' nation as benevolent. This dual process of identity formation produces and reproduces differences between 'them' (the Other/foreigner) and 'us as an us' (the norm/legitimate citizen). Discourses of foreignness are particularly virulent because, as Bonnie Honig (2001, 3) argues, they serve as devices "that give shape to or threaten existing political communities by marking negatively what 'we' are not" and because they also "allow regimes to import from outside (and then, often, to export back to outside) some specific and much-needed but also potentially dangerous virtue, talent, perspective, practice, gift or quality that they cannot provide for themselves." In other words, because foreignness is deemed to be outside of the nation (even when it is exoticized within the nation), it threatens the nation, and in the sense that foreignness defines 'us' as an 'us,' it is also instrumental in (re)founding the nation. In Canada, this has been especially evident in the concurrent ideas that immigrants are invading the borders of the nation and that the country is multicultural and tolerant. Such representations of the host country as benevolent are deeply troubled because they mask over the concrete ways in which Canadian governments have been instrumental in producing conditions of poverty, economic stagnation, and civil war in other countries, all of which contribute to migration patterns from poorer to richer countries.

Immigration practices and laws also have a particular role to play in Canadian nation building because Canada is a settler society in which British and French colonizers expropriated indigenous lands and suppressed indigenous ways of being and knowing, while also depending on immigration to expand the colonial project. Since the control of population inflows is a fundamental feature of the development of the nation, immigration policy and law have been and continue to be significant in determining the boundaries of Canada's political community. As Yasmeen Abu-Laban (1998, 71) says, although not limited to Canada, "the primary purpose of immigration policy is to deny Canadian citizenship to the majority of the world's inhabitants. Thus by its very existence, immigration policy – that is, the regulation of the movement and settlement of people – is about excluding. Immigration policy serves an important function in maintaining an inequitable world system because it involves the denial of citizenship and its attendant rights." Although all immigration practices inherently encompass processes of disjuncture, intermingling, and metamorphosis (hybridity) in that one is uprooted from a context and moves to another, those immigrants who do not conform to the status quo of the new context are directly subject to the denial of substantive citizenship.

To examine the various ways in which immigration policy functions to produce national borders of inclusion and exclusion, and also to produce representations of the 'good immigrant' (a cosmopolitan, adventurous contributor to the economy who replicates existing norms) and the 'bad immigrant' (who is dirty, selfish, backward, dangerous, and a financial drain on the nation), in the following analysis I argue that the limits and extent of state tolerance go beyond considerations of culture. More specifically, I explore how representations of those immigrants who do not easily, or for that matter ever, fit into a particular image of the nation are constructed through modes of normativity related to whiteness, ableism, and heterosexuality. By normativity, I mean the ruling or authoritative standard. I demonstrate that accounts of meaning-making can be put to work to deconstruct how variations of the-immigrant-as-Other are produced in ways that consolidate particular norms. These varied meanings of difference shape distinctions between citizens, potential citizens, partial citizens, and non-citizens (even if subjects have legal status as a resident or citizen), and are thus important to the study of identity/difference politics.

Discourses of whiteness, ableism, and heteronormativity are not typical lenses through which to examine 'the immigrant' in liberal political theory, but I encourage scholars who study the politics of identity/difference not simply to examine the character of groups and their relationship to the state, but to rethink the foundational categories and analytical frameworks that inform their studies. This kind of critical questioning not only challenges the many ways in which difference and dominance are constituted beyond the liberal multicultural scope of culture, but it also enables analysts to deconstruct the *relationship* between discourses that produce and operationalize varied norms of whiteness, colonialism, capitalism, gender, disease, family, disability/ability, and sexuality.

Whiteness and the Making of Settlers, Citizens, and Immigrants

White supremacy, whiteness, and subjects marked as white are not examined in any depth in liberal multicultural theories of identity/difference politics, even though white supremacy is a central organizing ideology of social relations of difference. Immigrants tend to be explicitly referenced in terms of their so-called different cultures, ethnicities, religions, languages, and nationalities (different for whom?). Within these discourses lies an unspoken and implicit assumption that immigrants are marked as non-white. Rosa Baaba Folson notes that, regardless of the length of time they live in Canada or the number of generations they produce there, non-white immigrants tend to be categorized as partial or non-citizens, whereas immigrants marked as white quickly become represented as natural citizens. In these representations, Folson (2004, 30) states, a "common notion of an immigrant is a non-white person, who is professionally challenged and speaks with an accent," and who has "a particular labour-market location." Whiteness thus haunts multiculturalism. Even when non-white immigrants gain legal citizenship status, they are still often characterized as immigrant foreigners.

The distinction between citizen and immigrant overlaps with that of settler and immigrant, although these do not map onto each other perfectly either. In Canada, some citizens are not settlers but the original people. As well, both immigrants and citizens can be settlers, although each kind of settler has a different relationship to the state and the nation. In particular, an important distinction exists between the white European settlers and more recent newcomers. Settlement that was historically driven by colonial goals of expanding the domain of specific white groups is distinct from more recent immigration that serves the ongoing neo-colonial model of expansion and more systematically includes non-white peoples. In modern terms, then, the settler is specifically one who arrives in the land of other people and takes claim of that land as 'new land' or a colony. Immigrants (whether white or non-white) are also settlers in that they also occupy land that has not been ceded or justly claimed by the state. Under Canadian law (rather than indigenous law), immigrants are deemd to be aliens who intend to make the country their domicile and are assigned the status of lawful permanent residents. Both kinds of settlers are implicated in the conditions that structure indigenous and non-indigenous relations (Lawrence and Dua 2005), although, importantly, in disproportionate and different ways. These differences exist because of the structural privilege of whiteness.

Significant legal, social, and material implications arise from having the status of a citizen or an immigrant (or refugee or illegal migrant), but all citizens, settlers, and immigrants are *subject* to power. "Citizens and subjects," comments Barbara Cruikshank (1999, 20, 22), "are not opposites ... Citizens are made and therefore subject to power even when they become citizens." Citizens are both subject to the authority of another and authors of their own actions; and those viewed as subjects are not signified *only* through constraining forms of power, because they also have agency to make meanings. In this sense, Cruikshank continues, the citizen is not the antithesis of the subject; rather, "although democratic citizens are formally free, their freedom is a condition of the operationalization of power." Accordingly, it is necessary to examine "how power works to make subjects out of citizens and citizens out of subjects."

Through accounts of the meaning-making processes that produce representations of the settler and the immigrant, in this section I explore how whiteness works to make subjects out of citizens and citizens out of subjects. By contextualizing the historical and varied processes in which some subjects benefit from whiteness and all are produced by it, I examine how the white Norm constructs itself by devaluing the non-white Other. I specifically take account of two trajectories of whiteness: the historical rivalry between white European settlers for control and ownership of territory, and the expropriation of indigenous land by white settler groups. Both European settlers and indigenous peoples carry their own historically constituted configurations of culture, but rather than analyzing these group histories through the primary lens of culture, I situate cultural differences in the context of colonial practices of white supremacy.

The rivalry between European settlers/colonizers in Canada entailed colonial tactics by the English to assimilate the French. In 1759, after years of fighting, Quebec fell under English control. Subsequently, the English authorities attempted to assimilate French settlers. The following excerpt from the 1839 Durham Report (Durham 1839) is particularly notable in this regard:

> It will be acknowledged by every one who has observed the
> progress of Anglo-Saxon colonization in America, that sooner or
> later the English race was sure to predominate even numerically

in Lower Canada, as they predominate already by their superior knowledge, energy, enterprise, and wealth. The error, therefore, to which the present contest must be attributed, is the vain endeavor to preserve a French Canadian nationality in the midst of Anglo-American colonies and states ... I believe that tranquility can only be restored by subjecting the province [of Lower Canada] to the vigorous rule of an English majority; and that the only efficacious government would be that formed by a legislative union.

Though the Durham Report also forecast a union between the English and the French (the 1840 Act of Union), this was not based on a partnership but on a need to encourage the assimilation of the 'troublesome Canadiens.' English dominance therefore produced representations of the French as white migrants who could be assimilated into Anglo norms.

Yet, long after Quebec ceased to be a French colony, several distinctive features of the French empire endured. Specifically, the Catholic Church gained a privileged position in the dominion with the regime of formal institutions, the seigneurial system was re-established under the Quebec Act of 1774, the Quebec Civil Code was entrenched within the legal structure, and, like other provinces, Quebec was granted jurisdiction over matters central to its cultural survival (such as education, health, and the solemnization of marriage). This contrasted with the attempts to destroy indigenous structures, practices, and bodies through disease, the reorganization of nations through the reserve system, bans against traditional practices, the residential school system, and control of band membership through the Indian Act. The French, like the indigenous peoples, resisted English tactics of assimilation, but the French differed from indigenous peoples in that their philosophies and norms resembled those of the English, and they were able to maintain many of their distinctive institutions and practices. Indigenous nations, on the other hand, faced annihilation and resisted it in ways that French settlers, as white settlers, did not. In this regard, though French settlers encountered English hostility, in relation to indigenous people they were also deemed to be tolerable and, to some extent, necessary to the peaceful development of the nation. Given this, though French settlers and indigenous nations share the common status of national minorities, the differences between them are deeply embedded in historical contexts of whiteness and colonialism.

As well as illuminating the relational economic, political, and social advantages of being historically racialized as a white French speaker in Quebec, and a white Anglo in the rest of the country, my account of meaning-making deconstructs the changing character of white dominance. This historical analysis of the processes of meaning-making that marked (and continue to mark) some settlers as privileged over others specifically demonstrates that the character of dominance is now not solely about the privilege assigned to English or French Canadians, but it has also extended to include other groups who replicate English and French norms. While the content of whiteness shifts, the privilege of whiteness as a marker of difference remains salient.

An account of the conditions under which whiteness is produced and transformed reveals that the authority of the two settler groups has been expanded to include immigrants who most easily fit into a racialized Euro-liberal representation of Canada. This expansion historically included the Scots, Irish, Americans, Germans, Scandinavians, Belgians, Mennonites, and Icelandic people. The hierarchy that privileged (and continues to privilege) Euro-liberal values and whiteness therefore explicitly favoured (and continues to favour) specific groups, groups that have adapted and been reconstituted through processes of white Euro-Canadianization. The English (and the French) therefore created an imagined community, one that hinged on the notion of a white man's country and the erasure of indigeneity (Dua 2000, 57). In this regard, processes of meaning-making that extended representations of white dominance were not simply the product of nation-building practices that favoured those who were British (nationality), ethnic Western Europeans (ethnicity), and who spoke English (language), but these practices also explicitly favoured those who were racially signified as white.

This changing character of white privilege is an aspect of difference that is important to analyze because the face of dominance is as much contingent and changeable as are representations of Otherness. This contingency and variation does not mean that whiteness is not locatable; rather, it suggests that accounts of dominance are needed on a continuous basis. A historically situated analysis of whiteness can illuminate how shifting representations of the desirable and undesirable citizen have been constructed around skin colour and biological superiority, as well as around language, religion, accent, culture, and national origin, or a combination of these dimensions. In his study of migration in Canada between 1896 and 1932, Donald Avery (1979, 7-8), for example, examines how and why Eastern, Central, and Southern European immigrants were candidates for Canadianization in contrast to blacks and Asians, but how they also remained marked as foreigners because of differences related to language, culture, occupation, and place of residence. As Avery (1979, 14) points out, these groups were defined as "persons thought to lie outside the country's Anglo-Saxon Protestant and French Canadian Roman Catholic communities." Although he notes that women immigrants also experienced modes of exclusion, his study highlights that the transatlantic capitalist labour market attracted male workers. Many of these workers, Avery (1979, 13) contends, were marked as dangerous foreigners because they engaged in "syndicalist, socialist, and communist activity." When the First World War broke out, national anxieties regarding the dangerous foreigner were fuelled by the Red Scare (communism) and international fears of Bolshevik-type activity, which threatened Canadian norms of industry, the family, and ownership of personal property. The Dominion (federal) government adopted guidelines and the 1914 War Measures Act to deal with 'enemy alien residents' in Canada, which included Germans, Ukrainians, Italians, Hungarians, and Bulgarians (and later also the Japanese and other Asians). Today, these same groups are assumed to be part of dominant society.

Avery's historical analysis remains salient today, for it illuminates that representations of the dangerous foreigner are produced through a simultaneous preference for whiteness (however historically defined), a specific set of liberal ideological values (as opposed to, say, socialist values), a system of free enterprise (in which, typically, the able-bodied and male foreigner must contribute to the growth of the national economy and its infrastructure), and the political status quo (the existing structures, policies, and laws of industry and the state).

The work of Vic Satzewich (2000, 2007) and David Roediger (2002) also provides important insights regarding groups who are now racialized as normal (white) but were not necessarily always racialized in this manner. Satzewich traces the ways in which Ukrainians in North America were considered peripheral Europeans throughout the 1800s right up to the 1920s. He argues that Ukrainians did not express an early desire to attach themselves to dominant English and French groups who were racialized as white but rather identified according to their countries of origin (Austria, Hungary, and Russia). Indeed, initially, the desire for inclusion in the larger white society, as Roediger (2002, 328-32) notes, was not the same for Irish and Italian immigrants, who were considered "the not-yet-white ethnics" but are now constructed as white. The shift clearly demonstrates that representations of racialized Otherness are far from static and that the processes of meaning-making that constitute this variation are themselves historically generated.

Furthermore, a deconstructive account of the processes that give meaning to whiteness directs attention to the ways in which racial difference can be inscribed onto the body and determinative of material differences, even though a person may not benefit from white structural privilege or identify as white. In the early colonial period, for example, the approach taken by Europeans to the Métis varied according to skin colour, as well as the status of the father (Stoler 2000, 331). Depending on how a Métis person fit into the standard of whiteness set by European settlers, they were treated as a charity case, as someone to be 'saved' and moulded into a colonial citizen, or as a subject to be abhorred and rejected. Although initially the 'mixing of races' was believed to bring some benefits to foreign traders (because women provided kinship links and knowledge of the terrain, as well as companionship in otherwise male-dominated outposts), by the early 1800s, for many Europeans the mixing of blood signalled European decay and a threat to white prestige. This was because "such mixing called into question the very criteria by which Europeanness could be identified, citizenship could be accorded, and nationality assigned" (Stoler 2000, 325). The gap, in other words, between so-called pure Europeans and hybrid Métis subjects was exposed as a social myth.

An account of the operations and effects of changing discourses of whiteness is hence crucial to an understanding of identity/difference politics. It provides a way to contextualize the changing face of domination and how racial discrimination and exclusion are differently experienced by those who are signified as becoming white, semi-white, not white enough, and non-white in different historical moments. An analysis of historically produced white/non-white binaries is especially telling because, even while non-whites were Othered in direct relation to those marked as white, they were also deemed necessary to the nation because of changing labour market needs. By taking an account of these dual processes of Othering and nation building, the analyst can critically examine various incarnations of whiteness and racialized Otherness, and also the *constancy* of white privilege. For instance, after the completion of the Canadian Pacific Railway in 1885, which was crucial to the economic development of the nation, the federal government introduced the Chinese Immigration Act, which imposed a head tax on immigrants and effectively prevented the migration of the Chinese, even though the railway across Canada had been built mostly by Chinese labourers (Abu-Laban 1998, 71). And, from the 1600s to about 1833, those marked as blacks were brought into Canada by white owners to be slaves both in the home and outside but were denied the right to freely migrate to Canada, unlike many white migrants who were free to settle across Canada to build its economy (Boyko 1995). In both instances, the nation-state was imagined as white despite the labour of non-white people.

Representations of the nation and of Otherness were specifically constituted through a matrix of meaning-making that linked norms of whiteness with those of capitalism. In the early 1900s, the entry of Asian migrants into Canada, for example, was shaped by the contradictory demands of capitalist expansion and nation building, and a simultaneous colonial project of claiming indigenous land and creating a sense of identity for established white settlers (Dua 2000, 57). At this historical moment, a shift occurred from a staples economy dominated by fur trade and fisheries to a capitalist economy that, dominated as it was by agriculture and industrial production, needed more workers. But, because Canadian governments could not attract enough of the right sort of British and European migrants to build the imagined community, they allowed for limited and controlled migration from Asia (Dua 2000, 57-59).

Historicized accounts of meaning-making that constructed the nation as white show that citizens marked as white and non-white were dialectically constituted. These accounts also draw attention to the ways in which practices of racialized Othering were resisted by those directly affected. In 1914, for example, a steamer called the *Komagata Maru* arrived at Vancouver harbour carrying 376 passengers, most of South Asian origin. When government officials denied them entry to British Columbia, the BC South Asian community mobilized to fight their decision (which also affected the ship's crew, most of whom were Japanese men). Local community members not only hired a white lawyer to force the immigration officials into court, they also challenged two Orders-in-Council that restricted entry into Canada. In one Order-in-Council, the sum that a potential migrant was required to possess was raised from $25 to $200; in the other, migrants were required to journey directly to Canada from their country of origin (this stricture was aimed specifically at Indians, for, in 1914, no passenger ship sailed directly from India to Canada) (Grace and Helm 1998, 90). As well, members of the community organized a *gurdwara* (Sikh temple) support committee led by Bhag Singh, Balwant Singh, Mit Singh, and Hussain Rahim. These community members held a meeting in which over $100,000 was pledged in support of those on the ship, and they raised the profile of the case across America, Canada, and India through a Punjabi-language newspaper, *Ghadar*. The *Ghadar* lambasted the

Canadian government for denying the passengers the right to enter Canada and for preventing the delivery of provisions to the ship, which were in short supply (Buchignani, Indra, and Srivastiva 1985, 51-57).

Meanwhile, on the *Komagata Maru*, Gurdit Singh Sarhali, who had originally chartered it and who remained aboard for the entire two months it was held at Vancouver, wrote to the governor general warning him that the forcible return of his passengers and crew would lead to serious disaffection in India (Buchignani, Indra, and Srivastiva 1985, 57). This was a situation that the British in both India and Britain wished to avoid. However, following negotiations and the threatening presence of the HMCS *Rainbow*, a Canadian government naval ship, the *Komagata Maru* was forced to leave the shores of BC, amid the cheers of thousands of Vancouver residents. This history remains important to many South Asians today, as a reminder of how white settlers differentiated the good and bad migrant on racial terms and also of acts of resistance by members of the South Asian community. In other words, this instance illustrates how the production of white superiority presented an occasion for domination as well as an avenue of resistance.

Immigration and Norms of Ableism

Discriminatory immigration policies and nation-building practices have not only produced representations of whiteness as a privileged and superior mode of difference, but these have also produced and instituted other modes of normalization. Accounts of meaning-making provide a critical examination of these variations. In this section, I consider how Otherness functions by constructing immigrants with socially defined disabilities through norms of ableism and how these norms interact with other norms through a matrix of meaning-making. Such an analysis transcends the liberal pluralist preoccupation with culture by focusing on the multiple interactive processes by which medical inscriptions of disability construct some subjects as imperfect and deviant Others while portraying others as physically, mentally, and physiologically superior. The norms of ableism, as legal scholar Judith Mosoff (1999, 174) observes, are especially significant to immigration policy because the "immigration system is one way that the Canadian state articulates rules about how an outsider can become an insider. But in addition, the immigration system is a means of further distinguishing insiders from outsiders through a policy that is made by 'us' but applies to 'them.'"

In historicizing representations of the 'immigrant,' an account of meaning-making can be deployed to locate and scrutinize how and why immigration law constituted and reconstituted stereotypical representations of disability. This includes the first immigration statute of the Confederation, An Act Respecting Emigrants and Quarantine (1859), which explicitly linked immigrants and disease and consolidated stereotypes about disability. Mosoff (1999, 155) remarks that "These stereotypes were based on ideas of people with disabilities as contagious, dangerous, not quite human, or non-persons." Stereotypical meanings of disability continued to apply in the 1869 Immigration Act, which required masters of sailing vessels to post a $300 bond to secure the landing of any person who was "Lunatic, Idiotic, Deaf and Dumb, Blind or Infirm" (Klein 2001). In this instance, hegemonic norms of class and ableism operated interactively, whereby wealth offset the burden of allowing entry to those signified as disabled Others.

Stereotypes of disability are rooted in liberal norms of rationality, industry, autonomy, and progress. Barbara Arneil evaluates these norms by identifying how major liberal thinkers, such as John Locke and John Stuart Mill, defined the liberal citizen and non-citizen by making links between imperfect and defective Others abroad (the idle, irrational, or custom-bound) and at home (the 'feeble-minded' or 'idle poor'). Arneil (2004, 3, emphasis in original) specifically traces "the profound connection between the colonized in America or India (the 'external' other) and the various groups of people *in England* (the 'internal' other), both of whom are seen to deviate from the same norms of liberal citizenship." As she argues, the liberal norm of reason required that deviants either be educated so as to bring them into conformity with norms of citizenship (potential citizens, who can be cured) or excluded if they could not conform (non-citizens, who must be segregated, contained, or repressed).

Although, within Canada, the approach was to cure the disabled, the eugenics movement also linked discourses of disability with immigration so as to exclude less aesthetically desirable immigrants (Jakubowicz and Meekosha 2003, 186-87). From 1906 to 1976, for instance, certain diagnoses made a person inadmissible, regardless of cost of treatment, severity, whether the condition could be controlled, or whether the state would be required to pay for treatment (Klein 2001). Section 29 of the 1906 Immigration Act banned all people with a mental disability, including anyone "who is feeble-minded, an idiot or an epileptic, or who is insane or has had an attack of insanity within five years." At that time, no amount of family support or proof of independent living could overcome meanings of abnormality. The standards of ableism therefore signified some subjects as irredeemable through what

Foucault characterized as the clinical gaze. Furthermore, under section 3 of the 1906 Immigration Act, immigrants could be deported after two (then three, then five) years if they were deemed a public charge, medically diagnosed as insane or handicapped, or simply characterized by infirmity.[1] Thus, though the population was controlled at the point of entry through strict limits in immigration legislation that entrenched norms of ableism, the same systems of meaning-making underlay corresponding efforts to assimilate or eliminate those marked as different who were already in Canada.

During the nineteenth and early twentieth centuries, through this clinical gaze, nation-building discourses led to such state practices as the imposed sterilization of those marked as feeble-minded, epileptic, insane, and congenitally deformed, as well as those who were deemed to have defective sensory organs, such as the Deaf and the blind. This practice was premised on dominant gendered constructions of disability, where, for instance, Alberta's 1928 Sexual Sterilization Act (repealed only in 1972) legalized the forced sterilization of women in mental health institutions who were deemed to be medically and socially deformed, as well as actual or potential criminals and deviants. Many of these women were placed in mental hospitals so as to prevent the reproduction of another 'deviant.' An account of the discourses that produced this characterization of deformity further reveals that ablest and gendered processes of Othering operated through processes of racialization. One historical example of this lies in the fact that sterilization policies disproportionately targeted indigenous women. Arneil (2004, 24) cites Owen Dyer's (1996) study of sterilization in Alberta, which shows that "of the 2832 'mentally defective' women who were sterilized under the Sexual Sterilization Act, a quarter were native Indians, although indigenous people make up only 2.5% of the province." In the US context, Myla Vicenti Carpio (2004) also examines how sterilization abuse affected indigenous women. This practice targeted them as a way to inhibit the reproduction of a next generation of indigenous peoples. These instances illustrate how a historically situated matrix of meaning-making constituted Otherness and also constructed a particular image of the able nation through interactive processes of differentiation that privileged norms of ableism, maleness, masculinity, and whiteness.

The interplay between discourses of ableism and racialization also informed the 1906 Immigration Act, which in turn simultaneously shaped characterizations of disability and race. This act continued the previous ban on admission of those seen as mentally disabled but also extended the meaning of mentally deficient people to include "persons who have been insane at any time previously ... persons of constitutional psychopathic inferiority ... persons over fifteen years of age physically capable of reading who cannot read the English or the French language or some other language and dialect" (Mosoff 1999, 156). Mosoff (1999, 19n34) states that, "besides the obvious effect of this provision on people with intellectual disabilities, the real intent may have been to exclude people of certain races and national origins." This is because the reference to literacy is directed to non-European non-white migrants who did not conform to the image of the ideal Canadian citizen. In this regard, negative representations of disability functioned through racist ones, and racist representations functioned through ideas about disability. To put it differently, repressive ideas about race and mental deficiency worked through one another to generate a broader notion of deviancy.

An account of this matrix of meaning-making shows that deviancy was concurrently spawned through market-driven preferences for the able-bodied worker. The 1976 Immigration Act, for instance, emphasized the need to foster the economy and encourage the entry of people involved in commercial activity, while also promoting the domestic and international interests of Canada and facilitating family reunification (Mosoff 1999, 153). Section 19(a) of the 1976 act specifically lays the medical, economic, and social grounds on which those marked as disabled could be refused immigration. This clause (emphasis added) targets restrictions to those

> (a) persons who are suffering from any disease, disorder, disability or other health impairment as a result of the nature, severity or probable duration of which, in the opinion of a medical officer concurred in by at least one other medical officer,
>   (i) they are or are likely to be a *danger to public health or to public safety,* or
>   (ii) their admission would cause or might reasonably be expected to cause excessive demands on health or social services.

This clause directly ties medical models of impairment, disease, disorder, and health to state-centred economic considerations. Section 19(b) repeats this link by constructing disability as a financial burden (rather than a responsibility), one that the person marked as disabled and his/her caregiver(s) must carry. Included in the class of people who can be refused admission to Canada are

(b) persons who there are reasonable grounds to believe are or will be unable or unwilling to support themselves and those persons who are dependent on them for care and support, except persons who have satisfied an immigration officer that adequate arrangements, other than those that involve social assistance, have been made for their care and support.

Section 19(b) therefore both privatizes and individualizes the care of those defined as disabled because the state does not want to incur the financial 'burden' of those who are constructed as abnormal. A deconstructive analysis of this characterization of abnormality identifies the priority assigned to market liberalism and how it generates representations of the unable and dependent subject through norms of ableism and capitalism simultaneously.

Although the Canadian government claims to have removed the criteria for inadmissibility evident in the 1976 legislation, the 2001 Immigration and Refugee Protection Act maintains the language of excessive demand, with the effect of regulating those who are designated as un-able. In particular, section 38 of the 2001 act states that

A foreign national is inadmissible on health grounds if their health condition a) is likely to be a danger to public health; b) is likely to be a danger to public safety; or c) might reasonably be expected to cause excessive demand on health or social services.

This provision is not unlike section 19(a) of the 1976 act, even though the language has shifted from disability to health grounds; in this regard, the criterion of excessive demand is effectively maintained. The definition of excessive demand is especially troubling because it is vulnerable to the opinions of medical officers who must follow guidelines that serve the best financial interests of the state, whereby health costs, equipment costs, supplies, and qualified personnel are key determinants. The government states that "In determining inadmissibility, a complex formula is used to project the cost of an applicant's health condition. The cost is considered as excessive demand if it is likely to exceed the average cost of caring for a Canadian citizen or permanent resident" (CIC 2004).

This notion of excessive demand thus continues to normalize and privilege able-bodiedness by legitimizing the idea that immigrant applicants with disabilities and Canadian residents/citizens with disabilities are disproportionately using state resources and goods. By contrast, the good immigrant is deemed to be able-bodied, independent, and an active agent in the expansion of a market economy. Given this, the criterion for judging excessive demand reiterates a preference for norms of ableism and capitalism. An account of how these norms produce and organize difference raises questions about the underlying normalizing paradigm of wealth and industry that demarcates the desirable and undesirable immigrant.

Such normalizing paradigms structure representations of Otherness through discourses of disability even before immigrant applicants become legal Canadian residents. This is evident in such immigration cases as *Thangarajan v. Canada*. This case started when Rajadurai Samuel Thangarajan (the respondent) applied for permanent residency for himself and on behalf of his dependants, including a son who was medically defined as being moderately mentally retarded. His son, William, had been refused entry by immigration officials on the grounds that he might reasonably be expected to cause excessive demands on social services in Canada.

The case went to the Federal Court of Appeal in 1999, when the appellant (the minister of citizenship and immigration) argued that subparagraph 19(1)(a)(ii) of the Immigration Act was intended to ensure access to health and social services for existing Canadian citizens and permanent residents, not for potential migrants. According to the appellant, admitting immigrants who made excessive demands on social services undermined the ability of current Canadians to access them. The appellant specifically argued that William Thangarajan created excessive demand because the special education costs of a mentally challenged student in the publicly funded provincial school system fell within the act's specification of burden on social services. In the end, the court agreed. An account of the processes of meaning-making that produced representations of William Thangarajan as an Other shows that medicalized interpretations of the body designated him as a financial burden and ultimately as an undesirable immigrant.

What is further illuminated through this analysis is that William was marked as an undesirable financial burden even though he applied under the family class category. This is notable because, though income would be expected to be a factor in the independent category, in family class applications there is a legal expectation that family sponsors would privately support the applicant for up to ten years, without any reliance on the state. The privatization of responsibility for new immigrants who immigrate under the family class is itself problematic but is further distorted by the fact that those immigrants who have family members signified as disabled Others are forced to justify their 'public' costs while also carrying the private (and legalized) financial responsibility for the immigrant. In short, the financial assessment of the medical condition of a person signified as disabled should simply be irrelevant to family sponsorship (Mosoff 1999, 166).

An account of the processes of meaning-making that defined William as an undesirable immigrant provides a way to examine how norms of ableism function through liberal norms of the ideal family, namely, one that is a collection of biologically related, independent, and *able* individuals.[2] This analysis reveals that hegemonic meanings of the family assume that family members have differing economic roles and that William could not fulfill his role. However, even if he were unable to work, this should not have been a consideration under a family class application, because employability, as noted above, is irrelevant to this particular category. Yet the interplay between economic considerations and conventional interpretations of the family reiterated medical representations of disability and thus regulated distinctions between the desirable and undesirable immigrant.

Overall, my analysis of this case shows that clinical constructions of disability as a deficiency were constituted and upheld through liberal capitalist norms regarding the ideal worker, the ideal (white) citizen, the means of production, and the family. This account thus exposes the complexities of a matrix of meaning-making, in which multiple processes interact with one another to legalize injurious meanings of disability. The Council of Canadians with Disabilities (CCD 2001) suggests that, in considering these kinds of cases, immigration officials continue to give no weight "to the individual needs, capacities, or merits of people with disabilities or the positive contributions made by people with disabilities in our society." These negative conceptions of disability have the effect of keeping 'the disabled' outside the borders of the nation; they also perpetuate the status of outsider for those currently within the borders of the nation-state. The CCD (2001) states,

> It is important to emphasize that not only potential immigrants
> are devalued and dehumanized but also Canadian citizens with
> disabilities are given the 'message' that a disability in itself is
> enough to prevent a person from becoming a landed immigrant
> in Canada. Furthermore, they are given the message that there is
> nothing a disabled person can contribute to our society[,] nor
> can they overcome the attitude that they are a 'burden' or have

'excessive demands' on our health care system. Therefore the
[Immigration] Act also has the effect of continuing to devalue
persons with disabilities who presently live in Canada and are
Canadian citizens.

In short, the privilege assigned to ablest norms is constructed and entrenched
by dominant notions of the ideal immigrant and the ideal citizen.

These conceptions of disability have been widely challenged by persons
with disabilities. For instance, before it became the CCD in 1980, the Coalition of Provincial Organizations of the Handicapped (COPOH) brought
together women and men with disabilities from across Canada to ensure that
disability was recognized in the equality clause of the then proposed Charter
of Rights and Freedoms. COPOH's motto was "A voice of our own," and its
stated purpose was to build an organization *of* not *for* persons with disabilities.
As the organization (CCD 1998b) observed, "This means that we as persons
with disabilities speak for ourselves on issues of concern rather than others
speaking for us." From its situated social location of marginalization, COPOH
enacted its agency and addressed the Special Joint Parliamentary Committee
on the Constitution 1980 to successfully argue that including disability in
section 15(1) was crucial. Thus, discourses of ableism gave rise to a group
identity and led to political action, as much as they discriminated against
people with disabilities. Since that time, the CCD (1998a) has advocated for
law reform, self-representation, and accessible transportation among other
issues, in order to redirect social meanings attached to disability and ability
that affect the material and lived realities of subjects.

The Immigrant and Norms of Sexuality, Gender, and Desire

To further deconstruct the processes by which representations of the undesirable and desirable immigrant are constituted in ways that consolidate dominant norms, in this section I take accounts of norms of sexuality, gendering,
and desire. Unlike liberal multicultural approaches, which obscure, ignore,
or overdetermine issues related to sexuality, gendering, and desire, my analysis
focuses on how specific discourses of criminality, disease, and family determine historically produce norms of sexuality, gender, and desire, and consequently signify lesbian and gay immigrants as deviant.

Although some of the formal prohibitions against gay and lesbian people
who wish to immigrate to Canada have been removed, historically, immigration law and practice have been instrumental in characterizing homosexuality

as a crime. From 1952 to 1976, Canada's immigration policies were blatantly homophobic. 1952 provisions added to the Immigration Act made "homosexuals" and "persons living on the avails of ... homosexualism" inadmissible to Canada, both as visitors and immigrants. Homosexuals were grouped together with other prohibited classes such as prostitutes, pimps, beggars, and vagrants; a visitor or immigrant could be deported from Canada on any of these grounds (Caswell 1996, 564-65). This tactic to bar homosexuals from entry into Canada paralleled the ways in which particular subjects were marked as disabled and as non-white subversives.

An effect of this penalizing meaning of homosexuality is that sexual minorities have faced legal disciplining. One such instance involved the deportation of a post-operative trans-sexual. In 1972, the *Sherwood Atkinson (Sheri de Cartier)* case went to the Immigration Appeal Board when a (male-to-female) trans-sexual was charged with pursuing sexual activities with a male and practising homosexualism, even though she had undergone sex reassignment surgery. The law (wrongly) recognized her as a male who had engaged in sex with another man and consequently signified her as an undesirable immigrant. This construction of difference as aberrant and abhorrent was thus produced through meanings about heteronormativity and homosexuality. In the end, she was denied entry into Canada on the basis of sexuality because, it was argued, she had engaged in homosexual conduct (Lahey 1999, 138).

Despite the "decriminalization of homosexuality in the Criminal Code in 1969, the federal government did not amend the Immigration Act to delete homosexuality from the list of inadmissible classes to Canada until a new Immigration Act was proclaimed in 1976" (Fisher et al. 1998). Yet even this amendment continued to negatively represent and exclude gays and lesbians by reinforcing links between meanings of homosexuality and criminality. Under the 1976 act, if lesbian or gay immigrant applicants had been criminally charged or convicted under the legal language of homosexual offences in other countries, they were denied entry to Canada on the basis of their criminal record. Regardless of the justifiability of the criminal record – the events that led to it could sometimes be highly questionable – all such instances entrenched the idea that criminal behaviour and homosexuality were intrinsically connected. Kathleen Lahey (1999, 139) notes one such 1992 case, in which "Immigration Canada denied a Dutch gay man's application for landed-immigration status on the basis of a criminal record that had

arisen out of charges laid against him for 'homosexual offences' by Nazi oc-
cupiers of Holland during the Second World War."

As well as unpacking how demeaning representations of homosexuality
are interpreted through discourses of criminality, my account identifies how
representations of sexual deviancy and criminality function by constructing
some immigrants as transmitters of disease. The co-functioning of these discourses has been especially salient with regard to lesbians, gays, queers, and
tran-sexuals since concerns about HIV and AIDS have entered the mainstream
public discourse; this is the case even though it is estimated that, worldwide,
a significant portion of HIV cases have been contracted through heterosexual
sexual contact (Entwisle 2000, 3). Under the 1976 Immigration Act, for example, gay and lesbian immigration applicants who had been diagnosed
with HIV or AIDS were deemed medically inadmissible if they were perceived
to represent a danger to public health or public safety or if it was believed that
they would cause or might reasonably be expected to cause excessive demands
on health or social services. Although, under the 1976 act, the minister of
immigration could issue exemption permits to gay and lesbian applicants on
humanitarian and compassionate grounds, this was both discretionary and
temporary. Indeed, as Donald Caswell points out in his seminal text *Lesbians,
Gay Men, and Canadian Law* (1996, 556), though most gay and lesbian immigrants apply to immigrate on these grounds, homophobia among immigration officials persists as a significant problem in a system that is highly
discretionary.

The 2001 Immigration and Refugee Protection Act made changes in immigration law. For example, *the act* recognizes sexual orientation, gender-
based persecution, and HIV/AIDS status as grounds for making refugee claims.
For some, the new law indicates that the government is shifting from the
construction of HIV and AIDS as dangerous and infectious illnesses to recognition that they are chronic conditions like cancer or heart disease (Klein
2001). Though the stigma attached to HIV and AIDS is quite different from
that of cancer and heart disease (in that HIV/AIDS has been constructed as
a widely contagious condition spread by homosexuals, whereas heart disease
and cancer do not have this stigma), the interactions between discourses of
disease, disability, and homosexuality continue to construct gays and lesbians
with HIV and AIDS as undesirable migrants.[3]

An account of the processes of meaning-making that construct the homosexual immigrant applicant as deviant (one whose sexual desires are abnormal

and therefore subject to criminalization, and who is a transmitter of disease) further exposes that such constructs are sustained through heteronormative meanings of the family. In these instances, difference is constituted through a matrix of meaning-making composed of discourses of heteronormativity, the conventional family, criminality, and disease. As Mosoff (1999, 163) notes, Canada's first formal definition of the family appeared in 1927 immigration legislation as father, mother, and children under eighteen years. "Subsequent definitions of family," she (Mosoff 1999, 163) continues, "maintained the vision of the nuclear family but were more explicit about the economic unit. For example, the Immigration Act 1952 s.2(g) defined family as the father and mother and any children who, by reason of age or disability, are in the opinion of an immigration officer, mainly dependent upon the head of the family for support." Here, disability is recognized as a category of difference that can lead to dependent familial relations, and the family is defined in heteronormative terms.

When historically generated traditional meanings of the family are critically analyzed, it becomes evident that a preference for heteronormativity underlies immigration legislation. Although lesbian and gay partners of Canadians have been allowed to immigrate to Canada since 1976, most have not entered under the family class category. Such is the case even though this category has clear advantages, whereby "family class applications are processed with priority, and the Canadian sponsor of an applicant who has been refused has the right to appeal the decision to the Appeal Division of the Immigration and Refugee Board" (Fisher et al. 1998). Before 2003, because under the 1976 Immigration Act gays and lesbians did not meet the established criteria of family, many were forced to apply on humanitarian and compassionate grounds. Indeed, most same-sex partners who were accepted as legal immigrants entered under this provision, thereby reiterating the idea that gays and lesbians were special (rather than usual) cases. The fact that the 'back door' route of humanitarian and compassionate applications was necessary at all is a reflection of the ways in which gay and lesbian migrants were signified as second-tier applicants.[4] For some same-sex partners who could not overcome the barriers of immigration law but wanted to live with their partners in Canada, the options have been even more limited. Some, desperate to join their partners, become immigrants by spending years on student visas, enduring opposite-sex marriages of convenience, sometimes living illegally underground, and working in exploitative conditions (Caswell 1996, 568).

Importantly, the production of negative meanings of homosexuality through discourses of criminality, disease, and the normal family leads to discrimination, but it also engenders resistance. Challenges have been made, for example, to heterosexist meanings of family. These challenges are important to note in the study of meaning-making because they illustrate the contested nature of subject formation and the agency of subjects marked by discrimination. One instance of this resistance is exemplified in a case involving two self-identified lesbians, Christine Morrissey and Bridget Coll, who challenged the Immigration Regulations' restrictive definition of spouse (Caswell 1996, 569). When Morrissey, a Canadian citizen, applied to sponsor Coll, her partner of fourteen years, she did so on the basis that Coll was her life companion. The Immigration Department refused to process her application on the grounds that the regulations limited sponsorship to those signified as opposite-sex couples.

In January 1992, Morrissey took a Charter of Rights and Freedoms challenge to the Federal Court. The challenge stated that the relevant provisions of the Immigration Regulations were unconstitutional in that they discriminated against lesbians and gays under section 15. Further, the challenge requested that "same-sex partners" should be read into the regulations or that the definition of spouse should include same-sex partners. The government responded by informing Coll that, because she had not filed for permanent residency, it would move for dismissal. Coll immediately applied for permanent residence. To her surprise, she did not have to attend the usual interview, and her application was quickly processed (Caswell 1996, 569). In September 1992, she was granted permanent residence. When she had initially applied, the Immigration Department had informed her that she was ineligible for the independent category; strangely enough, this was the very category in which she received her new status. This is notable because, rather than signifying Coll as a family member, the government placed her in a category that would not challenge the norms of a heterosexual family. As Caswell (1996, 570) suggests, the government chose to settle this case rather than risk losing it and have the courts rewrite the definition of a spouse. Thus the government initially rejected, then resisted, and ultimately grudgingly interpreted the meaning of "a spouse" as a same-sex partner but without having to expand the formal definition.

Recent changes in immigration law may create more accessibility for gay and lesbian immigrants, including under the family class. In 2002, the new

Immigration and Refugee Protection Regulations expanded the definition of a common-law partner to include an individual who is cohabiting with a person in a conjugal relationship or who had cohabited for a period of at least one year. The new regulations also allow family sponsorship through a "conjugal relationship"; this category includes a person who has been in such a relationship for at least one year but was unable to cohabit with his or her partner due to persecution or any form of penal control. Thus, under the category of family class, same-sex partners can now apply to immigrate to Canada as a spouse, common-law partner, or conjugal partner. However, the effect of the new rules on gays and lesbians is not entirely clear, especially because same-sex spousal applications have been consistently processed without transparency. The Lesbian and Gay Immigration Taskforce of Canada (LEGIT 2003) also points out that, though the definition of "partner" has expanded, there are concerns that the backdoor route of humanitarian and compassionate grounds is no longer readily available.

Even when sexual minorities become legal residents in Canada, hetero-normative processes of meaning-making continue to determine and limit the official capacities of lesbian, gay, bisexual, trans-sexual, and queer subjects, such that they still face what Lahey (1999, 171) calls "civil death." Thus, even if sexual minorities are successful in immigrating to Canada, they continue to be marked as deviants or partial citizens because the law continues to deny the full legal personality of all sexual minorities (Lahey 1999, xv). The legal personalities of lesbians and gays continue to be subject to restrictions, with the effect of limiting participation and free movement in the public sphere. Indeed, even after the battle to include sexual orientation in section 15(1) of the Charter had been won, winning a case prohibiting discrimination based on sexual orientation *(Egan v. Canada)* took over eight years.

Implications for the Politics of Identity/Difference: Differentiating Immigrants

The category of the 'immigrant' is clearly established as an important marker of difference in contemporary political theory, one that determines social, economic, and political life. Yet, as the above accounts of meaning-making demonstrate, it is necessary to rethink how immigrants are analyzed beyond the scope of culture. I have argued that to conceptualize the category of im-migrants solely or even primarily through the lens of culture, or for that matter, through any singular mode of difference, is to narrowly interpret social difference and to erase the ways in which Othering occurs through a matrix of meaning-making. Representations of immigrants vary according to how the matrix is operationalized in specific contexts through norms related to culture, language, accent, skin colour, disability/ability, gendering, whiteness, the market economy, disease, and criminality. Attention to these variations not only challenges the singular preoccupation with culture but it also enables better understanding of the ways in which representations of Otherness and of the nation are mutually constituted. When liberal multiculturalists declare one mode of identity as politically more important than another, it is crucial to examine what specific agenda is being advanced, which norms are being protected and privileged, and, accordingly, what is really at stake for the state in regulating a particular form of difference.

The key lesson in this chapter is not simply that analysts should extend the study of identity/difference to include a wider range of subjects. Rather, my primary point is that the analysis should radically contextualize the historically specific regimes in which social categories are constructed and positioned. This contextualization makes it possible to identify how to reinterpret meanings differently from those entrenched through dominant lenses. Reinterpretations are necessary in the case of calcified social categories that already have a place in mainstream theories of identity/difference politics, as I have argued in this chapter with regard to immigrants, and are also necessary so as to open up the study of social relations of difference that are currently largely ignored, as I will argue in the next chapter.

4

Regulating Difference: Accounts of Deaf and Trans-sexual Difference

In 2002, in the US, a Deaf lesbian couple's decision to conceive a child with a Deaf sperm donor in hopes that the baby would be born Deaf sparked national and international controversy because it challenged both hetero-sexual and hearing norms. In 1995, in British Columbia, a human rights case involving a male-to-female trans-sexual who was denied the opportunity to volunteer at a feminist rape relief centre sent shock waves across feminist or-ganizations in Canada because it challenged transphobia and norms of gender. In this chapter, through these cases, I demonstrate the value of analyzing modes of difference largely unexamined in the study of identity/difference politics. I take accounts of the meaning-making processes that produce rep-resentations of Deafness and trans-sexuality so as to explore how structures of difference are produced and regulated. This analysis specifically contributes to an understanding of how self-directed meanings are produced by a matrix of meaning-making in tandem with the production of, and resistance against, externally imposed meanings. There are, in other words, distinctive *structures of difference* that require contextualized analysis.

Two important theoretical insights are brought to bear through the study of structures of difference. First, this kind of study unveils the false logic of ontological conceptions of (Deaf and gendered) identity and subsequently sheds light on the relationality and contingency of difference. Second, putting the logic of identity categories into question makes it evident that there is no idealized notion of identity, for all modes of difference are circumscribed by a set of norms and touched by power. This does not mean that representa-tions of difference are meaningless or that all meanings of difference are equally troubled; rather, my analysis shows that power is productive in mul-tiple ways and at multiple levels in that it generates and governs various structures of difference, including those directed by subjects marked as Other. These conditions may generate subjectivities as well as subjection.

Meaning-Making and Representations of Deafness

When deconstructing representations of Deafness, accounts of meaning-making reveal a wide variety of representations. These may correspond with the ways in which self-identified Deaf subjects understand their own identities in an affirming manner and/or they may reiterate interpretations of Deafness as an abnormality. In this section, I consider three particular structures of difference that are generative of various meanings of Deaf identity: those that distinguish culture-based and oralist meanings, those that differentiate representations of Deafness and disability, and those that organize Deaf-centred norms.

CULTURE-BASED AND ORALIST NORMS OF MEANING-MAKING

An account of meaning-making can be put to work to deconstruct how norms of oralism (the privilege assigned to the hearing world) and those of Deafness are productive in differentiating Deafness as a disability and Deafness as culture. As I concluded in Chapter 1, it is critical to examine why and how culture gains meaning in specific ways *without* prioritizing it as the most salient form of difference. The analysis that I prescribe provides a way to interpret, describe, and explain how positive representations of a Deaf culture do not (necessarily) emerge through a commitment to a historical homeland or even a geographically intimate community (Ladd 2003, 175), but through a social distinction between normality (hearing) and abnormality (Deafness). In these latter instances, difference is produced through a medical system of meaning-making processes, in which Deafness is a defect that must be fixed (CAD 2002a). These clinical representations configure Deafness as a disability, an aberration, a social difference that may deserve empathy and charity (particularly if being Deaf is the result of nature) but one that is abnormal.

By contrast, meanings of Deaf identity grounded in culture constitute Deaf subjects as *linguistic* minorities. Paddy Ladd (2003, 17) calls the creation of cultural representations of Deafness an act of resistance to linguistic colonialism. To contextualize the effects of historical modes of linguistic colonialism and provide a counter-narrative to oralist hegemonies, Ladd (2003, 256) purposely draws parallels between the colonization of non-white peoples whose native languages were threatened and sometimes eradicated (as in the case of indigenous peoples), and the practices by which Deaf ways of communicating were disregarded and suppressed. Ladd understands colonization as a historical relationship between unequal groups of people, in which the dominant hearing group not only ruled Deaf ways of being, but also imposed its own norms in such a way as to create and sustain oralist privilege. Such practices included hiring requirements that effectively prohibited Deaf people from becoming teachers, as was the case in some Alberta and Newfoundland schools; the removal of Deaf teachers from schools and attempts to ban them from working with Deaf children; policies that prohibited the use of Sign in educational institutions, including Deaf schools such as one in British Columbia that, for twenty years, did not permit its use (Roots 2003); the erasure of Deaf histories (Gannon 1981; Lane 1984); and acts of what Ladd (2003, 17) calls "welfare colonialism," in which the Deaf were constructed as feeble-minded, in need of charity and help.

Ladd's analysis of the practices and discourses of exclusion that mark Deafness as deviant and abnormal is important because it illuminates the control and rule of oralist norms. But his interpretation of colonialism also tends to conflate the histories of white Deaf peoples and non-white peoples (whether Deaf or not). The terminology of colonialism has certainly been used in contexts that challenge traditional dichotomies of European/non-European and white/non-white (for example, some Chinese politicians and scholars have employed the notion of colonialism in reference to China's historical relationship with Japan). In European and North American contexts, however, there is some danger in collapsing all modes of cultural subjugation, specifically because *racialized* colonialism has a long and distinct history. Thus, it is important to situate a particular mode of domination in its historical context.

Of course there are intricate links between racialized experiences of European colonialism and Eurocentric constructions of Deaf cultures as immature and uncivilized. Indeed, the work of Barbara Arneil (2004) and Christopher Kliewer and Linda May Fitzgerald (2001) shows this to be the case. In Canada, however, colonialism is deeply embedded in modes of racialization, white supremacy, and imperialism. These aspects of difference are especially important in Canada because of the ways in which indigenous peoples continue to be subject to colonial discourses and because many people of colour within Canada continue to be marked by various histories of colonization. Furthermore, it is important not to universalize the experiences of all Deaf people. Because some people are both Deaf and non-white – rather than either Deaf or non-white – it is important to be precise about when and how oralist meanings are constituted through discourses of racialization. In short, in Canada's case, colonization is deeply embedded in racialized discourses. Even subjects who were never formally colonized by European powers, such as the Nepalese, display the same signs of the colonial condition as do people from India because of dominant ideologies of whiteness (Uprety 1997, 367). The constructed associations between race-thinking, skin colour, accent, language, ethnicity, national origin, culture, and history are what I emphasize in my understanding of colonialism.

Despite these misgivings about the conflation of different kinds of oppression, Ladd is right to identify that repressive representations of Deafness are constructed through oralist notions of normality. His argument is especially cogent in the context of ongoing linguistic oppression against those who Sign. Despite, for example, the landmark 1997 Supreme Court of Canada decision in *Eldridge v. British Columbia*, which stated that the failure of governments to provide Sign language interpretation in the delivery of health care services (where it was necessary for effective communication) violated the Charter rights of Deaf Canadians, most federal, provincial, and territorial governments have failed to take any steps to meet the obligations set out by the Supreme Court. Ultimately, in public life, the Deaf continue to experience the erasure of Deaf ways of being. An account of these discourses puts into question the structure of difference that gives meaning to the Norm/Other binary of hearing/Deaf.

MEANINGS OF DEAF CULTURE AND DISABILITY

Accounts of meaning-making can simultaneously be put to work so as to examine those modes of difference that are structured by marginalized systems of meaning-making. These create hierarchical representations of Otherness. I will characterize these as Other/Other so as to signify that meaning-making is always relational, that there are different Selves and Others, and that the Norm/Other is not a singular dominant-subordinate relationship but consists of various degrees of subjectivity and subjection. In this section, I specifically explore how contemporary meanings of disability as a positive quality constitute Deaf identity.

Leading disability advocate Vic Finkelstein (1991, 160) contends that Deaf people "have more in common with other disability groups than they do with groups based upon race and gender." According to Finkelstein, the disabled and the Deaf are both marked by signs of social abnormality and biological defectiveness, such that both social categories are constructed through inscriptions of disability. Rather than attending to which meaning is more legitimate – Deafness as a disability or Deafness as a culture – a contextual account of meaning-making critiques how these meanings are relationally differentiated and why, and what is at stake in these characterizations of Deafness for variously positioned subjects and groups. For Finkelstein, what seems to be at stake is the possibility of inclusion within mainstream society. Thus, rather than adopting what he sees as segregationist practices that isolate Deaf institutions (such as Deaf schools), he argues that it is necessary to eventually integrate those socially constructed as disabled and Deaf into mainstream society. His position is premised on the idea that the social differences between the Deaf and the hearing could be alleviated if those signified as Deaf embraced the need for oral assistance through captioning, lip-reading, assistive devices, oral interpretation, and most controversially, cochlear implants. An account of meaning-making can distinguish these responses to Deaf difference from those that see oral assistance as normalizing, thereby revealing the differences between representations of disability and Deaf culture.

Such an analysis illuminates that in culture-based understandings of Deaf difference, access to medical care, rehabilitation, and support services is not as directly relevant to the Deaf as it is to those marked by socially defined disabilities (Lane 1997, 161). This is because some rehabilitative devices have historically been used by hearing educators to oppress Deaf practices. In particular, whereas the model of disability defines a Deaf community in terms of hearing impairment, the model of culture rejects this characterization. Indeed, many of those who identify as Deaf understand themselves as having far more in common with other language minorities than with those signified as having a disability. On this basis, rather than wanting to integrate into societal norms, many subjects who self-signify as Deaf both desire and require separate and distinct Deaf-centred institutions and practices. Separation is necessary, they argue, because 90 percent of Deaf people are born to hearing parents and need socialization in Deaf systems of meaning-making by attending Deaf schools. This kind of claim is not universally made, for some Deaf people endorse legal provisions, such as those of the Americans with Disabilities Act, which pushes for the integration of those signified as disabled. Yet, as Harlan Lane (1997, 164-66) argues, though solidarity can exist between Deaf and disabled people in that both struggle for control of their destinies, both endeavour to promote their own constructions (or systems of meaning-making), and both have allied in creating services and commissions, there are still legal, material, and social implications of conflating the two.

An account of the processes of meaning-making that produce meanings of Deafness as a disability and Deaf identity as a cultural identity unmasks how these representations of difference are constituted through norms of oralism and ableism, and also through norms of disability. Though each characterization leads to social marginalization and exclusion, they are distinct in how they structure difference. In particular, my account suggests that Oralist and ablest norms produce a dichotomy between one kind of Norm/Other (the hearing/Deaf), as well as distinctions between a different kind of Norm/ Other (disabled/Deaf) or what I distinguish as Other/Other so as to signal relational hierarchies of Otherness and the incoherency of strict dualisms.

Deaf-Centred Norms of Meaning-making

As well as critically analyzing differing historically situated processes of meaning-making that produce binaries of Deaf/hearing, disabled/able-bodied, and Deaf/disabled, accounts of meaning-making identify how Deaf subjectivity is constituted through Deaf-centred norms. Thus, in addition to deconstructing the structures of difference between Norm/Other and Other/ Other, a critical analysis of Deafness attends to processes that produce differences *within* this category. This kind of analysis scrutinizes the characteristics and practices that normally ground Deaf-centred meaning about Deafness.

According to the Canadian Association of the Deaf (CAD), particular characteristics and practices constitute a healthy sociological community of Deaf people. This culture is distinct in that it has its own unique language (Sign), set of values (attitudes toward Deaf interests), forms of art (theatre, poetry, jokes, writings, paintings, magazines, journals, and books by and about the Deaf), educational institutions,[1] political and social structures (such as the CAD), and tools of communication (such as telecommunication display devices, caption decoders, and flashing alarms). In particular, the content of a Deaf culture is shaped by the significance accorded to Sign language. Sign distinguishes those who engage in language primarily through visual (rather than verbal) means. Thus, Sign language is determined by Deaf people to be a unique feature of Deaf culture; they do not conceive of it as an abnormality or the product of a subculture (Ladd 2003, 224).

While illuminating what typically gives meaning to a Deaf identity from a Deaf-situated standpoint (i.e., Sign language), my approach also critically examines the heterogeneity that defines this collective social identity. The importance of Sign language varies, for instance, according to national context. The CAD (CAD 2002a) uses American Sign Language (ASL) and la Langue des Sourds du Québec as its two official languages and recognizes English and French as its two secondary languages; those living in Britain take British

Sign Language (BSL) as their primary language; in Australia, Australian Deaf and non-vocal communities recognize Auslan, which is related to BSL, though not identical to it, and is distinct from ASL. This heterogeneity is not obscured through an account of Deaf-centred modes of representation, but rather, this analysis contextualizes how representations of Deafness are constituted and performed through differing constructions of nationhood.

In deconstructing such differences, an account of meaning-making also sheds light on how representations of Deafness are generated through modes of racialization and ethnicization. These variations, as Susan Foster and Waithera Kinuthia (2003) assert, are important to the ways in which Deaf Asian American, Hispanic American, and African American scholars and teachers understand their identities in ethnic and racial terms rather than through unidimensional modes of deafness and oralism. By acknowledging that Deafness is not always the primary mode of identification for all Deaf people, more careful analysis of difference can reveal when and why Deaf identity is overdetermined. Joseph Fischgrund and C. Tane Akamatsu (1993, 177) suggest that, on this basis, it becomes possible to see that "what is commonly referred to as 'Deaf culture' is in fact white Deaf culture, and what is commonly referred to as the 'Deaf community' is in fact narrowly defined as the community of white Deaf people." Indeed, identification with Deafness varies according to individual characteristics (gender, roles, beliefs, character), situation (geographic location, whether the Deaf person attended a Deaf school, and location of home/work/neighbourhood), social interactions (alienation, discomfort, sameness, difference), and societal conditions (institutionalized forms of stereotyping) (Foster and Kinuthia 2003, 271).

Although such heterogeneity is illuminated through my account of meaning-making, this analysis does not lead to a preference for homogeneous or heterogeneous social categories. Rather, it contextualizes why and how one mode of representation is preferred. Thus, rather than collapsing differences so as to re-present Deaf cultures negatively or positively or, conversely, emptying "Deaf culture" of all meaning, this analytic device deconstructs the conditions that produce both representations of difference in the first place. It moves away from the notion that ideal meanings exist, even when positive meanings are produced and even when meaning-making is self-directed. This is not to say that positive and Deaf-centred representations of difference are not crucial to an understanding of identity/difference politics and to practices of resistance. Rather, my point is simply that all processes of subject formation are structured by social, economic, and political context, and that all produce degrees of normalization. Accordingly, even where the desire is to promote a particular mode of difference in a positive way, it cannot be exempt from an account of meaning-making.

To elaborate on this point, I'll draw on Jane Berger's (2005) study of nineteenth-century Deaf schools in the US. This study shows that, even while Deaf schools were being created in order to promote Deaf language and intellectual and spiritual development, their founders were also appealing to discourses of charity by replicating ideas about Deafness as a defect. As Berger (2005, 160) notes, one of the founders of Gallaudet University, Reverend Thomas Hopkins Gallaudet himself, "described untutored deaf people as heathens to convince potential donors of the exigency of institutions." As well, though "founders of the institutions emphasized deaf people's intellectual and spiritual potential, they also uniformly described deafness as a calamitous tragedy." Berger goes on to argue that, as practices of market liberalism became widespread in the eighteenth and nineteenth centuries, advocates for Deaf schools emphasized representations of the Deaf as legitimate charity cases. In these instances, representations of Deafness were given meaning through a matrix of meaning-making composed of interactive discourses of ability and disability, charity, and productive labour. The Deaf, it was argued, were particularly deserving of charity because, for reasons beyond their control (being born 'abnormal'), they could not contribute to the competitive marketplace in the same way as hearing people. They simply did not meet the standards of "individualism that constituted each person as singly responsible for his well-being" (Berger 2005, 161).

Educators who favoured the promotion of Deaf ways of being effectively institutionalized these ideas of Deafness as a defect (however unintentionally) by officially categorizing schools for the Deaf as legitimate charities rather than educational enterprises. Berger (2005, 163) concludes that, in doing so, as well as providing students with religious and vocational education, and creating spaces to develop Deaf practices and to avoid the stigma attached to Deafness, these schools "taught children that there was something seriously wrong with deaf people that rendered them charity cases from whom even the most mundane of accomplishments were considered an extraordinary achievement." A value of Berger's study is that it reveals how representations of Deafness are shaped by temporal and spatial context. It also shows how meaning-making processes that legitimized Deaf subjectivity in positive ways were directly bolstered by meanings that signified Deafness as a defect, even by those who advocated for the Deaf. It is precisely this contradictory activity of generating and also normalizing positive and negative representations of Deafness that requires critical analysis in the study of identity/difference politics.

Currently, Deaf scholars and activists continue to constitute meanings of Deafness by forming and re-forming a specific set of Deaf-centred norms. These meanings are often self-directed and positive, but a set of norms is still at play for determining what a Deaf identity is. According to the CAD, for instance, being Deaf is distinct from being deafened: the latter, a medical and sociological term, refers to individuals who lose hearing later in life and who may not be able to identify with either the Deaf or hard-of-hearing communities. In this understanding, those who are deafened have lost some level of hearing, normally communicate via oral speech (CAD 2002b), and do not necessarily identify with the Deaf community. Accounts of meaning-making can be mobilized so as to assess the ways in which distinctions between deaf (small "d") and Deaf (large "D") determine the boundaries of a Deaf culture, and where, simultaneously, a Deaf cultural identity is not imposed on someone who does not participate in that culture.

What is especially interesting in this analysis is how subjects marked as non-Deaf can also be signified as members of a Deaf culture. The CAD (2002b), for example, states that inclusion in a Deaf culture depends on a person's status within it, attitude toward aspects of it, involvement in the local Deaf community, and skill in Sign language. A critical analysis of these differing ways of being represented as a member of a Deaf culture therefore demonstrates a distinction between externally imposed oralist representational discourses (in which a Deaf culture encompasses those who are signified as medically deficient) and community-driven discourses (in which the intensity and saliency of involvement determines membership), and how these are mutually constituted. Ladd (2003) takes a similar view and emphasizes that members of a Deaf culture can be the hearing children of Deaf parents (this will depend on whether they Sign and participate in Deaf culture), a person who marries a member of a Deaf culture, a parent of a Deaf child, someone who becomes Deaf in early life, or someone who works within the Deaf community over an extended period. Fischgrund and Akamatsu (1993) also contend that to be a member of a Deaf culture is to self-identify with the Deaf, to support the values of Deafness, and to be accepted as a member. Although the degree of membership in a Deaf culture and the intensity of feeling like a member may vary based on audiological (severity of hearing loss), political (whether one works with Deaf people to exert pressure on the state), linguistic (whether one Signs), and social factors (participating in a Deaf community and families), membership does not depend on being Deaf (Fischgrund and Akamatsu 1993, 171-72).

Accounting for the specific processes and conditions through which membership in a Deaf community is determined can reveal that oralist privilege is rooted in discourses of biology, that multiple meanings of Deaf identity are possible, and that dominant society and Deaf people create diverse kinds' of socially embedded meanings of difference. Such an analysis identifies key markers of Deaf culture and simultaneously provides a way to examine how these are not the same in character for all members of a Deaf culture, or shared in equal measure or in the same way (Ladd 2003, 260). Differences, in other words, are born out of relational and social contexts; and as such, there is no substantive logic to identity, only meanings as they are made in and through matrices of meaning-making.

On this basis, no matter which person occupies the centre of a particular meaning-making process (including one that is marked as Other), the process itself can always be subject to deconstruction. This is not only to avoid unqualified imposed meanings of difference, but also because self-directed processes of meaning-making are not free of discourses of power. In interpreting representations of difference, accounts of meaning-making show that there are no determinate standards for dictating what an ideal representation looks like. For that reason, it is not enough to argue that Deaf-centred meanings are automatically preferable, more legitimate, or more accurate because a Deaf subject created them (although they are also no less preferable, legitimate, or accurate than other-imposed meanings either). Instead, precisely so as to disrupt the production and regulation of difference, accounts of meaning-making are necessary to deconstruct how and why some meanings are treated as preferable, legitimate, and accurate, whereas others are not, and how these meanings determine relations of penalty and privilege.

DESIGNING DEAF BABIES: NORMS OF DEAFNESS, ORALISM, DISABILITY (AND HETEROSEXUALITY)

The interplay between oralist norms, meanings of disability/ability, and Deaf-centred understandings of difference can be illustrated through a brief analysis of one of the cases that opened up this chapter, a case characterized by H-Dirksen L. Bauman (2005) as "designing Deaf babies." Through a study of some of the media reports of this case, I take an account of the oralist and ablest processes of meaning-making that constitute and regulate Deafness as a disability and illustrate how these differ from discourses that constitute Deafness as a cultural identity.

The case involved a Deaf lesbian couple, Sharon Duchesneau and Candy McCullough, who chose a sperm donor with a family history of Deafness because they hoped to have a child who would be Deaf. They already had a Deaf daughter, Jehanne, who was conceived with the help of the same donor. Before their son, Gauvin, was born, the *Washington Post Magazine* (Mundy 2002) quoted Duchesneau as saying that "a hearing baby would be a blessing. A deaf baby would be a special blessing." The case received international attention and was controversial not only because it challenged mainstream representations of Deafness as a disabled identity, but because it also raised questions surrounding genetic technology and homosexual parenting. Representations of Otherness were thus constructed and governed within a matrix of meaning-making, whereby discourses of disability, culture, nature, heteronormativity, and gender all interacted with one another.

My analysis of this case exposes two central dynamics about the processes that produced representations of abnormality: first, there were marked differences between medical/disabling systems of meaning-making and social/culture-based systems of meaning-making; second, these respectively corresponded with other-imposed and self-directed/Deaf-centred meaning-making processes. Some reports, for instance, imposed the discourse of disability on the Deaf couple through headlines such as "Victims from Birth: Engineering Defects in Helpless Children Crosses the Line," "The Deaf Baby Cult," and "Lesbians Order Defective Baby." Reporters such as Wendy McElroy (2002) argued that reproductive technologies were being misused by the couple to reproduce a child with a "sensory defect." Chuck Colson (2002) also related clinical discourses with Deafness by likening the couple's decision to the practice of eugenics. He claimed that Deaf people wrongly understood themselves as a multicultural group and that they were really a disabled minority. Both reporters accused the couple of being morally irresponsible and selfish.

In some reports, Duchesneau and McCullough were said to be unprofessional, irrational, selfish, morally irresponsible, and uneducated, even though both were mental health specialists and therapists to Deaf people and their families. Other reports buttressed these demeaning representations by linking homosexuality and disability, and by claiming that the couple did not understand the compounded experiences of discrimination. Ken Connor, president of the US Family Research Council, is quoted as saying, "To intentionally give a child a disability, in addition to all of the disadvantages that come as a result of being raised in a homosexual household, is incredibly selfish" (Pyeatt 2002). By linking together norms of able-bodiedness, heterosexuality, and reproduction, and subsequently constituting Deafness as a disability, such statements had the effect of sustaining stereotypes and reinforcing the conflation of Deafness with disability.

By contrast, in other media reports (notably by the British Deaf Association, the Ethics Unit at the Children's Research Institute in Australia, and the BBC News), culture rather than physical abnormality was the battleground for signifying difference. In such headlines as "Couple 'Choose' to Have Deaf Baby" and "Deaf Lesbians Criticized for Efforts to Create Deaf Child," Duchesneau and McCullough were constructed as autonomous subjects rather than abnormal and deviant. Such reports included statements from the lesbian couple that disassociated Deafness from disability. In a British Deaf Association (BDA 2002) media release, for example, Duchesneau remarked, "While being deaf is experienced as a loss by people who become deaf later in life, for people who are born deaf there is no loss ... Being deaf is just a way of life." The two women stated that they viewed Deafness as a cultural identity, not a disability, one in which Sign language was central because it enabled "them to communicate fully with other signers as the defining and unifying feature of their culture" (Spriggs 2002). Both women emphasized that they were born Deaf and, having suffered from being raised primarily in the hearing world, wanted their children to share their culture. Both also attended Gallaudet University, which they said nurtured a lively Deaf intelligentsia (Spriggs 2002). In constructing their own subjectivities as cultural identities, Duchesneau and McCullough therefore took up Deaf-centred norms of subject formation.

An account of these conflicting characterizations of Deaf identity as a disability and as a culture shows how they relationally gained meaning through processes of subject formation that either re-entrenched oralist and ablest norms (based on the clinical gaze) or subscribed to Deaf-centred norms (based on culture). Moreover, such an account specifies that the point of disjuncture between these differing interpretations lies between medical and social meaning-making systems. Such a disjuncture, Bauman (2005, 314) argues, emerges "only within the contact zone between hearing and deaf worlds, between auditory and visual modalities ... It is only in the hearing/deaf contact zone where the site of disability [and oralism] emerges." In other words, in this case, the structure of difference that privileges and regulates oralism and denigrates Deafness becomes more visible when the point of disjuncture between other-imposed and self-directed systems of meaning-making is located. When one locates the site in which privilege is constructed, the sources of oppressive modes of meaning-making become starkly exposed.

An implication for political action that arises from such an account is that dominant norms can be refused. Thus, the choice made by Duchesneau and McCullough to have a child with a Deaf sperm donor actually distanced them and their children from a world organized by disablest and oralist norms. As Bauman (2005, 313) states, "having a deaf baby in a Deaf family distances the social site in which disabling conditions are most prevalent. Such an environment then opens the space for a visually centred episteme to emerge that results in lived experiences not predicated on the lack of a sense, but on the plentitude of a visual culture with its own norms of language acquisition and identity development." By choosing to have a Deaf child (insofar as reproductive technology could satisfy such a choice), Duchesneau and McCullough thus limited their contact with the conditions of oralism and disability – contact that would have been greater had they had a hearing child (Bauman 2005, 314).

Importantly, the position taken by Duchesneau and McCullough can also be read as one in which they did not simply refuse oralist and disablest meanings in favour of culture-based meanings, but in which they also refused the overall structure that gave rise to the tension between self-directed and other-imposed meanings in the first place. Such a refusal is specifically evident in that they did not aim to reconcile the set of conflicting meanings. Instead, their decision indicates that it is possible to reject the structure of the contact zone itself – namely, the zone in which culture-based, oralist, and disablest meanings conflict – by taking oralism and disability out of the picture entirely. This in itself can be understood as an act of resistance to hegemonic modes of meaning-making.

Making Meanings of Gender and Trans-sexuality

In this section I deploy an account of meaning-making to study a particular set of gendered structures of difference. I examine some of the processes of meaning-making that construct meanings of trans-sexuality, specifically those that form and de-form meanings of trans-sexuality and those that constitute counter-meanings. Following Jean Bobby Noble (2006, 17), I hyphenate "trans-sexuality" not to signify that this mode of difference transcends gender, but "to defamiliarize the way that these [gender] terms manipulate and produce gender difference by deploying ... an alibi of gender essence."

Three reasons lead me to focus on the processes that produce representations of trans-sexuality. First, trans studies are not optional extras to be included in the study of identity/difference politics; nor are they extraneous to a feminist analysis or reducible to queer studies. Rather, the study of trans-sexuality is constitutive to theories of misogyny, heteronormativity, homophobia, and racism (Noble 2006, 2) – all of which, in my view, fall under the rubric of identity/difference politics. Second, the symbolic, social, and material impact of gender, heteronormative, and transphobic norms structures the lives of trans-sexuals in discriminatory ways that are directly relevant to the study of difference and power. As the Canadian National Association of Women and the Law (NAWL) (Denike and Renshaw 2003, 5-6) observes, trans-sexuals face a series of interrelated socio-political issues, including hate violence, abusive treatment by law enforcement personnel, chronic underemployment, and lack of access to social services, the end result of which is public humiliation, derision, ridicule, marginalization, and exclusion. My analysis of trans-sexuality aims to highlight some of these systemic legal and health issues. Third, an account of the processes that produce meanings of trans-sexuality exemplifies that gender norms are not stable or fixed but subject to socially situated interpretations that transcend traditional binaries. In particular, trans-sexuality indicates that subject formation does not have to be constrained by normalizing processes of differentiation, because meanings of difference are socially constituted, both by state and non-state agents, and can therefore be remade.

The idea of an open-ended process of subject formation has been a central feature of trans-genderism, an umbrella category into which trans-sexuality sometimes falls. Indeed, the very meaning of "trans-gender" is in a constant state of becoming. In its initial usage, the word referred to persons who transcended gender norms (this included trans-sexuals, drag queens and kings, intersexed persons, transvestites, and people who do not identify with the categories of male and female). Since at least the 1990s, however, its meaning has been in a state of flux. Paisley Currah, Richard M. Juang, and Shannon Price Minter (2006, xiv) remark that, since 1995, it "is now generally used to refer to individuals whose gender identity or expression does not conform to the social expectations for their assigned sex birth. At the same time, related terms used to describe particular identities within that broader category have continued to evolve and multiply." Noble (2006, 3) sees the terms "trans-sexual" and "trans-gender" as essentially contested and free-floating but adds that, "at its most provocative, *trans-* and the space it references refuses the medical and psychological categorical imperatives through which it has always been forced to confess."

Various related terms (transvestite, cross-dresser, trans, female-to-male, male-to-female, and boyz) recode identity language, such that the category of trans-gender has expansive and contested meanings, although these too are subject to various kinds of normalizing processes of meaning-making (which is especially apparent in discussions about who is really trans). One particular area of tension is the inclusion of intersex people in the definition of trans-gender (Currah, Juang, and Minter 2006, xv). Although the terminology of trans-genderism may be insufficiently inclusive in some instances and imprecise in others, it has come to include the social category of trans-sexuality. This is the case though some trans-sexuals object to being included under the catch-all term "trans-gender" because it masks their specific health care and social service needs, and because trans-genderism can be overdetermined by a lesbian/gay framework (Namaste 2005, 2).

DIFFERENCE: NATURAL OR SOCIAL?

An account of the processes that de-form affirming representations of trans-sexuality deconstructs how gender norms reinforce a preference for naturalized representations of subject formation over social understandings. The former are rooted in the idea that an intrinsic link exists between identity and nature, in which male and female identities are assigned at birth. Here, primacy is assigned to the male and female anatomical bodies (read: normal, natural, God-given body), whereby a gender identity is given meaning through a naturalized and fixed relationship between the physical and social body. These prevailing norms of gendering are premised on two kinds of sexed bodies in which the pre-cultural male or female body matches cultural maleness or femaleness. These binary-based norms of gender determine the standard by which to represent bodies (feminine, masculine, too feminine, too masculine, not feminine enough, not masculine enough), with the effect of signifying trans-sexuality as deviant and abnormal. Trans-sexuality is specifically deemed abnormal in that it does not conform to a 'true' sex, according to the presence or absence of a 'proper' penis or the capacity of the vagina.

Accounts of the processes of meaning-making that produce these portrayals of trans-sexuality are especially effective in illuminating that the binary of male/female (as anatomically sexed bodies) does not provide a permanent foundation of gender. This is because, as Foucault (Hoy 2005, 69) showed in his studies of sexuality and discipline, "talk about the natural body is historically conditioned by the discursive need to talk about something natural to which the norms [of sexuality] are applied." In other words, the very idea of a natural body being authentically one way or another comes into being through social forms of disciplinary power. Understanding of the body is therefore not pre-discursive or pre-normative (Hoy 2005, 69). Indeed, meaning-making processes can and do produce representations of gender, sexuality, and desire that transcend the conventional naturalized binary. As Judith Butler (1990, 10) says, "When the constructed status of gender is theorized as radically independent of sex, gender itself becomes a free-floating artifice, with the consequence that *man* and *masculine* might just as easily signify a female body as a male one, and *woman* and *feminine* a male body as easily as a female one." Indeed, Butler (1990, 184) continues, hegemonic processes of gendering that characterize subjects as women/feminine and men/masculine are rule-generated in that they "rely on the consistent and repeated invocation of rules that condition and restrict culturally intelligible practices of identity." In short, dominant processes of gendering are premised on a sex-equals-gender equation, as opposed to a sex-is-gender equation.

REGIMES OF SCIENCE

One way in which these rule-generated gender norms are consolidated is through strands of science that naturalize the conventional male/female binary, heteronormativity, and the sex-equals-gender equation. These particular regimes of science are instrumental in creating and upholding a structure of difference in which trans-sexuality is hyper-visible in some instances and invisible in others. At the same time, as I explain later, these disciplining discourses also give rise to forms of subjectivity that refuse scientifically driven normalizations of gender. Let me say more about how science transphobically governs structures of gender difference.

Though he does not use the language of meaning-making, Andrew Sharpe (1998, 29) traces various scientific processes of subject formation to illustrate that the medical profession has produced two broad narratives for conceiving of trans-sexualism. Both of these regulate gender norms, sexual choices, and desires through a heteronormative lens. The first is the discovery story in which the true trans-sexual is one who undertakes surgery. According to this story, when surgery transforms the anatomy it also transforms sexual desire, for as long as the subject is anatomically one sex it is inappropriate for him/

her to desire someone who has the same anatomy; that desire becomes more acceptable when it can be characterized as heterosexual after surgery. In the case of male-to-female trans-sexuals, the effect of this is that the subject is constituted as homosexual prior to surgery and heterosexual after it. Accordingly, the sexual desire of the male-to-female trans-sexual is legitimized only once heterosexual status is achieved. In this first scientific narrative, then, trans-sexual desire is regulated by heterosexual norms of desire.

The second medical narrative, Sharpe continues, has emerged as the number of sex reassignment surgeries has grown. Sex reassignment is without doubt an important step for some trans-sexuals. Yet, in dominant narratives of sex reassignment, trans-sexuals are not only signified as biological inversions, but they are also constructed as psychologically inverse (Sharpe 1998, 29-30). The scientific language of gender dysphoria specifically entrenches the idea that trans-sexuality is a psychological disorder, in which trans-sexual subjects are deemed to be born in the wrong body. Since the role of science is to cure disorders, sex reassignment surgery is deemed necessary so that the psychological gendered self can match the correct bodily gender. These psychological traits are, in turn, determined by sexual desire, such that lesbians and heterosexual and bisexual male-to-female candidates are considered poor risks for surgery; this is because the latter two are most likely to be psychologically designated as transvestites or heterosexuals with impotence problems (Sharpe 1998, 30). Surgery therefore "emerges in medical practice as a prize ... conferred upon those who have successfully accomplished pre-surgical medical rites of passage, thereby satisfying medical experts that they will blend into society post-surgery" (Sharpe 1998, 32). Undergoing surgery does not erase the idea that trans-sexuality is deviant and abnormal, but it does satisfy hegemonic representations of heteronormativity, sex, and sexual desire/capacity.

In sum, these science-based narratives are produced by heterosexual and binary-based processes of gendering, and both reproduce them. These narratives reflect and perpetuate normalizing gendered systems of meaning-making, and they reveal a crisis about the ways in which identities are conceptualized. The crisis emerges, as Marjorie Garber (1992, 11) argues, because trans-sexuality (and cross-dressing) represents a third sex or a third term. Garber states that the "third" "is a mode of articulation, a way of describing a space of possibility. Three puts in question the idea of one: of identity, self-sufficiency, self-knowledge." It is not, she contests, a limited mode of representation in that it does not merely describe those subjects who are deemed to be outside the heteronormative system of gendering. Rather, thirdness destabilizes the "stable, unchallengeable, grounded and 'known'" (Garber 1992, 13). Transvestism destabilizes such binaries as male/female and sex/gender, and it also destabilizes other definitional distinctions and signs of over-determination such as black/white (Garber 1992, 16-17).

An account of the meaning-making processes that produce representations of thirdness enables the destabilization of dominant modes of representation. In this instance, by deconstructing the very structure of difference (in this case, a binary), the analysis reveals specifically that the very ontology and substantive logic of identity is troubled. When gender is troubled (to borrow from Butler), the assumed conditions of authenticity that organize difference are disrupted. And in the disruption of these conditions, it becomes possible to consider and produce modes of gendering that go beyond traditional binaries. Not only can conventional gender categories be reversed (if this is desirable at all), but trans-sexuality can also be given meaning through discourses that fundamentally challenge a binary structure of difference. Garber's notion of a third sex may be one example of such an alternative. Another is Gloria Anzaldúa's (1999) conception of mestiza, which anchors subjectivities in particular places with distinctive histories (Alsop, Fitzsimons, and Lennon 2002, 214) and welcomes what liberal conceptions of identity perceive as ambiguous, conflicted, and threatening.

REGIMES OF LAW

In conjunction with science, the law produces meanings of trans-sexuality and acts to operationalize gender norms. For example, birth registration requirements and census provisions permit a choice only between two variants, male and female (Findlay 1999, 6). In Canada, the law also requires that trans-sexuals register a 'change' in their gender following surgery. Although such legal recognition of a gender 'change' can be significant on a political and individual level, it is important to understand that Canadian law has a minimal capacity to recognize it, for only after surgery does such a gender identity assume legal status. This legal regulation can have serious implications for trans-sexuals. In *Kavanagh v. Attorney General of Canada*, for example, the Canadian Human Rights Tribunal ruled that upon being convicted of a crime, Corrections Canada was justified in refusing Synthia Kavanagh access to a women-only prison, despite the fact that Kavanagh, a male-to-female trans-sexual, identified as female. The tribunal based its decision on the fact that

Kavanagh had not undergone sex reassignment surgery and was not therefore legally registered as female under the Vital Statistics Act, even though she identified as female, underwent hormonal therapy, and presented herself as feminine (Denike and Renshaw 2003, 8-9).

Provincial laws in Canada also determine meanings of trans-sexuality. In Quebec, for example, the Direction de l'état civil (Office of Civil Status) states that "a male-to-female transsexual must undergo a vaginoplasty – the construction of the vagina – in order to change name and sex" (Namaste 2005, 5). Viviane Namaste notes that, in 1997 and 1998, with regard to female-to-male trans-sexuals, this office invoked a vague criterion for changing genital organs. Whereas sex and name changes for female-to-male trans-sexuals required hormone therapy and such surgeries as a hysterectomy and a double mastectomy, for female-to-male trans-sexuals it was unclear whether a phalloplasty (the construction of a penis) was necessary at all.

As well, my account of transphobic meaning-making processes provides a critical analysis of how hegemonic gender norms are fashioned, however unintentionally, through equity-related laws. In Canadian human rights and Charter law, for example, it is not entirely clear what enumerated ground trans-sexuals should employ to make legal claims of discrimination, because the law determines trans-sexuality to be ambiguous. Some trans-sexuals have deployed "sex" as a default category because no other ground effectively covers discrimination based on gender transition (Denike and Renshaw 2003, 8). However, this option of making a claim based on sex discrimination is limited to those who have undergone surgery and is not open to pre-operative trans-sexuals.

As an enumerated ground, sexual orientation, which is predicated on the hetero/homo dualism, may or may not be relevant to trans-sexuals because they can be heterosexual, lesbian, gay, bisexual, queer, or asexual. Certainly, if they are heterosexual, trans-sexual people are impacted by laws that discriminate on the basis of sexual orientation (such as marriage laws), but sexual orientation remains uncertain ground for protection (Denike and Renshaw 2003, 9). This is especially because sexual orientation itself gains meaning from relatively stable systems of sex and gender in which the relationship between sex, gender identity, and gender expression maintains the hegemonic framework of the proper female and male subjects (Currah 2001, 185, 191). Moreover, even in gay law reform movements, "transsexual homosexuals come to represent a threat not only to heterosexual hegemony but also to homosexual and transsexual 'coherence'" (Sharpe 1998, 27). This is because the social category of trans-sexual homosexuals disrupts heterosexual norms of opposite-sex desire as well as the (already threatened) coherency of gay and lesbian desire.

In Canada, it has also been argued that trans-sexuals could make claims on the enumerated ground of disability, specifically because trans-sexuality is linked to illness or gender disorder. This contrasts with what is possible in other countries: in the US, for example, the Americans with Disabilities Act explicitly excludes transvestism, trans-sexualism, and gender identity disorders that do not result from physical impairments (Currah 2006, 6). But even where disability might be a chosen enumerated ground, it is difficult terrain to navigate. On the one hand, disablest representations of trans-sexuality (as a gender disorder) reinforce notions of Otherness, in which the abnormality is seen as being scientifically treatable through sex reassignment and hormone therapies (Denike and Renshaw 2003, 8-10). On the other hand, despite the enormous financial and personal costs of seeking health care, the ground of disability provides an important outlet for trans-sexuals and can enable (rather than constrain) political and legal claims (Levi and Klein 2006). In particular, health care policies on disability open up access to hormone treatment, therapy, and sex reassignment surgery as necessary health care items. As well, those who undergo surgery may experience significant post-surgical constraints and complications, ongoing physical pain and discomfort, and concerns about genital functioning. Hormone treatment, too, may cause problems (Kessler 1990, 68).

Legal meanings of sex, sexual orientation, and disability are thus not clearly or self-evidently appropriate for claims regarding trans-sexuality. Indeed, though some human rights claims have been won on the basis of sexism, homophobia, and disability/ability, the law does not always have the capacity to address discrimination outside the listed enumerated grounds. On this basis, trans advocates such as the Trans Action Society (an organization based in Canada that promotes equality rights, social justice, and health care for trans-sexuals and their families) have argued that "gender identity" should be added as a ground of protection under human rights legislation (Denike and Renshaw 2003, 10). Trans Action defines the prohibition of discrimination on the grounds of gender identity as the "protection against discrimination for anyone who, temporarily or permanently, is, or is perceived to be, a member of the gender other than his or her assigned gender" (Denike and Renshaw 2003, 10).

Although it is important to remember that definitions of "gender identity" have tended to be English-centred and marginalizing of francophone interpretations (Namaste 2005, 114-15), this enumerated ground could be useful. "Gender identity" could potentially unmask the web of power in which discrimination against trans-sexuals takes place and could also offer protections to those who are excluded because they do not conform to the norms of sex and gender. NAWL takes the position that the ground of gender identity is "not over-determined by previous jurisprudence, as might be the case for sex, sexual orientation, and disability, and it would potentially protect a greater range of gender variant people than do the existing categories" (Denike and Renshaw 2003, 10). The meaning and use of "gender identity" thus presents an alternative way of approaching trans-sexuality because it challenges the structures of difference that constitute norms of gender, homophobia, and transphobia.

This enumerated ground has, to some extent at least, been taken up in parts of Canada. The Northwest Territories has recently added "gender identity" to its human rights code. As well, the British Columbia Human Rights Commission (BCHRC 1998) has proposed including gender identity as a formal ground for protection in its human rights law, and the Ontario Human Rights Commission (OHRC 2000) has taken the position that human rights complaints of discrimination and harassment based on gender identity will be accepted under the ground of sex. The UK also passed a Gender Recognition Act in 2005, "which allows transsexual people to apply for legal recognition of their new gender" (Currah, Juang, and Minter 2006, xxi). This act arose from a European Court of Human Rights decision that concluded that the UK violated the European Convention on Human Rights in denying trans-sexuals the right to obtain new birth certificates or to marry in their 'new' gender. These kinds of legal changes may or may not be effective in dealing with transphobia, but they do signal the potential of the law to reconfigure difference in less injurious ways.

REGULATING NORMS OF GENDER AND SEXUALITY: *NIXON V. VANCOUVER RAPE RELIEF SOCIETY*

I now turn to a legal case to show that an account of meaning-making is effective in illuminating and critiquing how historically conditioned streams of repressive scientific and legal discourse generate meanings of trans-sexuality. I specifically examine how and why, and with what effects, these discourses were adopted by a feminist organization in Canada. The case – *Nixon v.*

Vancouver Rape Relief Society (henceforth referred to as *Nixon*) – is now well known in some fields of study (some feminist theories, queer theory, trans studies) but has not been taken up in liberal theories of identity/difference politics, at least not as far as I am aware.

Nixon involved the rights of Kimberley Nixon, a male-to-female trans-sexual.[2] The case entered the legal realm in 1995 when Nixon, a post-operative trans-sexual woman, was prohibited from volunteering in a peer counselling training program run by Vancouver Rape Relief and Women's Shelter (VRRWS), a self-declared feminist organization. Nixon, who was born with male physiology in 1957, realized at the age of five that her male physical attributes did not correspond to her sense of self as female. Until 1989 she lived publicly as male and privately as female. That year, she began living full time as female, and in 1990 she had sex reassignment surgery. Her birth certificate was subsequently amended to change the sex designation pursuant to section 27(1) of the Vital Statistics Act. She had been living as a woman for sixteen years and had undergone surgery five years prior to the incident at VRRWS. After successfully completing the pre-screening process to ensure that she did not disagree with VRRWS collective political principles, Nixon attended the training session. There, a VRRWS facilitator immediately identified her as someone who had not always lived as a girl or woman; after confirming this with Nixon, the facilitator asked her to leave. Nixon filed a sex discrimination complaint with the British Columbia Human Rights Tribunal in August 1995. On this enumerated ground of "sex," Nixon was effectively claiming that she had suffered sexual discrimination as a woman and that her new legal identity as a woman was not recognized by VRRWS.

In January 2002 the Human Rights Tribunal decided that Kimberley Nixon was a woman and that VRRWS had discriminated against her. She was awarded $7,500 for "injury to dignity," the highest Human Rights Tribunal award ever in British Columbia. VRRWS appealed the tribunal decision to the BC Supreme Court in August 2002. In December 2003, the court overturned the tribunal decision on the grounds that it had not correctly interpreted the hardships faced by VRRWS and because it had erred in holding that VRRWS did not have a primary purpose of providing services to women in the political sense understood by the organization. In particular, in its decision (*Vancouver Rape Relief v. Nixon et al.*), the Supreme Court concluded that VRRWS had the right to define its clientele and membership, and that in doing so, it could legitimately exclude male-to-female trans-sexuals. Invoking *R. v. Powley,* which outlined a test to determine who was a member of the

Sault Ste. Marie Métis community, the judge applied the test to Nixon. This is interesting because a test intended for racialized Others was applied to a gender Other as if race-thinking and gender-thinking were interchangeable. The test had three criteria for membership – self-identification, ancestral connection, and community acceptance. According to the judge, Nixon met the first of these. However, because her genetic characteristics and life experience did not satisfy the ancestral connection requirement and because VRRWS was deemed to be analogous to a community, she did not qualify under the other two.

Nixon's lawyer appealed the BC Supreme Court decision in January 2004, and the BC Court of Appeal reviewed the case in April 2005. The review included submissions from intervenors such as Equality for Gays and Lesbians Everywhere (EGALE, a national organization committed to advancing equality and justice for lesbian, gay, bisexual, and trans-identified people, as well as their families throughout Canada), who supported Kimberley Nixon's position. In December 2005, the BC Court of Appeal dismissed the appeal. Explaining what had motivated her legal battle, Nixon remarked, "I felt less than human and I didn't want to be here anymore. I felt I wasn't part of society; I wasn't wanted. I thought about the Lions Gate Bridge. But I've spent my whole life surviving, so I filed the human-rights complaint instead" (Rupp 2005).

At the initial tribunal, VRRWS and Kimberley Nixon both agreed that gender categories were socially constructed although experientially real and that sex itself was not a binary. Both also supported the need for women-only organizations to provide services to women who are victims of male violence. And both took the position that trans-gendered people are marginalized and disadvantaged in Canadian society. However, VRRWS also gave a particular meaning to gender, one that was premised on predictable relations between gender and sex, whereby natural sex identity produced a corresponding social gender identity. The VRRWS also argued that Kimberley Nixon was not entitled to protection from discrimination on the basis of sex, because the BC government had not agreed to add gender identity to its Human Rights Code. Moreover, they argued that even if she were discriminated against on the basis of sex, the lifelong experience of being treated as female was a bona fide occupational requirement and a justifiable basis to exclude trans-sexual women from the VRRWS program (Findlay 2003, 2). VRRWS asserted that, as a feminist organization, it was structured on principles of common sexual experience as related to childhood socialization, life-long experience of being raised as female, social and physical relationships to reproduction, and particular kinds of subordination (Denike and Renshaw 2003, 13). The VRRWS lawyers maintained that women suffered oppression from birth and that they should resist male violence by working together with other women who also experienced oppression as a product of having life-long experiences as female. In effect, norms of gendering determined the arguments advanced by VRRWS.

Interestingly, VRRWS representatives stated that to disallow men and trans-sexual women from counselling rape victims was not to take a position on what a woman is but to acknowledge the differences in life experiences that led to female subordination. Yet, as Namaste (2005, 66) points out, VRRWS invoked the criterion of experience only with regard to trans-sexual women who volunteered. The society's volunteers also counselled prostitutes and women with physical disabilities who had been sexually assaulted but were not required to have personal experience of prostitution or disability. VRRWS also claimed that, within the meaning of the BC Human Rights Code, participation as a volunteer was neither a service nor employment (Findlay 2003, 11), and that it should benefit from section 41 of the code, which allows organizations to exempt some people from participating because doing so promotes the interests and welfare of an identifiable group characterized by a common sex or political belief. Yet even here, the meaning of an "identifiable group" depended on how the category of woman was defined.

Of itself, the adoption of these conventional gender meanings does not indict VRRWS. Rather, as an account of meaning-making brings to light, VRRWS relationally privileged processes of gendering that produced categorical distinctions between men/male and women/female over processes of gendering that left open the meaning of gender. As Noble (2006, 7) says of the Nixon case, the essentializing assertions of VRRWS, "whether trans-phobic in intention or 'only' in consequence, attempt to fix not only the limits of gender but also the intelligibility of what counts as the experiences of the appropriately gendered body." Specifically, in privileging traditional binary-based categories and thus effectively closing off gender meanings, VRRWS re-entrenched a set of gender norms.

An account of these norms shows that Nixon's difference was explicitly constructed by linking conventional meanings of natural identity to conventional meanings of social identity, thereby reinforcing the notion that sex produces gender (and rejecting the idea that sex is gender). Although it is true that representational distinctions do exist between subjects marked as male-to-female trans-sexuals and females who are born females, such distinctions were not neutrally conceived by VRRWS. In other words, it preferred one system of gendering to another without adequately subjecting the foundations of that system to critique. The effect was that legally institutionalized gender binaries that were operationalized through medical and pathological discourses of disability were given legitimacy by a feminist organization. These discourses constructed Kimberley Nixon as an unauthentic woman. In particular, such representations were justified by VRRWS on the basis that Nixon's physiological body did not correspond to its conventionally signified social body. A claim to authenticity was thus dictated by the hegemony of a meaning-making system premised on a naturalized relationship between identity and culture, and a conventionally understood sex binary.

One could argue that Nixon herself reiterated gender norms because she deployed the enumerated ground of sex and the category of woman. And indeed, she did self-signify as a woman on the grounds that she was medically and legally a woman (under the Vital Statistics Act); nor, she added, could she be treated as a man simply because she had not always been anatomically signified as a woman. She also held that, although she was once deemed anatomically male, she had been female (in a non-anatomical way) since birth. In this sense, she relied on a system of gendering that was predicated on the conventional difference between men and women. Yet the important point is not that she self-identified as a woman – this was a choice for her to make – but that she was excluded by VRRWS because she did not conform to a deeply entrenched set of gender norms.

In particular, Kimberley Nixon's gender identity challenged the relationship between sex assignment at birth and gender expression. She rejected legal and scientific conceptions of gender that governed the varied regimes in which conventional meanings of men (those born with male genitals) and women (those born with female genitals) are legitimized, and in doing so she produced a gender identity alternative to that advanced by VRRWS. Although she did not revoke the category of woman, she gave meaning to it without naturalizing the relationship between gender identity and anatomy. Nixon questioned the presumptive stability and pre-given relationship between sex and gender. Her lawyer argued that a corresponding relationship between biological and social representations was not a precondition for producing the category of woman. On the contrary, in the moment that Nixon recognized herself as a woman, her social location was very much informed by histories of patriarchy and sexism.

The regulation of gender norms by a feminist organization is steeped in a history of patriarchy, so perhaps we should not be particularly surprised that VRRWS held a traditional meaning of woman. The category "woman" has been *the* constitutive feature of many feminist organizations, and any foundational change to it destabilizes feminism itself, or so it is argued. This, however, is a false conclusion precisely because, as a theoretical tool and ideology, feminism offers a way to challenge how subjects are produced through relations of gender. This is not to suggest that an emancipatory politics necessitates the rejection of conventional social categories. On the contrary, I advocate the idea of taking an account of meaning-making so as to critically analyze why and how such categories are circumscribed through particular conventional discourses and to consider what other interpretations of difference are possible through this critique. In other words, I am arguing for a form of politics that involves opening up, rather than closing, the processes by which difference is constituted. And because VRRWS closed such a process, its actions to exclude Nixon served to perpetuate gender norms and reinforce disciplinary scientific and legal meanings of trans-sexuality.

In specifying that gender norms structured meanings of difference in ways that deemed Nixon's subjectivity to be unrecognizable and unauthentic, an account of meaning-making draws attention to the very crisis in identity production that Garber (1992) names. In the case of Nixon, one expression of that crisis was evident in the ways in which Nixon's public identity was in jeopardy. Another crisis arose because Nixon formed representations of her identity by challenging the established bound of gender formation, and in doing so she ruptured the foundations of conventional systems of gender. One of the impacts of disrupting the gender norm for Kimberley Nixon (as she herself explained at the Human Rights Tribunal) has been the narrowing of her work opportunities: she experienced a series of dismissals once her employers learned of her sex change. As Nixon said, "This case has been a lot to endure: to be attacked around my identity. But if I had walked away, I couldn't continue to live. It's hard for a transgendered person who seeks support and help ... I am so afraid that Rape Relief will turn away a transgendered person from accessing services and that may cost a life" (Rupp 2005). The impact of the case on her life is no doubt enormous, for the law, which promised to be a site of recognition, ended as a source of judicial disciplining. This account of judicial disciplining not only provides a way to document such modes of regulation, but it also shows how Kimberley Nixon produced her gender identity by challenging conventional binary-based meanings of gender that justify heteronormativity and transphobia.

Alternate Directions of Study: Mapping Structures of Difference

The examples of Deafness and trans-sexuality discussed in this chapter show that accounts of meaning-making can expand and enrich the terrain of identity/ difference politics. This occurs not only by virtue of encompassing modes of difference that go beyond the scope of culture, but also in terms of, first, analyzing how institutionalized discourses like science and law are circumscribed by ablest and gender norms and how these norms are replicated and modified in the processes of subject formation, and, second, in terms of situating various meaning makers (such as health care professionals, disability organizations, self-identified Deaf people, a feminist organization, and Kimberley Nixon) in the analysis, and not solely the state.

Overall, these two accounts expose the myth that identities naturally pre-exist. This is not to say that the body politic and identity politics are irrelevant. Nor do I claim that identities are essentially fluid and subsequently without significance. Let me repeat that this would be contrary to my argument that processes of meaning-making produce representations of difference that variedly determine socio-political positions, material and social opportunities, and subjective experiences. It is precisely because processes of meaning-making produce representations of subjectivity and subjection that are circumscribed by contexts of difference that accounts of meaning-making are useful. Specifically, my analysis reveals the fallacy that subjects *have* identities and shows that they are produced *as* identities through meaning-making processes. In this regard, accounts of meaning-making deconstruct *how* identities *become* institutionally, structurally, and symbolically significant through meaning-making processes that are created by and generative of privileging and penalizing relations of difference.

Furthermore, my analysis demonstrates that self-directed and externally imposed meanings (such as Deaf versus disabled, biological versus social) are not always reconcilable; indeed, my intent is not to resolve conflicting meanings. Conclusive resolution is not only unrealistic, but such a goal is also premised on eradicating difference itself. To reiterate an earlier point, the production of self-affirming meanings of difference does not necessarily emerge from repressive conditions; nor are these assumed to be better because they are formed in heightened contexts of contestation. Rather, my point is that, through critique, counter-meanings of difference can be produced even in repressive conditions. In addition, the above accounts do not necessarily lead to the conclusion that representations of difference simply need to be reversed – although this analytic tool does not categorically dismiss this strategy either. Thus, I do not suggest that Deaf-centred modes of meaning-making should be privileged over oralist versions, or that conventional meanings regarding the male and female subject should be switched with each other. Such strategies would ultimately obscure the ways in which marginalized subjects enact their agency. They would also maintain the logic that some modes of representation are *intrinsically* better than others, leave too much room open to exchange existing formations of dominance for new representations of dominance, and fail to fundamentally destabilize the structure in which norms function. Although transforming meanings of abnormality into meanings of normality does change the structure of difference, the entire structure that gives rise to this distinction needs to be fundamentally critiqued.

By critically mapping the ways in which difference is structured, analysts can challenge the specific practices, institutions, and agents that create, sustain, and regulate relations of penalty and privilege. In particular, the analyst can locate points of intervention at which to make social change; subsequently, change can occur by resisting injurious representations of difference and interpreting difference beyond the regulated terrain of the contact zone in which conflicting meanings arise. Such interventions potentially open up other ways of making meanings of difference while also destabilizing those processes that limit an understanding of difference to such conventional binaries as Deaf versus hearing, Deaf versus disabled, biological sex versus social gender, and male versus female. In the next chapter, to get beyond these one-dimensional binaries, I identify in more detail how to deconstruct a matrix of meaning-making through relational accounts.

5
Accounts of Racialized Gendering: Domination and Relational Othering

In 2003, through the Canadian Society of Muslims, the Islamic Institute of Civil Justice (IICJ) put forward a proposal to establish Islamic arbitration tribunals that would allow Muslims living in Ontario to resolve family-related disputes using the principles of Shariah, or Islamic personal law. The ensuing debate was fraught with strong concerns about the application of Muslim law in the Canadian context, even though other religious communities, including Mennonites, Catholics, Jews, and Ismaili Muslims, already organized arbitration services for their members (Eisenberg 2007, 211). As well, suspicions were voiced concerning the ways in which Shariah law would make Muslim women vulnerable (as if they are not already vulnerable in contexts of Islamophobia). In late 2005, the Ontario premier went against the recommendations of the Boyd Report (Boyd 2004), which had, in consultation with various stakeholders, outlined some ways to regulate the application of religious laws in arbitration disputes. The premier went further to say that faith-based arbitration for family law disputes would no longer be permitted.

The debate about the application of Shariah law is a striking example of the ways in which some identity-related claims emerge as competing claims. In particular, the debate was set up as one between claims of culture and claims for sex equality rights. Those who supported the IICJ proposal were viewed as pro-culture and anti-feminist; conversely, those who opposed it were seen as modern, progressive equality-seekers and bad Muslims. My intention in this chapter is not to enter into a discussion about the tension between so-called conflicting liberal rights, or to explore alternative ways to publicly assess identity-related claims, or even to examine the need for a "third space" in which it is possible to think through ways to implement Shariah law and simultaneously protect the rights of women.[1] All of these are important projects, both theoretically and politically. But my reason for invoking the Shariah case is to focus attention on the ways in which a choice between cultural rights and sex equality rights is demanded when aspects of difference are conceptualized as separable rather than relational, mutually constitutive, and co-implicative.

To illustrate this dynamic, I draw directly on feminist intersectional-type theories, which, as I noted in Chapter 2, have complicated an understanding of difference and power. They have shown that the production of difference is complex rather than reducible to one or more dimensions. On this basis, difference cannot be fully understood through unidimensional approaches, because these eclipse other modes of difference. This, of course, has been one of my critiques of liberal multiculturalism. But nor is an additive approach satisfactory, even though it has been deployed by the Canadian government, as seen in policy documents on gender mainstreaming (SWC 1998, 2001, 2003, 2004), in which issues of race and class are appended to questions of gender. As well, a hierarchical approach is inadequate because it continues to assume that one or more aspects of identity are primary, whereas others are nominally relevant. Although not all aspects of difference are equally salient in all contexts, even some feminist theory has shown a tendency to assert that "woman" needs to be de-centred but has then continued to privilege it as a site of analysis. In particular, even when multiple differences are ana-lyzed together, the race-class-gender trinity tends to be reproduced. This trinity approach leads to the exclusion of other aspects of difference such as sexuality (Fogg-Davis 2006) and disability (Garland-Thomson 2002).

Underlying these unidimensional, additive, and hierarchical approaches is the assumption that aspects of difference can be quantified, categorized, and ranked in bounded ways (Collins 1990, 225). By contrast, an intersectional-type approach starts from an understanding that, because representations of difference are performed through integral systems of identification and power, they cannot be separated out and ranked. This is not to say that they are in-distinguishable, but it is to recognize that 'competing' systems of oppression and privilege interactively function to enable one another (Fellows and Razack 1998, 340).

My goal in this chapter is to analyze the operations and effects of a dom-inant matrix of meaning-making, namely the interactive processes that produce and organize representations of difference. I specifically take accounts of meaning-making processes that make and mark representations of indigenous women and women of colour in Canada as Other. I am interested in particular about how these categories become totalized by relationally distinguishing forms and degrees of Otherness. These two social collectivities are relationally distinct and internally diverse, but both are constituted by dominant vehicles of power in marginalizing and oppressive ways. The framework of the matrix of meaning-making is especially valuable because it shows that difference is constituted relationally; in particular, both the interactions between processes and the relationship between different sets of interactions matter. So, for instance, analysts must look beyond a single set of interactions between racialization and gendering (which construct such categories as non-white women) to examine the interactions that occur between different kinds of racialized forms of gendering (which relationally produce such categories as indigenous women and women of colour) and also between discourses of racialized gendering and other discourses (which produce relational differences among indigenous women, and among women of colour). It is precisely the production and organization of these variations that I discuss in this chapter.

Although indigenous peoples and immigrants are often the subjects of study in liberal multicultural discourses – in that claims regarding land, treaty rights, and religious practices are typically examined through the lens of culture – the interactions between multiple processes of differentiation remain underanalyzed in mainstream political theory. Furthermore, though the categories of immigrants and women of colour may seem synonymous, not all women of colour have the legal status of immigrant: some are citizens, others are residents, and yet others (refugees, temporary workers) may have unequal legal status or no legal status at all (undocumented subjects).

Relational Processes of Othering

To unpack the complexities of a matrix of meaning-making, I take accounts of the relationships between different sets of processual interactions. Although having only a partial perspective on the operations of a matrix of meaning-making is possible, by examining specific relational forms and degrees of penalty and privilege, I seek to achieve a better understanding of how meanings are circumscribed by various interactive norms and how similar kinds of interactive processes produce varied representations of difference.

Relational processes of Othering, I suggest, function through interactions between such signifying binaries as Oriental/Occidental (Said 1978), Third World woman/Western woman (Mohanty 2003), and outside/inside (Fuss 1991), as well as through representations of hybridity and thirdness (Anzaldúa 1999; Bhabha 1990, 1994; Garber 1992). Although binaries have been much maligned over recent years, especially because they overdetermine difference and eclipse the ways in which it functions on the borders of binaries or in between them, I am of the view that they are useful in elucidating some central dynamics of the relationship between domination and subordination. But rather than examining binaries in isolation from one another (and thereby collapsing into essentialized characterizations of identity), my approach involves taking an account of the *interactive relationships* between binary modes of signification. Thus, I seek to move away from looking solely at characterizations of the Norm/Other dichotomy, in which subjects are either dominant or subordinate, to examining hierarchies of Othering. As I stated in the previous chapter, I will refer to these degrees and forms of Othering as Other/Other, but it is important to remember that Otherness itself assumes that a Self or Norm is already implicated in its production. This relational way of analyzing binaries in the context of a matrix of meaning-making has the potential to address the porous spaces of borderlands and in-betweenness that exist amid binaries, without overdetermining or downplaying the significance of such systems of domination as white supremacy, patriarchy, heteronormativity, and ableism.

The importance of relationality has been explored by numerous feminists, including Susan Friedman, who speaks of relational narratives and relational positionality. Relational narratives, Friedman (1995, 7) states, describe "the agonistic struggle between victim and victimizer." This struggle "requires acknowledging how privilege and oppression are often not absolute categories but, rather, shift in relation to different axes of power and powerlessness." For Friedman, this kind of analysis shows the value of examining relational narratives as complements to binary-based narratives. I want to push Friedman's insights further to suggest that relational forms and degrees of penalty and privilege actually substantially create, organize, and sustain such binaries as white/non-white, male/female, and heterosexual/homosexual. In other words, my claim is that an analysis of relationality does not simply complement an analysis of binaries: rather, it punctuates the fact that binaries produce relational differences, and vice versa.

In the accounts of meaning-making that follow, I argue that, in contemporary Canada, representations of the dominant white, heterosexual, Western European, financially secure, able-bodied male – all of which are constituted through interacting systems of racialization, sexuality, gendering, colonialism, and disability/ability – form the standards of a dominant matrix of meaning-making. The dominant matrix gives rise to, and is constituted by, binary-based representations of the non-white, homosexual, non-European, poor, disabled gendered subject. These matrices are not fixed, precisely because, as the previous chapters indicated, systems of whiteness, gendering, heteronormativity, and disability/ability are changeable. Accordingly, I explore Canada's current dominant matrix of meaning-making in a strategically essentialist way, whereby I examine how these systems specifically interact in particular social relations, how they do so differently depending on the vehicles of power at play, and what the resultant effects are for particular social arrangements.

Theoretically, accounts of the interactive processes of meaning-making provide a way to critically examine how representations of privilege and penalty are constructed by (violently) constituting various Others as abnormal not only relative to a dominant norm, but relative to one another as well. Such representations of Otherness are of course highly varied and sometimes even competing (that is, they may consist not only of "I am non-white because you are white," but, relatedly, of "My non-white identity is *better/worse* than yours because of your gender, or your sexuality, or your class position"). But it is precisely this variation that can be contextualized through a critical analysis of meaning-making.

Critiques of a Dominant Matrix of Meaning-Making

DOMINANT REPRESENTATIONS OF INDIGENOUS WOMEN

An account of meaning-making processes that produce significations of indigenous women as Other is critical in foregrounding the impact of colonial discourses, especially because it illuminates a binary between settler/indigenous or colonizer/colonized.[2] By situating this binary in the specific historical context of colonial Canada, the analyst can examine how white colonizers signified their own superiority through the criminalization and attempted eradication of indigenous peoples and how the very construction of Canada as a nation-state is rooted in colonial demarcations of territory, citizenship, and national identity. This kind of analysis shows, for example, that the Otherness of Status Indians is what Dennis H. McPherson (2006, 9) calls a "legal fiction," one produced through a highly formalized reserve system, legal control of specific indigenous people as wards of the state, the residential school system, child welfare agencies, and formal exclusion from citizenship. The interplay between nation building and colonialism specifically led to the attempted annihilation of indigenous cultures and the continuing denial of sovereignty and government refusal to honour treaties and resolve land claims (Razack 1998, 59).

An effect of this colonial legacy was to create a racialized and cultural indigenous identity that was previously organized on the basis of nationhood. Although, for many indigenous people, a shared mode of identity now reflects a unification of epistemologies rather than the homogenization of a victimized collective identity, and it also points toward shared practices of resistance against colonialism, dominant discourses have interpreted representations of indigeneity in terms of a totalizing category of Otherness. The consequence is that dominant nation-building practices have determined standards of citizenship and nationality according to hegemonic criteria set by white European male settlers, even though this was, and continues to be, resisted by indigenous peoples.

When accounts of meaning-making are taken through an intersectional-type lens, it becomes evident that colonial discourses of Othering operated (and still operate) through various binaries, not solely those that function through representations of colonizer/colonized. This analysis provides a way to examine how colonial and racial systems of meaning-making interactively function through other constitutive processes so as to differentiate indigenous women as Other, from both the white Norm and other marginalized social groups. Attending to the variation in Othering is therefore not simply a matter of complicating the analysis by scrutinizing how one kind of difference interactively functions through another to produce demeaning representations of indigenous women. Rather, it is a way to highlight that one set of interactions is constituted and regulated in relation to another set. In the case of dominant representations of indigenous women, it is important to examine how racialization operates through gendering and vice versa, and how it does so in various ways so as create distinctions between indigenous peoples.

For example, this kind of analysis provides a way to evaluate how the racialized binary of settler/indigenous works in tandem with, and is upheld by, the gendered binary of male/female, and how patriarchal norms thereby create distinctions between indigenous men and women *within contexts of white supremacy*. Through this analysis, the historical and institutionalized practices of colonialism come under scrutiny. This includes the impact of the 1876 and 1884 Indian Acts, which Ottawa implemented in order to produce a nationalist representation of white Canada, and which indigenous people resisted. Colonial domination was not 'simply' implemented through a racialized and expansionist discourse of colonialism but also through the control of indigenous women's legal identities (A. Smith 1999; Smith and

Ross 2004). The Indian Act aimed to discipline Status Indian women who married non-status men, and who thus did not remain within the legal confines of the colonial definition of "Indian," by denying them their status. Through section 12(1)(b), such women could be prevented from inheriting property, taking part in band business, accessing amenities for themselves and their children within the community, returning to live with family members on a reserve, and even being buried there – all of which had dire social, political, and economic consequences for them (Jamieson 1978, 1; Suzack 2007, 218-19). Although representations of difference that distinguished the social location of indigenous men from that of settlers were also constituted through processes of gendered racialization and racism, this clause of the Indian Act afforded colonial authorities a direct legal way to relationally differentiate Status Indian women from Status Indian men.

Importantly, the legacy of this structural and disciplinary patriarchal law still interacts with existing colonial discourses. As Patricia Monture (2007, 205 and 206-7) observes, indigenous women continue to experience forms of violence and face higher rates of involvement in the criminal justice system; those living on reserves still cannot access a matrimonial property law regime. As well, despite amendments to the 1985 Indian Act, which removed some restrictions to status, the legal status of Status Indian women is still regulated by the state. In particular, the act continues to discriminate against Status Indian women who marry non-indigenous men through provisions that effectively deny Indian status to their grandchildren (McIvor 1995; Monture-Angus 1999; Napolean 2001; Suzack 2007).

Even were the Indian Act changed so that it no longer discriminated against women, it would remain an undesirable way of structuring social relations, for in itself it is a tool of colonial regulation. The Act certainly affords some rights to indigenous peoples, but it also maintains the legitimacy of colonial law (Alfred 2005; Coulthard 2007). As such, the Indian Act structures a complicated relationship between indigenous peoples and the Canadian state. Aside from highlighting this fraught relationship, my analysis indicates that through the continued regulation of subjects marked as Status Indian women, the differences between men/women and settler/indigenous are produced and solidified through interactive gendered, colonial, and nationalist discourses in such a way as to sustain the privilege of the white male Norm. In other words, according to the colonial standards of nation building – namely, those that generate and function through a dominant matrix of meaning-making – the binaries of male/female and settler/indigenous work through one another to produce differing degrees and forms of Otherness.

To further analyze the inner workings of Canada's dominant matrix of meaning-making, it is useful to take an account of the processes of Othering that compose relational differences between indigenous women and another totalized category of subjects who are penalized through processes of gendered racialization: women of colour. Dominant representations of both these social groups are given meaning through interactive processes of Othering (racialized gendering), but each group is constituted in distinct ways, such that they are differently situated within Canada's dominant matrix. The construct of "women of colour" specifically emerges as a *contested* identity, especially to reveal that, as a historical construct, it provokes uncomfortable and strange meanings for many women (Bannerji 2000; Jhappan 2006; Mahtani 1994). As Himani Bannerji (2000, 28) rightly contends, the category of "women of colour" is entrenched in troubling historical meanings of "coloured" and the depoliticization of whiteness as a marker of privilege. Given this, Bannerji (2000, 34) asserts that the terminology of "women of colour" has "the power to erase or empty out actual social relations and forms of power – 'race,' gender and class – while creating an aura of concreteness or meaning whose actual relevances or coordinates are located within the state's discourse of ruling." Bannerji argues that it is critical to challenge the ideological workings of diversity politics that erase the interactions of gendered, racialized, and class politics in order to expose the underlying ideologies of whiteness. In doing so, she concludes that she prefers the term "non-white women" rather than "women of colour" because it does not evade the politics of whiteness.

In my view, Bannerji's critique is correct, but it is worth considering why the women of colour category remains salient – in both theoretical and activist circles. In this instance, an account of the relational processes of Othering indicates that the category has political efficacy in Canada because, in the context of a colonial history of nation building, interactive processes of racialized gendering have produced relational differences between indigenous women and other non-white women. Hegemonies of gendered whiteness function by constructing a relationship between two different forms of racialized gendering. These are different in that the category of women of colour was constructed through racist representations grounded in earlier ideologies of European colonialism in which non-white Others were viewed as inferior, and the cultures of indigenous women (and men) have faced the possibility of eradication in Canada. The violence that has shaped the social position of indigenous women has been especially configured through the desire of white colonizers not only to dilute or inferiorize, but also to annihilate those who represent indigenous bodies and ways of knowing (Razack 1998, 59).

These two forms of difference are relational in that they are constitutive of each another. By this I mean that the dominant matrix of meaning-making takes shape according to different historical legacies that explicitly and implicitly signify various gendered and racialized Others in relation to one another. The production of representational and material distinctions between women of colour and indigenous women thus serves to uphold the dominant matrix, whereby privilege is assigned to the white male Norm in both instances. In this regard, an account of the different ways in which representations of Otherness are produced shows that disparate histories are related in that they create and sustain gendered modes of whiteness through one another.

As well as providing an understanding of how dominant representations of indigenous women are constituted by differentiating them from those that constitute indigenous men and women of colour, my account of the relational interactive processes of meaning-making provides a way to critically examine how a dominant matrix is created and upheld through processes that produce relational distinctions *between* indigenous women. This analysis illuminates that socially driven modes of racialized gendering function through discourses of the white nation, but in varying ways. Despite the fact that there are shared experiences of the colonial legacy and common struggles against gendered whiteness, as well as some shared cultural norms, colonialism has constructed specific kinds of differences between indigenous women. As well as producing differences along the lines of geography (urban/rural and reserve/non-reserve), class, skin colour, and sexuality, the colonial imaginary has created legal distinctions between First Nations, Inuit, and Métis subjects. I briefly examine these legal differences among indigenous women as a way to highlight the work of relational processes of Othering within groups, although many other kinds of differences can be examined.

In the 1800s, to affirm the Otherness of indigenous bodies, identities, and practices, colonial governments legally defined "Status Indian" in ways that split indigenous peoples into distinct categories; these formations were imagined according to the terms of Canadian nation-building. These categories erased legal representations of indigeneity for Métis and Inuit people, who then fell into the status of a unitary form of Canadian citizenship. This colonial wish to legally render Inuit and Métis indigeneity invisible existed in tandem with the desire to discipline and eradicate those who were marked as Status Indians. Although they are related, these dual practices operated as distinguishable ways of differentiating Others in relation to white settler society and *in relation to one another as well*. Thus, through colonialism, the notion of an ideal white national citizen was (re)produced and consolidated by marking various indigenous subjects differently, but always as aliens on their own territory. In this sense, the dominant matrix of meaning-making historically operated by producing relational distinctions between First Nations, Métis, and Inuit identities (Other/Other) in ways that solidified the colonizer/colonized (Norm/Other) dichotomy. These varied forms of subjection were thereby constituted in direct relation to representations of white subjectivity.

The Canadian government has since reimagined this white nationalist discourse by constitutionally recognizing First Nations, Inuit, and Métis identity in the 1982 Canadian Charter of Rights and Freedoms. Yet these constructions are also productive and reflective of relations of privilege and penalty. On the one hand, this constitutional acknowledgment of all three categories produces a different legal status for indigenous people than was the case earlier in Canadian history. It symbolizes recognition of the differences among indigenous peoples. This has been both legally and symbolically important because, as some Inuit women have argued, though being indigenous is central to making constitutional claims for land and inherent rights, the state must also recognize the uniqueness of differing groups of indigenous people and their respective distinct historical rights (SWC 2000, 13).

On the other hand, though these categorizations are important for legal and cultural reasons, they can also reinscribe significations of indigeneity that were produced through interactions between colonial, gendered, and nationalist discourses. While colonial power historically worked to repress indigeneity and to legitimate white settler superiority, and then to re-form the legal identities of indigenous peoples through constitutional recognition in 1982, it did so without displacing the legitimacy or legal foundations of white settler subjectivity. In this regard, even while constitutional recognition produces some legal and substantive changes for indigenous people, as Glen Coulthard (2007) argues, it does not fundamentally transform the structure of difference that gives authority to a settler state. Certainly, First Nations, Inuit, and Métis people have generated and continue to generate their own understandings of these identities, but nonetheless indigenous men and women continue to be subject to state-sanctioned colonially rooted discourses of racialized gendering.

Overall, my analysis shows that a dominant matrix of meaning-making is structured by interactions between processes of meaning-making that produce and operationalize various forms and degrees of Otherness. In short, relationality is always at play. Representations of indigenous women as Other are produced not only through colonial systems that differentiate indigenous subjects and white settlers, but also by differentiating indigenous women and indigenous men, indigenous women (as original inhabitants) and women of colour (as settlers), and various groups of indigenous women. An analysis of relational Othering therefore indicates that no form of representation is untouched by relations of privilege and penalty, or interpretable in a fixed way.

I want to make clear that I do not assert that indigenous women cannot and do not self-signify or relationally signify in positive ways, or that constitutional recognition of First Nations, Inuit, and Métis lacks any value. Rather, as Wendy Brown (1995, 121) argues, it is critical to incessantly query why some group identities are repeated in claims for and by Others. Although she does not seek to critique the general worth or accomplishments of identity politics, Brown (1995, 74) warns that a politicized identity that "enunciates itself, makes claims for itself, only by entrenching, restating, dramatizing, and inscribing its pains in politics" cannot cease to exist as an injured identity. For Brown (1995, 73), "a practice that reiterates the existence of an identity whose present past is one of insistently unredeemable injury ... cannot be redeemed *unless* the identity ceases to be invested in it, and it cannot cease to be invested in it without giving up its identity as such." As I understand Brown, this does not mean that wounded attachments should not be examined, for these tell us something about the construction and operation of social hierarchies of difference. Instead, it is important to be mindful of the ways in which identity claims evoke and re-perform past and continued suffering.

In terms of such representative categories as First Nations, Métis, and Inuit women, it is therefore important to take accounts of when, why, and by whom these categories are deployed, how they reflect and/or challenge racialized forms of gendering produced through historically constituted colonial discourses that continue to operate, and how indigenous people generate their own meanings of difference in the context of this history and their own traditions. The turn away from a victim-based representation of indigeneity has been and continues to be central to many indigenous people. Patricia Monture, for example, subverts colonial meanings attached to indigenous women and calls for reindigenized self-representations of difference.

This, Monture (Monture-Angus 1999, 89) states, can emerge by rejecting colonial categories of identity (such as "Indian") and adopting instead the identity of one's family, community, and nation so as to be recognized as a Mohawk or Cree or Tlingit or Mi'kmaq or Saulteaux woman/mother/sister/ elder. Taiaiake Alfred and Jeff Corntassel (2005, 609) also propose ways to decolonize and reindigenize by turning toward indigenous sacred histories, ceremonial cycles, languages, ancestral homelands, decolonized diets, and kinship networks. Such strategies point toward alternative meaning-making processes whereby the relations of difference that structure a dominant matrix are resisted and rejected.

DOMINANT REPRESENTATIONS OF MUSLIM WOMEN

To further highlight the various manifestations and relationships of Othering, in this section I examine how specific forms of gendered racialization regarding Muslim women are produced and how they operate through interactive discourses of Orientalism, Islamophobia, and Eurocentric sexism so as to uphold a dominant matrix of meaning-making. These are not the only discourses at play, but, as will become clear, they are useful starting points through which to draw out other kinds of difference.

Eurocentric sexism consists of emphasizing Western European-based values of male superiority and white supremacy. Sexism and patriarchy are undoubtedly prevalent within Muslim communities but no more so than in other communities. Moreover, by linking together Eurocentrism and sexism, I seek to emphasize that, in the historical contexts of Western domination, sexism works in particular ways that may well be distinct from other spatial and temporal contexts. Orientalism, as Edward Said (1978, 5-12) showed, is a relationship of domination between Occident and Orient in which European-Atlantic dominance, rather than the Orient itself, is created and sustained through political-intellectual culture (in aesthetic, scholarly, economic, sociological, historical, and philological texts). Islamophobia functions by representing Islam as a fundamentalist religion rather than a variedly interpreted faith, a source of spirituality, an element of ethno-cultural identity, a marker of geography, an oppositional ideology, and an official state ideology for a number of countries (Ashgharzadeh 2004, 130). Although Islamophobia is not new, since the events of 11 September 2001, it has functioned in specific ways to justify the so-called war on terror and to regulate Muslim and Arab peoples (as well as those who appear to be Muslims and Arabs) through discourses of nationalism and security.

In recent years, manifestations of Orientalism and Islamophobia have served to further re-entrench the binary of 'them' (Muslims) and 'us' (the West). One Canadian expression of this can be seen in the security certificate program, which was introduced under a 1978 immigration law and has been used twenty-seven times. It allows for the preventive arrest and indefinite detention of non-citizens (including legal residents of Canada), without charge, under secret evidence. The program also allows for the deportation of non-citizens on the basis of secret intelligence presented to a Federal Court judge at closed-door hearings. Detainees can choose to be deported to their country of origin, but this is not an option for those who might face torture or death on their return. This program has been described by Amnesty International Canada (2006) as being fundamentally unjust. The United Nations Working Group on Arbitrary Detention and the United Nations Committee against Torture have also questioned Canada's use of it. Yet, under the guise of national security, the program has been activated to directly target Muslims and Arabs. For example, Hassan Almrei has been detained since October 2001 and remains indefinitely detained. Four others who have family in Canada have been re-leased under confining bail conditions, even though none have been charged with a specific crime or convicted. They include Egyptian-born Mohammad Mahjoub and Mahmoud Jaballah, Algerian-born Mohamed Harkat (detained for three and a half years without charge), and Moroccan-born Adil Charkaoui (arrested in June 2003). All were held at the Kingston Immigration Holding Centre in Ontario (which was run by the Canadian Border Services Agency), itself specially created for security certificate detainees.

On 23 February 2007, the Supreme Court of Canada unanimously ruled that the security certificate program violated the Charter of Rights and Freedoms. However, though the court concluded that continuing to detain prisoners without review was arbitrary, it allowed Parliament to maintain the law and rewrite it within one year. Ottawa duly passed Bill C-3 in February 2008, so as to amend the Immigration and Refugee Protection Act. But arguably, Bill C-3 worsens the effects of the security certificate program, for it does not strengthen the rights of detainees, even though it implements the appointment of a special advocate to represent the interests of a person named in a security certificate. Furthermore, it preserves secret trials, secret evidence, and the impunity of the state agencies of repression, especially the Canadian Security Intelligence Service. These kinds of "legally authorized zones of non-law" (Razack 2007, 13) ultimately constitute and reconstitute differences between Islam and the West.

An account of the matrix of meaning-making, as it relates to Muslims in Canada, shows that the story of difference is broader than the Islam/West dichotomy might first suggest. As during the debates about Shariah law in Ontario, popular media depictions of Western superiority reinforce sexist Eurocentric representations of Muslim women as victims of their oppressive culture, in which only white men can save brown women from brown men (Jiwani 2005a; Mohanty 2003; Razack 2005; Spivak 1988). In these conceptions of difference, "images of mutilation, barbaric customary rites, severe penalties for adultery, forced veiling, and polygamy are all highly powerful symbols of the barbaric East or South and, correspondingly, the civilized West or North" (Razack 1998, 125). This construction of Islam and Muslim women is not constituted solely by making monolithic meanings about Muslim women and white men, for difference is also constituted by creating distinctions between Muslim women and white women. In these instances, in contrast to representations of the 'good' white woman (who is defined as good on the basis that she lives according to heterosexual norms and is able-bodied, ideally a mother, and a worker outside the home), 'the' Muslim woman is represented as being contrary to liberal modernity, neither progressive nor secular – aspects deemed central to the project of Western nation building. This is especially so if she covers her head and/or body. Whereas, in reality, the history of veiling is more complex and multi-layered than its current association with oppression and Islamic fundamentalism suggests, for the West the veil symbolizes the oppression of all women and its own superiority over the non-West (Alvi, Hoodfar, and McDonough 2003; Bullock 2000, 2002; Shirazi 2001; Zine 2006). Indeed, as Afsaneh Najmabadi (2006, 242) comments, in the West, "It would be an understatement, then, to say that the veil of a Muslim woman is an overdetermined sign. As a sign of belonging to a religious community and thus already disqualifying the woman as a liberal autonomous subject, a sign of extranational belongings that constitutes a civilizational threat, a sign of religious challenge to the secularism of modern states, and finally a sign of women's oppression, it is hard to imagine how this sign can be successfully renegotiated."

Through dominant meanings about the veil and other religious and cultural symbols, Muslim women are deemed to be strange and strangers, regardless of their legal status in Canada. In particular, they are marked as subjects who must be pitied because they are culture-bound, without agency, and unable to help themselves. Through popular media discourses of gendered

Orientalism and Islamophobia, culture is not represented in terms of a context of choice but as a confining patriarchal instrument of control. These constructions of Islamic culture merely serve to reiterate hidden gendered Orientalist significations of Muslim and Arab women as universal dependants and victims of Muslim male violence, Arab familial systems, Islamic and religious codes, and non-Western national economic structures (Mohanty 2003, 17-42). Moreover, these depictions reinforce the preference for whiteness that is associated with liberal freedom, rights, choice, self-determination, and secularism, without appreciation for the ways in which Orientalist signs of difference are produced through the West's own understanding of itself. Indeed, in recent years, these representations of Muslim women have become ever more salient because they provided a guise for 'the coalition of the willing' to invade Afghanistan and Iraq.

An account of the interactive processes of meaning-making that produce such characterizations of Muslim women critically examines how a dominant matrix of meaning-making functions through these representations of Otherness by privileging white femininity and white masculinity, and simultaneously masking over histories in which white European colonizers restricted and regulated the freedom, rights, choices, and self-determination of white women and colonial Others through violence and imperialism. In this instance, the mutually constituted binaries of power at work are those of male/female and white/non-white.

My analysis also reveals the conditions of Othering that relationally differentiate Muslim women and other non-white women. This account of the relational processes of Othering contextualizes how Orientalist ideas, Islamophobia, and Eurocentric sexism construct Muslim women through various modes of Othering, in which some women racialized as Other are preferred. Sherene Razack (1998, 158) describes this process in the following way: "In identifying the multiple narratives that script women's lives, we come to see that women are socially constituted in different and unequal relation to one another. It is not only that some women are considered to be worth more than other women, but that the status of one woman depends on the subordinate status of another woman in many complex ways." Precisely because of these complexities, it is important to critically analyze the conditions that produce socially unequal relationships between Others. In particular, it is important to explore the ways in which interactive processes of subject formation construct Otherness differently but always in relation to the norms that privilege the dominant white male. Let me elaborate.

In recent years, dominant society has signified some Muslim women as model minorities. The definition of "model minority" varies according to what norms are preferred by dominant society, but on the whole, though the model minority is archetypically male, those Muslim women who are non-practising, educated, English-speaking (with a particular accent), wealthy, and unveiled can also be included in this category. On Canadian nation-building terms, the presence of the model minority is not ideal but is warranted for reasons of social and economic capital. Here, the model minority construct is "predominantly a reference to economic exceptionalism, upward class mobility, and educational excellence" (Puar and Rai 2004, 77). To put it differently, the model minority is one who can most closely replicate the ideal white male worker. By deconstructing the processes of meaning-making that give shape to this category, the analyst can question the assumption that this ideal worker is an active, able-bodied contributor to the means of production. When the minority conforms to hegemonic gendered, heterosexual, class-based, ablest, and racialized norms simultaneously, she is deemed to be the model Other.

A deconstructive analysis demystifies the vehicles of power that produce representations of the model minority Muslim woman to show that these are not only produced in relation to the dominant white majority culture, but also in relation to those of the less desirable indigenous or black woman, even though *all non-white women fall short of the preference for the citizen-subject who is white and male*. In Canada's case, these representations are rooted in nineteenth-century government policies aimed at preserving white British national identity, and in contemporary neo-liberal policies related to social services, the prison system, and crime. In particular, the interactions between different modes of gendering, racialization, and capitalism relationally and homogeneously construct indigenous and black women as poor citizens who don't and can't integrate. Thus, without referencing the historical conditions that produce differences between indigenous and black women, dominant discourses constitute representations of black women as welfare mothers who cannot alleviate their poverty, as aggressive matriarchs who emasculate their husbands and lovers, and as Jezebels who are sexually loose and hostile (Collins 1990, 67-90); and indigenous women are signified as prostitutes or sexually promiscuous, as overreliant on social services, and as drawn to criminal activity (Monture-Angus 1999; Razack 2002).

A critical analysis of the conditions in which these representations are produced and given authority shows that they materialize not only through processes that signify white men and white women as superior, but through a matrix of meaning-making that simultaneously produces differing representations of non-white women. So, whereas the Muslim woman remains constructed as the non-white Other (who is deemed subject to the oppressive ways of her husband, father, brother, and son), in contrast to those women signified as indigenous and black, the good Muslim woman is also signified as more pliable and obedient, highly driven by the desire for education, and committed to the institutions of heterosexual marriage and motherhood. In these instances, the model minority Muslim woman is represented in more 'positive' ways as a more suitable citizen than the indigenous or black woman. This is especially so if she is viewed as modern, secular, progressive, and a contributor to the economy – values that are used to distinguish the good and bad Muslim (Mamdani 2004), whereby the good subject is more closely aligned to a specific set of Western liberal values.

Negative representations of Muslim women are also constructed through this matrix of meaning-making. An account of both positive and negative characterizations shows that, on the one hand, gendered racialization marks some Muslim women as preferable, and that, on the other hand, these same kinds of processes mark other Muslim women as undesirable. There are, in other words, important variations in meanings assigned to Muslim women. These hierarchies of difference can be unpacked through an account of the processes of relational Othering.

In particular, an examination can be made of how some Muslim women are marked as dangerous in relation to other social groups. Although tropes of danger are not unique to the post-9/11 world but historically rooted in Orientalism, Islamophobia, and Eurocentric sexism, they have taken on a particular manifestation through recent discourses of terrorism. Recent constructions of the dangerous Muslim woman does not exist in isolation but in the context of relations between those signified as white Canadians *as well as between other subjects marked as women of colour.* Thus, though Eurocentric sexist discourses produce significations of many women of colour as backward, culture-bound, and non-secular, and even threatening to the nation, the Muslim body has been intimately associated with terrorism, danger, and fear.

Many instances can be found to illustrate the problems that arise from homogeneously characterizing all Muslims as potential or actual security threats, not least of which is the case of Maher Arar, who, while travelling through the US on his Canadian passport, was accused by American officials of being an Al-Qaeda member and subsequently deported to Jordan. Despite the fact that he has Canadian citizenship, because he held Syrian citizenship as well he was ultimately sent to Syria where he was imprisoned and tortured for over a year. After his release and return to Canada, systematic pressure (led by his wife, Monia Mazigh) resulted in a public inquiry, which concluded that Arar was not involved in illegal or terrorist activity and that the Royal Canadian Mounted Police had in fact abused its power. Following further pressure, in 2007 the prime minister of Canada publicly apologized to Arar and extended him $10.5 million in compensation.

Although it is true that some other religious and cultural groups marked as non-white, such as Sikhs, have been subject to violence and hate because they have been misread as Muslim, the discourse of Islamophobia is specifically directed toward those who are Muslim (whether theologically or secularly). Indeed, the law directly targets those who identify as Muslim rather than those who are read as Muslim. This does not mean that other people of colour have not been signified as equally threatening. In 1985, for example, after the Air India bombing and the lengthy trial that followed, the media constructed Sikhs in Canada as terrorists who were using Canadian resources as a way to further the nationalist agenda for Khalistan. And in 2002 and 2003, following the arrival of Chinese migrants on the shores of British Columbia, the Chinese were constituted as a menace to the nation. Alongside these tropes of danger, Islamophobia functions to construct Muslims as potential and actual enemies of the nation.

Itrath Syed rightly argues that Islamophobia is highly gendered. In her study of Shariah law debates in Canada, Syed (2006, 8) observes that, whereas the Muslim male body is constituted through discourses of colonialism and Islamophobia as dangerous and threatening, "the Muslim female body is correspondingly constructed to be, not fearsome, but loathsome. The Muslim female body, particularly when it is covered, is seen as consummately pitiful and disgusting. But in its loathsomeness, the Muslim female body is still that which pollutes, which does not belong and which has no right to claim belonging. In fact, it is in the act of claiming a right to belong to the Nation that the Muslim female body becomes threatening."[3] As I noted earlier, the Muslim female body is especially feared and loathed if it is hidden by the veil, such that the veil itself is feared and loathed. This was starkly exemplified in Canada in 2007, when Prime Minister Stephen Harper challenged the decision of Elections Canada to allow women to vote while having their faces covered by burkas or *niqabs*. The Elections Canada ruling stated that veiled women who wished to keep their faces covered for religious reasons were to present two pieces of identification, one of which gave their address. If only one piece of government identification was provided, another voter registered in the same district could vouch for them, and veiled voters would have to show their faces to confirm their identity, which, as some Muslim women's organizations pointed out, Muslim women already do at banks and border crossings. Yet depictions of the dangerous Muslim woman were rife in the media and on the internet, both when Elections Canada made its ruling and when Stephen Harper objected to it. As the work of Yasmin Jiwani (2005a, 2005b), Shanaz Khan (1993, 2002), Sherene Razack (2007, 2008), and Sunera Thobani (2007), among others, has shown, these representations of Muslim women are not only produced at the level of the state (through security legislation and immigration regulations) but at the societal level as well (via the media and everyday interactions).

These representations of Otherness perform through a dominant matrix of meaning-making so as to constitute meanings about Muslim women *and* non-Muslim women of colour through constructions of Otherness that are relational to one another and to dominant norms. Thus, for instance, the racist, sexualized, sexist, heterosexist, and ablest representations of Japanese women's bodies and identities – representations that were produced in eighteenth- and nineteenth-century Canadian immigration and citizenship policies – as submissive, shy, exotic, and hyper-feminine are reiterated by differentiating Muslim women as political, frenzied, and potential threats to the social order (while at the same time, they are also traditional and oppressed by their cultures). In this sense, dominance operates by relationally marking some women of colour as less threatening to the nation than are some Muslim women. Given this, interactive processes of meaning-making that produce representations of non-Muslim women of colour are instrumental in constituting the *conditions* by which Muslim women are constructed as Other.

Overall, my account of the conditions that give rise to these relationally constituted differences contextualizes the ways in which Muslims in general are subject to Islamophobia, how negative and overdetermined representations of Muslim women are constructed in the context of those processes of racialized gendering that privilege white men and white femininity, and how differences are simultaneously made among Muslim women and other non-white women through norms of gender, race-thinking, ability, and capitalism so as to produce the model minority, who, though still not part of the majority, comes as close to it as dominant standards permit. The interconnected nature of differentiation clearly extends beyond culture or, for that matter, beyond a list of multiple differences. This kind of analysis receives little, if any, attention in theories of liberal multiculturalism because the focus is on how to accommodate minority cultures rather than on how differences *between* Othered cultures are regulated through the norms set by a dominant culture. Culture is important to Muslim women (as it is to indigenous women) but a critical analysis of relational Othering can help to avoid the liberal trap of overdetermining the character and boundaries of a social group identity.

As I discuss in the next chapter, one of the major implications of analyzing the interactions between processes of meaning-making and their relationship to one another is that no neutral position exists within a matrix of meaning-making. This is the case because differing representations of Muslim women come to exist by virtue of producing differences between variously situated non-white women, and white subjects come to be reinstated as dominant through these same categories. These differences are mutually constituted and operationalized, in diverse ways and in varying degrees, which becomes apparent through a critical analysis. The point of recognizing this non-neutral aspect of subject formation is not to argue that women of colour produce oppression in the same way as do white women or white men, or conversely, that women of colour are innocent. Instead, it is to note that processes of meaning-making function relationally in ways that implicate one form of difference in the production of another form of difference.

Moreover, the above accounts of meaning-making provide a way to contextualize how a dominant matrix of meaning-making is constituted and upheld by relationally differentiating Others in ways that *sustain the privilege assigned to whiteness, masculinity, capitalist norms, and able-bodiedness.* To put it differently, though dominant interpretations of difference produce relational distinctions between Others, domination simultaneously operates by collapsing differences between various Others. The result is that the political, geographic, social, economic, religious, and ethnic differences between Muslim women are erased, as are the differences among black, indigenous, and Asian women. There is, in other words, a repeated reduced dichotomy between Norm/Other in which social categories are overdetermined by the logic produced by modes of dominance. Such dominant lenses are troubling not simply because they sustain privilege, but because they may also be adopted by Others who are constituted in the (mirror) image and wake of dominance. In sum then, my analysis of the relationship between different sets of interactive processes shows how the relativity of Otherness supports the conditions of a dominant matrix.

Relational Othering, Dominance, and the Study of Identity/Difference Politics

Accounts of meaning-making are always relational. By foregrounding this relational aspect through an intersectional-type approach, the complexities of difference can be examined in at least three important ways. First, by deconstructing the operations and effects of different interactions simultaneously, this analysis describes and explains various degrees and forms of dominance and subordination. Rather than treating all members of a social group as equally dominant or equally subordinate, this mode of analysis attends to the production of differences within and between social categories. A critical examination of these interpretations of difference alerts analysts to the ways in which meaning-making operates through multiple forms of relative dominance (such as inferiorization, discrimination, annihilation, erasure, criminalization, and pathologization). To expose this multiplicity of subjugating effects is at once to disrupt the operation of power in its putative univocality.

Second, while demystifying the conditions that produce different degrees and forms of dominance, accounts of relational processes of Othering provide a way to examine what is at stake in producing an undifferentiated category of Otherness, in which a multiplicity of political effects is masked. The study of relational Othering not only therefore indicates that dominance manifests itself in many ways – whereby the conditions of dominance are established through interactive systems of normativity that are irreducible to any one relation of difference – but it also shows that meanings (or standards) of Otherness are productive in re-entrenching a specific set of interactive norms that privilege whiteness, masculinity, capitalist values, able-bodiedness, and heteronormativity. To put it simply, this form of analysis attends to the very conditions by which a dominant matrix of meaning-making is organized and upheld.

Finally, through accounts of relational Othering it becomes evident that social hierarchies are deeply embedded in one another, such that it is not possible to undo a particular mode of subordination without addressing them all (Fellows and Razack 1994, 1998). To dismantle, for example, racist or sexist systems of meaning-making, it is necessary to simultaneously dismantle manifestations of dominance that arise from homophobia, heteronormativity, ableism, class privilege, and so on. Although systems of meaning-making are distinguishable in character and even effect, race-making, for example, intrinsically involves processes of gendering and class differentiation. This is not to argue that gender or class are reducible to race, whereby race-thinking is another name for other modalities of difference; as I have said, differences are not ontologically the same in character and effect. Instead, my argument is that to organize around only one or two modes of oppression or to claim that one system of meaning-making is universally more significant than another is to misunderstand the ways in which a matrix of meaning-making is structured by and productive of relational processes of Othering. Indeed, when the relationships between interactive processes of meaning-making are foregrounded, analysts can examine differences without entering into what Elizabeth Martinez (1993) calls the "Oppression Olympics." In the Oppression Olympics, "groups compete for the mantle of 'most oppressed' to gain the attention and political support of dominant groups as they pursue policy remedies, leaving the overall system of stratification unchanged" (Hancock 2007b, 68). If the overall system of stratification is not confronted, privileging and penalizing representations of difference will remain intact.

A major political implication of this analysis is that one cannot assume that all women of colour and indigenous women will automatically be allies or, conversely, that they are inevitably different and therefore remote from one another. Accounts of meaning-making provide a way to detect potential political alliances without assuming that all struggles are fundamentally similar in character or goals, or that all non-white women are sisters. Although many commonalities exist between women of colour and indigenous women in contexts of whiteness and patriarchy, and a desire for community and solidarity is felt, accounts of meaning-making indicate that marginalized women should care about the oppression of Others because they are relationally signified and therefore implicated in the conditions that structure and uphold a dominant matrix of meaning-making. Socio-political change, in this regard, does not lie with state recognition of minorities, or with the assignment of differentiated rights, or even with radicalizing practices of inclusion. Instead, radical change arises by disrupting the ways in which representations of difference are relationally constituted in and through a matrix of meaning-making, whether this is shaped by the state or not. This notion of disruption is the theme of the next chapter.

6
Possibilities for Democracy: Toward Disruption

This book began with a call to rethink the study of identity/difference politics so as to directly locate and contextualize the ways in which power shapes interpretations of difference, and interpretations of difference shape the forces of power. This, I have argued, requires a theoretical-conceptual shift away from liberal multicultural conceptualizations of culture. These not only narrow the scope and depth of the field of identity/difference politics but can lead to a form of politics that reiterates and legitimizes the regulatory role of the state, effectively leaving intact the conditions that determine the boundaries of inclusion and exclusion. By contrast, I have taken an approach that shifts the focus from the politics of culture to the politics of meaning-making so as to centre an analysis and critique of power. As I have argued in the previous three chapters, accounts of meaning-making provide a way to simultaneously rethink key categories of analysis, expand the scope of analysis, and complicate how the politics of identity/difference is theorized.

In this final chapter, I explicate the normative dimension of taking accounts of meaning-making. I focus in particular on the *work* of democracy, as opposed to theorizing an ideal democratic regime, practice, or principle. The idea of an ideal democratic regime, practice, or principle suggests that political change and liberation lie in the diminishment of power, or at the very least, in a renewed social contract that minimizes its abuse. But the logic of this conclusion is premised on the reduction of power to its repressive dimensions, whereby an ideal democratic condition is one in which power can be mastered or even eradicated. In this understanding of democracy, the ideal democratic model is a final end that exists outside of power. But precisely because all existing regimes, government types, ideologies, and practices always, and necessarily, differentiate between subjects (such as citizens and non-citizens), a democratic regime, like all others, will consist of capitalist, patriarchal, gendered, disablest, and racist systems of authority, systems that support and perpetuate economic and social inequities (Mansbridge 1996, 56). This is not simply an effect of imperfect practice, for in principle too, it remains that all democratic regimes, government types, and ideologies consist of repressive and productive power. As Barbara Cruikshank (1999, 2) suggests, "Like any mode of government, democracy both enables and constrains the possibilities for political action." "Democratic modes of governance," she continues, "are not necessarily more or less dangerous, free, or idealistic than any other. Even democratic self-government is still a mode of exercising power – in this case, over oneself." Indeed, a democratic mode of governance still entails the production and contestation of difference, and is, as such, essentially political.

On this basis, rather than examining democracy as an entity (a regime, a government type, an ideology, a society, or a nation-state) or discussing what overarching values can make it more inclusive (recognition, differentiated rights, representation, intercultural dialogue, civic virtue), I approach democracy as the practice of meaning-making. Insofar as democracy is understood as a form of politics that is concerned with the rule of the people, its unending work is to produce meanings about "the people" and, simultaneously, meanings regarding those deemed not to be "the people." Ideas about the people, as Margaret Canovan (2005, 39) argues, "have been used, adapted and extended in the course of past political struggles" but remain ambiguous and amorphous. This ambiguity arises, Canovan (2005, 60) says, because the concept of "the people" is inherently politically contingent. Representations of the people are, as such, not pre-determined and permanent, but are given meaning through historically rooted discourses, including those of law, politics, citizenship, nation, gender, racialization, and capitalism. Due to this contingency, particular groups in society claim the authority to determine who the people are – supposedly in the name of the people – and do so by constituting differences between subjects. These differences create the boundaries of "the sovereign people" and therefore shape the realities of social, economic, and political life along various lines of difference – both for those included in this definition and regulated by it, and those who are excluded from it. In this sense, claims about "the people" are changeable myths but with real political implications.

Accordingly, what lies at stake for democracy when questions of identity/difference politics arise is not simply the relationship between the majority and the minority, the state and the people, social/national unity and fragmentation, or 'our' culture and 'yours.' Rather, first and foremost, the ways in which practices of meaning-making constitute "the people" through power are at stake. This is not only in the sense that some are included and others excluded from this defining imagined idea but also in the sense that "the subject of democracy – 'the people' – is always unfinished, always in the process of coming into being" (Ferguson 2007, 42). The political potential of understanding democracy as unfinished business is that because meanings about the people are in a constant state of being made, they can be remade or made differently.

Overall, then, rather than considering democracy as a passive fixture of life, I perceive it as an activity through which meanings about difference are produced and reproduced, as a mode of action rather than an entity, and as a pervasive aspect of political life rather than an institutional regime. The practice of meaning-making is obscured when democracy is overdetermined as an entity or ideal rather than seen as an activity, for meaning-making remains unacknowledged and/or normalized. This practice is, however, examinable and radicalized by taking accounts of meaning-making. I conclude this book by signalling the normative value of this radical praxis.

Radicalizing Democracy: Disrupting the Forces of Power

As a mode of analysis and critique, accounts of meaning-making make visible the capacity of power to produce some subjects as "the people" (theory) and simultaneously deconstructs that power (practice). As such, an account of meaning-making can be understood as a form of political praxis, whereby theory (mode of analysis) and practice (mode of critique) come together. As a form of political praxis, accounts of meaning-making *disrupt*, at the root, the conditions that structure a matrix of meaning-making (rather than merely one dimension of difference or a binary of otherness/normality) and the ways in which differences are relationally signified in and through such a matrix to produce forms and degrees of penalty and privilege. As a form of critique, an account of meaning-making is *intrinsically disruptive* in that it puts into question and subverts a particular structure of difference and the calcified meanings of difference that are produced and operationalized through this structure. In short, here, theory is a form of action. The disruptive character of an account of meaning-making lies in questioning the terms of authority, the ontology, stability, and character of a form of representation. This praxis acknowledges the very real material effects of discourses of difference, which are in turn constructed by material conditions. For instance, dominant discourses of racialization produce employment discrimination, and practices of employment discrimination shape meanings of race. Material reality and discourse thus constitute one another. Discursive disruption is thereby necessary for generating material disruptions. To change actual practices of, for example, employment discrimination, the discourse itself must be disrupted, and vice versa.

This disruptive quality of taking accounts of meaning-making is specifically action-oriented in two key ways. First, it invites individuals and members of a social group, as participants and agents of meaning-making, to critically examine their own positions of difference in the matrix and how the matrix is constituted and upheld through meanings attached to these positions in relation to those of others. As Patchen Markell (2003, 7) argues, in order to "bear our share of the burden and risk involved in [the] uncertain, open-ended, sometimes maddeningly and sometimes joyously surprising activity of living and interacting with other people," we must acknowledge our own basic situation and circumstances. This does not require that we recognize and know all people as they really are; instead, it necessitates that we refuse to reduce subjects to "any characterization of his or her identity for the sake of someone else's achievement of a sense of sovereignty or invulnerability, regardless of whether that characterization is negative or positive, hateful or friendly" (Markell 2003, 7). This refusal is, in part at least, made possible by taking an account of the meaning-making processes that constitute our own individual and collective differences.

As a self-reflexive act rooted in critique, the praxis of taking accounts of meaning-making does not produce something that does not already exist; nor does it provide an ideal alternative account of who one authentically is and what one ought to do. Rather, it denaturalizes and disrupts the conditions that produce privileging and penalizing characterizations of subjectivity and subjection and that determine the boundaries of "the people." As Michel Foucault (1984, 46) says of historical critique, "criticism ... will separate out, from the contingency that has made us what we are, the possibility of no longer being, doing, or thinking what we are, do, or think." This disruption does not necessarily lead to the rejection of a representation of difference, although it can; this is because meaning-making is contested and sometimes deeply ambiguous. Nor is disruption always or necessarily overtly violent and rupturing; rather, it is varied in character and form precisely because, as accounts of meaning-making show, meanings are contextually and relationally produced, contingent in nature, and shaped by the specific forces of power at play. Disruption of a historically entrenched process of meaning-making that produces tightly bound conceptions of privileged subjectivity will, for instance, differ from the disruption of a process that operates in the borderlands of marginalized hybridity. This variability need not lead to the rejection of all meanings: instead, it is possible that self-reflexive accounts of meaning-making can give legitimacy to self-directed affirming modes of representation, whether these are adopted by an individual or by a social group. This is not to claim that critical analysis of meaning-making does not include judgments, for all interpretations include judgment to some extent. But even when processes of meaning-making that generate self-directed affirming representations of difference are critically analyzed, this deconstructive praxis does not automatically reject them. Instead, it seeks to examine what they represent, why, and with what effect, and how subjects understand their own place and that of others in the matrix of meaning-making.

Accordingly, rather than undermining positive or friendly meanings of difference, accounts of meaning-making enable self-reflection about one's own identity and can strengthen the grounds on which a form of difference is positively claimed by directly contextualizing its relevance. This varies, of course, according to the conditions under which self-reflexivity is expressed and received, and the asymmetrical relations of power in which self-reflexivity occurs. But, in general, this praxis deconstructs the basis on which self-affirming modes of difference are constituted and defended. This disruption specifically renders transparent the grounds on which an interpretation of difference is made meaningful. As Wendy Brown (2005, 16) says, "Critique passionately reengages the text, rereads and reconsiders the text's truth claims. In doing so, critique [can reassert] the importance of the text under consideration (whether a law, nation, principle, practice, or treatise), its power to organize and contain us, its right to govern us."

The second way in which accounts of meaning-making are action-oriented is that they actively engage subjects in the disruption of social processes of meaning-making. This social level of disruption is central to democratic politics because of how meanings shape representations of "the people." More precisely, since the very practices of individual meaning-making are structured and made available in social contexts, disruption of one's own position necessarily disrupts the social process of meaning-making in which that meaning operates. Thus, as well as examining our own contexts of meaning-making, the praxis of taking accounts of meaning-making demystifies and disrupts the broader circumstances and situations that create and organize representations of difference, and not simply those that structure one's own identity. Accounts of meaning-making are, as such, not person-centred but power-centred. Individualized person-centred inquiries into blame and culpability serve to idealize subjects as potentially transcendental entities (Gaon 2004, 109), generate essentialist conceptions of identity, and obscure an understanding of how and why differences become relevant to social hierarchies. In centering power rather than individual subjects, I am not claiming that no one is implicated in creating and perpetuating relations of penalty and privilege, for meaning-making obviously involves and needs agents, even when the individual (or set of individuals) does not believe in the meanings that are produced or disagrees with them. Rather, my point is that the condition of being implicated indicates that subjects have differing types and degrees of privilege, for difference has many manifestations and is relationally varied.

Power-centred accounts of meaning-making also help to avoid universalizing notions that that the individual is (necessarily) evil, or even intentionally oppressive, because he or she is implicated in a process of meaning-making that produces domination. As Sarita Srivastava (2005, 46) suggests, being implicated is not simply an individual condition, for implication primarily entails a structural relationship. Although there are individual psychological and emotional dimensions to recognizing one's own implication in sustaining oppression or privilege, and critical individual self-reflection may provoke empathy, trauma, and the desire for innocence and salvation (Srivastava 2005), the condition of being implicated is not simply about individuals. Rather, meaning-making is a practice that implicates us all in the social conditions that structure relations of penalty and privilege.

Thus, regardless of whether or not individuals or groups deliberately enact forms of domination, because different representations of subjectivity and subjection are constituted in relational ways, there is no process of subject formation that is void of power. Subjects are therefore implicated in a matrix of meaning-making by virtue of producing and enacting relational interpretations of difference and because subjectivity and subjection are conditioned relationally through such a matrix. Sometimes, individuals and groups become complicit in this complex web of power, particularly if they are invested in a particular conception of difference and particular conception of "the people." In these instances, they may fail to recognize how differently situated subjects oppress others. This failure often arises, as Mary Louise Fellows and Sherene Razack (1998, 339-40) point out, because of the need to protect a familiar way of producing identity, because of fear of erasure, and because dominant narratives about Others overdetermine how difference is seen. Indeed, for subjects marked by calcified forms of marginality, the very act of understanding "our complicity in the oppression of others ... not only *feels* like a risk: it *is* a risk. Our own claim for justice is likely to be undermined if we acknowledged the claims of Others, competing claims that would position us as dominant" (Fellows and Razack 1998, 340, emphasis in original). Given this, taking an account of how we become implicated in social relations of domination is not always easy. It requires an ethical commitment to accountability and responsibility to disrupt the conditions that make us complicit in normalizing processes of subjection.

One way of mobilizing this ethical commitment is to create alliances so as to collectively respond to various manifestations of domination. Moreover, collective disruption can provide a basis for alliances and resistance, and it helps to keep allied individuals and groups accountable and responsible to one another. A commitment to disrupt the processes of meaning-making that mobilize, reiterate, and legitimize dominant social norms and that we bear through representations of ourselves can enable differently signified subjects to recognize specific axes of alliance and specific points of disjuncture between them. Although alliances can be and are built between differently located subjects on the basis of shared struggles, humanistic claims of universality, similar experiences, overlapping concerns, strength in numbers, empathy, guilt, and a commitment and desire for community and solidarity, my analysis indicates that the need for individuals and social groups to build alliances also arises because of the shared condition of being implicated in a matrix of meaning-making. Alliances are necessary in order to disrupt the relational conditions that give rise to our own differences and those of others/Others. Disruption is not the only way to respond to the production and effects of dominant meanings, but such action strengthens the grounds by which alliances are created, and it also provides a way to counter dominant ways of organizing and governing difference. Disruption, in this regard, is a form of action that can defy the conditions that implicate subjects in the structure of a matrix of meaning-making.

Let me elaborate with some examples. Subjects signified as immigrants of colour in Canada can challenge racism not only by disrupting racialized processes of meaning-making that directly affect them, but by disrupting the varied meanings of racialized difference precisely because racialization and racism take on many forms and degrees. Since differences exist not solely between non-white and white immigrants, but also *among* non-white (as well as white) immigrants as a consequence of interactive discourses of gender, sexuality, and disability/ability, and so on. Collective accounts of how these interactions operate and are constituted provide a way to respond to social inequities by challenging the idea that racism is a monolithic experience and practice. Accordingly, the very content of racialization requires an anti-racist approach that is feminist, queer-centred, anti-disablest, and anti-capitalist because modes of racism, patriarchy, homophobia, heteronormativity, transphobia, and ableism are productive of one another and therefore implicated in each other. Alliances are thereby necessary between anti-racist, feminist, queer, and disability movements so as to disrupt the overall conditions of a dominant matrix of meaning-making that produces discriminatory and exclusive representations of "the people."

Disruption of the inner workings of the matrix is also necessary. Again, accounts of meaning-making can be put to work to disrupt the relational processes of Othering that uphold a dominant matrix, namely, the particular processes that implicate Others in the subjugation of other Others. For example, because dominant processes of racialization constitute relational differences between people of colour and indigenous people in ways that reaffirm a preference for whiteness, alliances are necessary between these two groups because one form of difference gives shape to the other. In Canada, people of colour are specifically implicated in the Othering of indigenous people because they occupy settler status. Sites of privilege and penalty will, of course, vary between both social groups, depending on how processes of meaning-making interact, such that some indigenous individuals are privileged in relation to individual people of colour on grounds of legal status, gender, class, ability, or sexual identity. But through the deconstruction of relational processes of Othering, the praxis of taking accounts of meaning-making disrupts how the production of one social position is implicated in the other and, simultaneously, disrupts the norms of neo-colonialism and white supremacy that are implicated in the Othering of both immigrants of colour and indigenous peoples. When these relations of co-implication are critically analyzed, alliances between people of colour and indigenous peoples can be built on the basis of disrupting the conditions that organize a dominant matrix of meaning-making, without minimizing the relevance of distinctive relations and degrees of difference.

In sum, the deconstruction of meaning-making is action-oriented in two ways. First, it is a self-reflexive mode of questioning meanings on the individual and group level. This self-reflexivity disrupts how subjects understand their own social positions and clarifies why a particular meaning of difference is of value to an individual or social group. Second, the praxis of taking accounts of meaning-making fosters active engagement in politics. It does so by making visible and disrupting the ways in which power produces difference in repressive and agency-inducing ways. This activity of disruption also acts as a response to dominant matrices of meaning-making, and as such, it is a form of resistance.

As a self-reflexive and politically engaged praxis, an account of meaning-making is not limited to those who are secure in knowing that disruption will not lead to (new or further) material loss and insecurity, and that there is some alternative ideal to the meaning that is disrupted. To make this claim would suggest that those in precarious situations are without choice and agency regarding the terms and effects of disruption, and as Foucault argued, "Individuals are both *subject to* the constraints of social relations of power and simultaneously enabled to take up the position of *a subject* in and through those constraints" (Allen 1999, 33, emphasis in original). Given this, to take account of the meaning-making processes that operationalize and generate a dominant matrix is to enact our capacities of shaping representations of "the people."

Constituting New and Alternative Kinds of Difference through Disruption

As a disruptive praxis, accounts of meaning-making do not seek to rescue subject formation from contestation – from difference itself – for this would be to mistake "the irreducible conditions of social and political life for pathologies that might someday be overcome" (Markell 2003, 4). Disruption is not directed toward erasing or pulling back power. Instead, the significance of conceptualizing democracy as the practice of meaning-making, and of radicalizing this practice through the disruption of meaning-making, is that, by confronting meaning-making processes that create and sustain relations of domination, new and alternative ways of constituting difference can be opened. Domination therefore needs to be resisted not least because it constrains the range of possibilities for interpreting difference in new ways. New ways of constituting difference are opened up by critiquing the repetition, re-enactment, and reinstitution of various encounters of dominance, and by subsequently also subjecting these new interpretations to critique.

New interpretations must also be subject to critique because they too are laced with power. Indeed, the "logical undecidability [that] emerges from rigorous critique" (Gaon 2004, 106) specifically indicates that meanings are perpetually deferred, always subject to other interpretations in other socio-political contexts. In this regard, meanings are never *fully* known but always interpreted through various lenses of dominance. These may be adopted by the self and by others/Others but, importantly, can also be re-encoded because there is no ideal meaning. In other words, the praxis of taking accounts of meaning-making does not foreclose how difference is interpreted but through disruption invites resistance to dominant meanings and opens up alternative ways of interpreting difference from those entrenched in dominant systems. If representations and structures of difference can be imagined beyond the scope of what seems entrenched and natural, it is possible for new forms of subjectivity (including new ways of imagining "the people") to emerge. Disruption therefore has normative capacity because it provides an impetus for this possibility.

Since new meanings and alternative kinds of difference are also circumscribed by various norms, it is important to identify how to distinguish between better and worse meanings. As I have argued, there are no ideal meanings of difference, for the notion of an ideal meaning is premised on the supposition that symbols of difference have essences and can be definitive, pre-determined, natural, and permanent. This supposition sits on faulty foundations precisely because forces of power shape meanings. As such, the choice is not between non-ideal meanings of difference that are produced through power and those that are ideal because they are free of power (for no choice exists at all in this instance!): rather, it lies between better and worse meanings of difference.

Developing a principle or criterion for distinguishing better meanings from worse ones is a challenging task because meaning-making always and already entails the requirement to give shape to a meaning, command one interpretation over another, and assign authority or legitimacy to it. The repression, negation, and constraint of a meaning is therefore intrinsic to the production of meanings. As David Theo Goldberg (1993, 9) states, "to name the condition [of meaning-making], to define it, to render it not merely meaningful but actually conceivable and comprehensible" is at once to constitute "power over it, to determine after all what it is (or is not), to define its limit." To make a meaning is thus to repress as well as produce the limits of that meaning. To be sure, there is a capacity to resist or make meanings in ways that are not coercive, but these too are circumscribed by the very parameters of meaning-making, such as cultural context and language rules. But the fact that meaning-making is always circumscribed by techniques of power does not uphold the idea that interpretations of difference are indistinguishable. Although differences between better and worse meanings are not self-evident in an account of meaning (because these are subject to interpretation and therefore not universally generalizable or a priori), the level of *responsiveness* to disruption is a useful indicator for distinguishing better and worse interpretations of difference.

On this basis, worse meaning-making processes are not those that name, define, and render conceivable and comprehensive representations of identity by constituting power over a meaning and determining the limits of it. The very practice of meaning-making necessarily entails these limits, not least because we psychologically and politically understand ourselves and others through this practice. There are, as Gayatri Chakravorty Spivak (1997, 361) says, essences that we are written into all the time because of history and language. Accordingly, boundaries around claims of difference do not in themselves constitute a worse meaning. Indeed, because difference is constituted through limitation of itself (that is, difference is produced relationally, by constituting distinctions between X and Y), subject formation is always constrained to some extent.

Yet worse meaning-making processes can be distinguished because they unreflectively close off the possibility of constituting other legitimate meanings by refusing contestation and critique. They function through dominant lenses that interpret meanings as if they were not subject to critique/disruption. For instance, while capitalism produces changing meanings regarding different kinds of workers, owners, and consumers, it simultaneously entrenches and authorizes dominant representations of difference as if these were not disruptable. Capitalist discourses may produce various manifestations of difference, but, because the capitalist system per se is so entrenched – even large-scale mobilization against its structures, institutions, and actors cannot seem to undo it – it is not responsive to fundamental critique/disruption. When such is the case, the system of capitalism closes off the possibility of constituting difference in new and alternative ways. This attempt to master difference by blocking and/or negating other interpretations is what characterizes a worse system of meaning-making.

Conversely, better meaning-making processes are those that are responsive to critique/disruption. These enable the contestability of one's identity even as one commits to some interpretation of that identity. Openness to disruption leaves space open for contestation and a plurality of sometimes conflicting interpretations of difference. Indeed, contestability is important because a subject may well commit to one interpretation of difference in one context and adopt another interpretation in another context. The praxis of taking an account of meaning-making may not in the end displace a particular meaning of difference and in fact may further legitimate that meaning. But when the conditions under which such a meaning is produced are themselves disruptable, and therefore not deemed to be constituted as fixed or final or inherently superior, they are preferable.

On this basis, the praxis of taking accounts of meaning-making is normatively valuable not only because it points to fields of plural, open-ended, indeterminate, and contingent meanings, and not only because it directly disrupts oppressive meanings. This praxis is also normatively valuable because disruption of meaning-making processes opens, rather than forecloses, a way of being *responsive* to critique. And responsiveness occurs by critically re-examining how, when, and why interpretations of difference are foreclosed or opened up.

Conclusions

The form of politics advocated in this book is premised on the disruption of vehicles of power that produce and secure relations of domination. It is not premised on the eradication or minimization of power, because power generates meanings of subjectivity as well as subjection and is enacted through meaning-making practices. Indeed, power links the terms of subjectivity to those of subjection (Cruikshank 1999, 23). Moreover, as Foucault asserted (1988, 95), power makes resistance possible, for resistance/critique/deconstruction involves using the very mechanisms of power that produce relations of domination. As such, power is central for democracy and to democracy.

The idea that power cannot be eradicated may seem defeatist, cynical, and gloomy, if not controversial. Bonnie Honig (1996, 258) likens it to giving up "on a dream of a place called home, a place free of power, conflict, and struggle." Yet, the dream of a place free of power is as dangerous as it is appealing. As Honig (1996, 270) adds, this dream "animates and exacerbates the inability of constituted subjects – or nations – to accept their own internal differences and divisions, and it engenders zealotry, the willingness to bring the dream of unitariness or home into being. It leads the subject to project its internal differences onto external Others and then rage against them for standing in the way of its dream – both at home and away." To acknowledge the impossibility and danger of such a dream is not, however, to resign in despair, for though there are no ideal meanings (ones that are outside power) and no ideal model of democracy (one in which there is an end to difference), it is possible to identify, evaluate, and mobilize meanings that do not create or perpetuate relations of domination. Disruption of the forces of power that produce meanings of privilege and penalty gives reason to hope for fundamental social transformation. And it is for this reason that a shift is needed away from liberal multicultural approaches to identity/difference politics, which do not seek fundamental change.

Ultimately, the shift from culture to meaning-making broadens and enriches identity/difference politics. This is the case in both theory and practice. As a *deconstructive analytic method* driven by an examination of power, an account of meaning-making demystifies and critiques the complex, multilayered, and interactive conditions under which differences are produced, organized, and governed. As a *disruptive political praxis*, it opens up avenues to interpret difference in alternative and new ways so that the work of democracy – the practice of making meanings about the people – is neither foreclosed nor free of critique. This praxis specifically promotes a liberatory form of politics in the following ways: it fosters self-reflexivity in the work of democracy; it provides transparent grounds for affirming, changing, or rejecting a self-directed mode of identification (whether this be on an individual, group, or institutional level); it gives shape to active and engaged practices of meaning-making beyond the scope of the state, without making the state irrelevant; and it provides a basis for creating and sustaining alliances. Not only do accounts of meaning-making therefore offer theoretical insights about the study of identity/difference politics, but these also provide some direction for how to navigate the lived politics of identity/difference.

Notes

PREFACE

1   The concept of Otherness refers to a socially constructed mode of relational difference that is denigrated, discriminated, and pathologized; the capitalization of this concept specifically symbolizes its constructed meaning as an object of difference, namely difference that is constituted by contrasting it with what is deemed to be essential and normal in a (falsely) totalizing way.

INTRODUCTION

1   There are some exceptions to the primacy assigned to culture in liberal multicultural thought. Tariq Modood (2007), for example, places an emphasis on religion rather than culture in his liberal theory of civic multiculturalism.

2   In *Multicultural Nationalism: Civilizing Difference, Constituting Difference* (2005, 6-7), Gerald Kernerman points out that, though in Canada the conversations regarding liberal and nationalist ideologies tend to focus on Kymlicka and Taylor, the 'Canadian school' to which they belong includes other liberal thinkers such as Joseph Carens, Simone Chambers, Michael Ignatieff, and Jeremy Webber. Kernerman's book is noteworthy because it seeks to analyze the dynamics and effects of past and present debates rather than resolve the terms of national unity and diversity.

3   The idea that Canada is an ideal model of multiculturalism has been contested by a number of thinkers. Yasmeen Abu-Laban and Christina Gabriel (2002) contend that in conjunction with immigration and employment equity policies, multiculturalism has transformed ethnic minorities into trade-enhancing commodities that are judged as valuable according to how well they suit the market economy. Melanie C.T. Ash (2004) argues that rather than always promoting respect for difference, multiculturalism can create further distance between those deemed to be 'real' Canadians and those who come from elsewhere. This notion of distance is also taken up by Minelle Mahtani (2006), who criticizes the two-nation model that underlies Canadian multiculturalism, specifically with regard to mixed-race

identities. Richard Day (2000) traces the way in which Canadian multiculturalism is a recent reproduction and proliferation of state-sponsored attempts to design a unified nation rather than a diverse one. Sneja Gunew (2004) draws out the colonial legacies that continue to haunt multiculturalism, both to situate different forms of multiculturalism and to challenge the separation between histories of racialization and cultural diversity. Like Elizabeth Povinelli (2002), Taiaiake Alfred (2005, 248) argues that multiculturalism "is still only an accommodation of the ethnic power of colonial Euroamericans and their more recent immigrant allies." Shauna McRanor (2006) follows suit and argues that Canadian liberal multiculturalism effectively undermines the capacity of indigenous peoples to pursue life in their own chosen ways.

4   Some theorists have thoughtfully reflected on the relationship between liberalism and diversity so as to foreground issues of power without actually displacing the privileged place of liberal political thought. In *Postcolonial Liberalism* (2002), for example, Duncan Ivison draws on post-colonial critiques of liberalism to argue that political arrangements should emerge out of the complexity of local environments and frameworks. Although Bhikhu Parekh, author of *Rethinking Multiculturalism* (2000), ultimately approves of many basic liberal doctrines, he also criticizes the "inegalitarian" side of liberalism – its support for capitalism, self-proclaimed superiority, demand for unity of mankind, intolerance, and dogmatism – through a careful analysis of the work of John Stuart Mill and John Locke (Parekh 1995). While concluding that the social contract ideal is not intrinsically faulted but historically corrupted, in *The Racial Contract* (1997) Charles Mills masterfully critiques white supremacy in liberal contract theory from an anti-racist perspective.

CHAPTER 1: THE PROBLEM WITH 'CULTURE'

1   Taylor may well contest the idea that his defence of culture is instrumentalist, but he does not fully explain what he means by recognition of culture as a vital human need. For further discussion on Taylor's defence of culture, see James Johnson's article "Why Respect Culture?" (2000).

2   The same could be said with regard to the relationship between culture and ethnicity. As Charles Mills (2007, 102) notes, though "ethnicity" is sometimes seen as a more neutral term than "race" and thus more respectable, like the concept of culture the "ethnicization of race" runs the risk of conflating the histories of ethnic groups racialized as non-white with those of groups racialized as white.

CHAPTER 2: THE POLITICS OF MEANING-MAKING

1   Rather than using the concept and terminology of intersectionality, feminists have developed such concepts as "interlocking oppressions" (Razack 1998), "multiple jeopardy" (King 1988), "discrimination-within-discrimination" (Kirkness 1987-

88), "multiple consciousness" (King 1988; Matsuda 1992), "multiplicity" (Wing 1997), "multiplex epistemologies" (Phoenix and Pattynama 2006, 187), and "translocational positionality" (Anthias 2001).

2 I would like to thank Bruce Baum for pointing out to me that Collins' idea of the matrix of domination appears to be distinct from Marxian theories of one over-arching system of domination. Whereas Collins argues that various systems of domination work together and simultaneously rather than hierarchically, some Marxist theories suggest that systems such as gendering and racialization follow from capitalist systems. This perspective is offered by Immanuel Wallerstein in his important book *The Modern World-System* (1976).

CHAPTER 3: RETHINKING ACCOUNTS OF THE 'IMMIGRANT'

1 A report by Janet Dench (2000) for the Canadian Council for Refugees observes that, from 1930 to 1934, 16,765 immigrants were deported on the grounds of being declared a public charge, insane, handicapped, and infirm (more than six times as many as in the previous five-year period). The number of deportations on the grounds of medical causes and criminality also increased.

2 Other meanings regarding this ideal family have emerged through racist and homophobic systems of meaning-making. In the 1800s, for instance, Canadian immigration legislation set out the rules for a head tax for those of Chinese origin, with the intent of limiting the numbers who could afford to emigrate and effectively curtailing the reunification of immigrants with their families. Further, immigration law from the 1920s and 1980s narrowly defined the family through conservative notions of father, mother, and children. These laws did not allow for common-law or same-sex sponsorship of immigrants.

3 The idea that immigrants carry and bring dangerous diseases to Canada is not, of course, uniquely related to sexual or gender difference. In 2003 and 2004, Severe Acute Respiratory Syndrome (SARS) was directly associated with Chinese and other Asian immigrants who had brought 'their' communicable disease to 'our' country. Stories about immigrants from India, China, the Philippines, and Vietnam who bring disease to Canada have also been promulgated by mainstream media, with such headlines as "Immigration Fuels Soaring TB Rate," which appeared in the *Victoria Times Colonist* (Li 2004, 25). Such instances exemplify the widespread and general association between representations of the non-white immigrant and disease. At the same time, by critically analyzing how these representations are determined through norms of sexuality and gender, analysts can reach a better understanding of hegemonic forms of Otherness and particular modes of nation building.

4 For refugee applicants who want to immigrate to Canada because of persecution based on their sexual orientation, the process is not only long and arduous, but

fraught with homophobia. Applicants must establish fear of persecution rather than of prosecution or discrimination; they must convince refugee board members that men sexually assault gay men; and, in a manner that appears not to be 'self-serving,' they must provide evidence that sexual orientation persecution takes place in their country of origin (Caswell 1996, 589-602). In *Tchernilevski v. Canada (Minister of Citizenship and Immigration)*, for example, the concept of persecution was narrowly defined. The court denied an appeal brought against the board by a gay man who sought refugee status on the grounds that, if he was forced to return to Moldova, he would be tried under the Moldovian penal code, which outlawed homosexuality. The board found that his fear was not objective, because the relevant code section was slated for repeal (Lahey 1999, 140).

CHAPTER 4: REGULATING DIFFERENCE

1 This includes the Ernest C. Drury School for the Deaf in Milton, Ontario, the Newfoundland School for the Deaf in St. John's, the Robarts School for the Deaf in London, Ontario, the Sir J. Whitney School for the Deaf in Belleville, Ontario, and Gallaudet University in Washington, DC.

2 In Canada, other human rights decisions dealing with male-to-female trans-sexuals on the grounds of sex include *C.D.P. (M.L.) c. Maison des jeunes* and *Mamela v. Vancouver Lesbian Connection*. *Maison des jeunes* involved a male-to-female pre-operative trans-sexual who was dismissed when she told her employer she was a trans-sexual and of her intent to transition with sex reassignment surgery. The Montreal Human Rights Tribunal ruled that trans-sexuals are protected against discrimination on the basis of sex. *Mamela v. Vancouver Lesbian Connection* involved the suspension of a pre-operative trans-sexual lesbian from volunteering as a librarian for Vancouver Lesbian Connection after a queer newspaper revealed that she identified as a lesbian but not as a woman. The British Columbia Human Rights Tribunal held that discrimination on the grounds of gender identity is discrimination on the basis of sex.

CHAPTER 5: ACCOUNTS OF RACIALIZED GENDERING

1 The tension between so-called conflicting rights has been explored by numerous thinkers, including Arneil et al. (2007), Monique Deveaux (2000a, 2000b, 2006), Marion Boyd (2004), Avigail Eisenberg (2002), Avigail Eisenberg and Jeff Spinner-Halev (2005), Susan Moller Okin (1994, 1998, 1999), Anne Phillips (2003, 2007) and Ayelet Shachar (2000, 2001, 2005). Alternative ways to publicly assess identity-related claims have been developed by Avigail Eisenberg (2006, 2007). Arguments supporting the need to question the division between cultural rights and sex equality rights through a "third space" have been considered in the work of Natasha Bakht (2004), Itrath Syed (2006), and Sherene Razack (2008).

2 I use the binary of colonizer/colonized cautiously, for though it signals a historical racialized relationship, it can also be read in ways that erase the acts of resistance of indigenous people. Further, it can suggest that colonialism took a single form, such that it is assumed that indigenous peoples seceded land through treaties whereas in fact this did not occur in parts of Canada (as, for example, in much of British Columbia). But because this term signals a historical and racialized relationship, where I do use it, I seek to foreground the distinction between white settlers and indigenous peoples.

3 I would like to thank Itrath Syed for granting me permission to quote from her master's thesis, completed at the University of British Columbia in 2006.

References

Abu-Laban, Y. 1998. "Keeping 'em Out: Gender, Race, and Class Biases in Canadian Immigration Policy." In *Painting the Maple: Essays on Race, Gender, and the Construction of Canada*, ed. V. Strong-Boag, S. Grace, A. Eisenberg, and J. Anderson, 69-84. Vancouver: UBC Press.

Abu-Laban, Y., and C. Gabriel. 2002. *Selling Diversity: Immigration, Multiculturalism, Employment Equity, and Globalization.* Peterborough, ON: Broadview Press.

Adhikari, M. 2004. "'Not Black Enough': Changing Expressions of Coloured Identity in Post-apartheid South Africa." *South African Historical Journal* 51 (November): 167-78.

Ahmed, S. 2007. "The Language of Diversity." *Ethnic and Racial Studies* 30, 2: 235-56.

Alfred, G.R. 1995. *Heeding the Voices of Our Ancestors: Kahnawake Mohawk Politics and the Rise of Native Nationalism.* Toronto: Oxford University Press.

Alfred, T. 1999. *Peace, Power, Righteousness: An Indigenous Manifesto.* Oxford: Oxford University Press.

–. 2005. *Wasáse: Indigenous Pathways of Action and Freedom.* Peterborough, ON: Broadview Press.

–. 2007. "Pathways to an Ethic of Struggle." *Canadian Dimension* 41, 1: 35-39.

Alfred, T., and J. Corntassel. 2005. "Being Indigenous: Resurgences against Contemporary Colonialism." *Government and Opposition* 40, 4: 597-614.

Allen, A. 1999. *The Power of Feminist Theory: Domination, Resistance, Solidarity.* Boulder, CO: Westview Press.

Alsop, R., A. Fitzsimons, and K. Lennon. 2002. *Theorizing Gender.* Oxford and Malden, MA: Blackwell.

Alvi, S.S., H. Hoodfar, and S. McDonough, eds. 2003. *The Muslim Veil in North America.* Toronto: Women's Press.

Amnesty International Canada. 2006. "Canada: Security Certificates – Time for Reform." *Take Action*, 14 February. http://www.amnesty.ca/take_action/actions/canada_certificates.php.

Anthias, F. 1998. "Rethinking Social Divisions: Some Notes towards a Theoretical Framework." *Sociological Review* 46, 3: 557-80.

–. 2001. "Beyond Feminism and Multiculturalism: Locating Difference and the Politics of Location." *Women's Studies International Forum* 25, 3: 275-86.

Anthias, F., and N. Yuval-Davis. 1983. "Contextualizing Feminism: Gender, Ethnic, and Class Divisions." *Feminist Review* 15: 62-75.

–. 1992. *Racialized Boundaries: Race, Nation, Gender, Colour and Class and the Anti-racist Struggle.* London and New York: Routledge.

Anzaldúa, G. 1999. *Borderlands/La Frontera: The New Mestiza.* San Francisco: Spinsters/ Aunt Lute.

Arat-Koc, S. 2005. "The Disciplinary Boundaries of Canadian Identity after September 11: Civilizational Identity, Multiculturalism and the Challenge of Anti-Imperialist Feminism." *Social Justice* 32, 4: 32-49.

–. 2006. "Whose Transnationalism? Canada, 'Clash of Civilizations' Discourse, and Arab and Muslim Canadians." In *Transnational Identities in Canada,* ed. V. Satzewich and L. Wong, 217-40. Vancouver and Toronto: UBC Press.

Arneil, B. 1996. *John Locke and America: The Defence of English Colonialism.* Oxford: Clarendon Press.

–. 2004. "The Constitutive Norms of Liberal Citizenship and the Legacy of Cultural Colonization." Paper presented at the Conference for the Study of Political Thought, University of Chicago, Chicago, 23-25 April.

–. 2007. "Cultural Protections vs. Cultural Justice: Post-colonialism, Agonistic Justice and the Limitations of Liberal Theory." In *Sexual Justice/Cultural Justice: Critical Perspectives in Political Theory and Practice,* ed. B. Arneil, M. Deveaux, R. Dhamoon, and A. Eisenberg, 50-69. London and New York: Routledge.

Arneil, B., M. Deveaux, R. Dhamoon, and A. Eisenberg, eds. 2007. *Sexual Justice/ Cultural Justice: Critical Perspectives in Political Theory and Practice.* London and New York: Routledge.

Ash, M.C.T. 2004. "But Where Are You REALLY From? Reflections on Immigration, Multiculturalism, and Canadian Identity." In *Racism, Eh? A Critical Inter-disciplinary Anthology of Race and Racism in Canada,* ed. C.A. Nelson and C.A. Nelson, 398-409. Concord, ON: Captus Press.

Ashgharzadeh, A. 2004. "Islamic Fundamentalism, Globalization, and Migration: New Challenges for Canada." In *Calculated Kindness: Global Restructuring, Immigration and Settlement in Canada,* ed. R.B. Folson, 130-50. Halifax: Fernwood.

Avery, D. 1979. *Dangerous Foreigners: European Immigrant Workers and Labour Radicalism in Canada, 1896-1932.* Toronto: McClelland and Stewart.

Azoulay, K.G. 1997. *Black, Jewish and Interracial: It's Not the Color of Your Skin but the Race of Your Kin, and Other Myths of Identity.* Durham and London: Duke University Press.

Bakht, N. 2004. "Family Arbitration Using Sharia Law: Examining Ontario's Arbitration Act and Its Impact on Women." *Muslim World Journal of Human Rights* 1, 1. http://www.bepress.com.mwjhr/vol1/iss1/art7.

Bannerji, H. 1995. *Thinking through Essays on Feminism, Marxism and Anti-racism*. Toronto: Women's Press.

–. 2000. *The Dark Side of the Nation: Essays on Multiculturalism, Nationalism and Gender*. Toronto: Canadian Scholars' Press.

Bannerji, H., S. Mojab, and J. Whitehead. 2001. "Introduction." In *Of Property and Propriety: The Role of Gender and Class in Imperialism and Nationalism*, ed. H. Bannerji, S. Mojab, and J. Whitehead, 3-33. Toronto: University of Toronto Press.

Barry, B. 2001. *Culture and Equality: An Egalitarian Critique of Multiculturalism*. Cambridge, MA: Harvard University Press.

Bauman, H.-D.L. 2005. "Designing Deaf Babies and the Question of Disability." *Journal of Deaf Studies and Deaf Education* 10, 3: 311-15.

BCHRC (British Columbia Human Rights Commission). 1998. *Human Rights for the Next Millennium*. http://www.bchrcoalition.org/files/.

BDA (British Deaf Association). 2002. "Deaf Couple's Deaf Desire." Media release. http://www.britishdeafassociation.org.uk/print_out.php?page=48@news=. Accessed 2003; website now discontinued.

Beltran, C. 2004. "Patrolling Borders: Hybrids, Hierarchies, and the Challenge of *Mestizaje*." *Political Research Quarterly* 57, 4: 595-607.

Benhabib, S. 1995. "Cultural Complexity, Moral Interdependence, and the Global Dialogical Community." In *Women, Culture and Development: A Study of Human Capabilities*, ed. J. Glover, 235-57. Oxford: Clarendon Press.

–. 2002. *The Claims of Culture: Equality and Diversity in the Global Era*. Princeton: Princeton University Press.

Berger, J. 2005. "Uncommon Schools: Institutionalizing Deafness in Early Nineteenth-Century America." In *Foucault and the Government of Disability*, ed. S. Tremain, 153-71. Ann Arbor: University of Michigan Press.

Bernasconi, R. 2008. "Before Whom and for What? Accountability and the Invention of Ministerial, Hyperbolic, and Infinite Responsibility." In *Difficulties of Ethical Life*, ed. S. Sullivan and D. Schmidt, 131-46. New York: Fordham University Press.

Bhabha, H. 1990. "The Third Space." In *Identity: Community, Culture, Difference*, ed. J. Rutherford, 207-21. London: Lawrence and Wishart.

–. 1994. *The Location of Culture*. London and New York: Routledge.

Bolan, K. 2006a. "A-G Calls for Fight against Spousal Abuse." *Vancouver Sun*, 3 November. http://www.canada.com/vancouversun/news/story.html?d=f625ceef-ed82-44ff-8236-ac6c8bb04ae6.

–. 2006b. "Family Appeals for Daughter's Safe Return." *Vancouver Sun*, 24 October. http://www.canada.com/vancouversun/news/story.html?id=5c651821-01ce-46e4-b8cd-b3dc1b8a17a2.

–. 2006c. "Who Murdered Manjit and Her Unborn?" *Vancouver Sun*, 27 October. http://www.canada.com/vancouversun/news/story.html?id=22534bbd-4e87-4496-9263-eee1a51668e6.

Bouchard, G., and C. Taylor. 2008. *Building the Future: A Time for Reconciliation (Abridged Report)*. Consultation Commission on Accommodation Practices Related to Cultural Differences, Government of Quebec. http://www.accommodements.qc.ca/index-en.html.

Boyd, M. 2004. *Dispute Resolution in Family Law: Protecting Choice, Promoting Inclusion*. Ontario Ministry of the Attorney General. http://www.attorneygeneral.jus.gov.on.ca/english/about/pubs/boyd/.

Boyko, J. 1995. *Last Steps to Freedom: The Evolution of Canadian Racism*. Winnipeg: Watson and Dwyer.

Brah, A., and A. Phoenix. 2004. "Ain't I a Woman? Revisiting Intersectionality." *Journal of International Women's Studies* 5, 3: 75-86.

Brown, W. 1995. *States of Injury: Power and Freedom in Late Modernity*. Princeton: Princeton University Press.

–. 1997. "The Impossibility of Women's Studies." *Differences: A Journal of Feminist Cultural Studies* 9, 3: 79-101.

–. 2004. "The Agony of Being Liberal." Paper presented at the American Political Science Association, Chicago, 3 September.

–. 2005. *Edgework: Critical Essays on Knowledge and Politics*. Princeton and Oxford: Princeton University Press.

Brubaker, R., and F. Cooper. 2000. "Beyond 'Identity.'" *Theory and Society* 29: 1-47.

Brumann, C. 1999. "Writing for Culture: Why a Successful Concept Should Not Be Discarded." *Current Anthropology* 40 (Supplement): S1-27.

Buchignani, N., D.M. Indra, and R. Srivastiva. 1985. *Continuous Journey: A Social History of South Asians in Canada*. Toronto: McClelland and Stewart in association with the Multiculturalism Directorate, Department of the Secretary of State and the Canadian Government Publishing Centre.

Bullock, K.H. 2000. "The Gaze and Colonial Plans for the Unveiling of Muslim Women." *Studies in Contemporary Islam* 2, 2: 1-20.

–. 2002. *Rethinking Muslim Women and the Veil: Challenging Historical and Modern Stereotypes*. Herndon, VA: International Institute of Islamic Thought.

Butler, J. 1990. *Gender Trouble: Feminism and the Subversion of Identity*. New York: Routledge.

–. 1993. *Bodies That Matter*. New York: Routledge.

–. 1995. "Contingent Foundations." In *Feminist Contentions: A Philosophical Exchange*, ed. S. Benhabib, J. Butler, D. Cornell, and N. Fraser, 35-58. New York and London: Routledge.

–. 2005. *Giving an Account of Oneself*. New York: Fordham University Press.

CAD (Canadian Association of the Deaf). 2002a. "A Position Paper: Deaf Culture vs. Medicalization." http://www.cad.ca/en/issues/deaf_culture_vs_medicalization.

–. 2002b. "A Position Paper: Definition of Deaf." http://www.cad.ca/en/issues/definition_of_deaf.asp.

Canovan, M. 2005. *The People.* Cambridge: Polity.

Carens, J.H. 2000. *Culture, Citizenship and Community: A Contextual Exploration of Justice as Evenhandedness.* New York: Oxford University Press.

Carpio, M.V. 2004. "The Lost Generation: American Indian Women and Sterilization Abuse." *Social Justice* 31, 4: 40-53.

Caswell, D.G. 1996. *Lesbians, Gay Men, and Canadian Law.* Toronto: Emond Montgomery.

CBC. 2006. "2 Teens Guilty of Manslaughter in Senior's Death." CBC News, British Columbia. http://www.cbc.ca/canada/british-columbia/story/2006/11/10/bc-teens.html.

CCD (Council of Canadians with Disabilities). 1998a. "About Us." http://www.ccdonline.ca/about-us/index.htm.

–. 1998b. "The Disability Rights Movement and the Present Constitutional Challenge." http://www.ccdonline.ca/law-reform/analysis/rightsandconstitution.htm.

–. 2001. "Immigration Challenge in 'Equality Matters.'" http://www.pcs.mb.ca/~ccd/emches~1.html.

CCSG (Chicago Cultural Studies Group). 1994. "Critical Multiculturalism." In *Multiculturalism: A Critical Reader,* ed. D.T. Goldberg, 114-39. Cambridge, MA: Blackwell.

Chakravarti, U. 2001. "Wifehood, Widowhood, and Adultery: Female Sexuality, Surveillance, and the State in Eighteenth-Century Maharasta." In *Of Property and Propriety: The Role of Gender and Class in Imperialism and Nationalism,* ed. H. Bannerji, S. Mojab, and J. Whitehead, 223-44. Toronto: University of Toronto Press.

Christensen, K.M., and G.L. Delgado. 1993. "Section 1: The Issues." In *Multicultural Issues in Deafness,* ed. G.L. Delgado, 1. New York: Longman.

CIC (Citizenship and Immigration Canada). 2004. *Immigrating to Canada as a Skilled Worker.* Government of Canada. http://www.cic.gc.ca/english/skilled/index.html. Accessed 2004; website now discontinued.

Collins, P.H. 1990. *Black Feminist Thought: Knowledge, Consciousness, and the Politics of Empowerment.* Boston: Unwin Hyman.

–. 2000. *Black Feminist Thought: Knowledge, Consciousness and the Politics of Empowerment.* New York and London: Routledge.

Colson, C. 2002. "Lesbians Order Defective Baby." *Connection Magazine,* August. http://www.connectionmagazine.org/2002_08/co_colson.htm.

Coulthard, G. 2007. "Subjects of Empire: Indigenous Peoples and the 'Politics of Recognition' in Canada." *Contemporary Political Theory* 6, 4: 437-60.

–. Forthcoming 2009. "Resisting Culture: Seyla Benhabib's Deliberative Approach to the Politics of Recognition in Colonial Contexts." In *Realizing Deliberative Democracy,* ed. D. Kahane, D. Leydet, D. Weinstock, and M. Williams. Vancouver: UBC Press.

Cowlishaw, G. 1987. "Colour, Culture and the Aboriginalists." *Man* 22, 2: 221-37.

Crenshaw, K.W. 2000. *Background Paper for the Expert Group Meeting on the Gender-Related Aspects of Race Discrimination,* meeting held 21-24 November, Zagreb, Croatia. http://www.wicej.addr.com/wcar_docs/crenshaw.html.

Cruikshank, B. 1999. *The Will to Empower: Democratic Citizens and Other Subjects.* Ithaca and London: Cornell University Press.

Currah, P. 2001. "Queer Theory, Lesbian and Gay Rights, and Transsexual Marriages." In *Sexual Identities, Queer Politics,* ed. M. Blasius, 178-99. Princeton: Princeton University Press.

–. 2006. "Gender Pluralisms under the Transgender Umbrella." In *Transgender Rights,* ed. P. Currah, R.M. Juang, and S.P. Minter, 3-31. Minneapolis: University of Minnesota Press.

Currah, P., R.M. Juang, and S.P. Minter. 2006. "Introduction." In *Transgender Rights,* ed. P. Currah, R.M. Juang, and S.P. Minter, xiii-xxiv. Minneapolis: University of Minnesota Press.

Danius, S., and S. Jonsson. 1993. "An Interview with Gayatri Chakravorty Spivak." *Boundary* 20, 2: 24-50.

D'aoust, V. 1999. "Complications: The Deaf Community, Disability and Being a Lesbian Mom – A Conversation with Myself." In *Restricted Access: Lesbians on Disability,* ed. S. Raffo, 115-23. Seattle: Seal Press.

Dauvergne, M., K. Scrim, and S. Brennan. 2006. Hate Crimes in Canada. Canadian Centre for Justice Statistics. Statistics Canada. http://www.statcan.ca.english/research.

Day, R. 2000. *Multiculturalism and the History of Canadian Diversity.* Toronto: University of Toronto Press.

–. 2004. "On Dialogue and Differends: On the Limits of Liberal Multiculturalism." *Canadian Diversity* 3, 2: 36-38.

Deb, K. 2002. "Introduction." In *Mapping Multiculturalism,* ed. K. Deb, 13-67. Jaipur and New Delhi: Rawat.

Dench, J. 2000. "A Hundred Years of Immigration to Canada 1900-1999: A Chronology Focusing on Refugees and Discrimination." Canadian Council for Refugees. http://www.web.net/~ccr/history.html.

Denike, M., and S. Renshaw. 2003. "Transgender and Women's Substantive Equality: Discussion Paper." National Association of Women and the Law. http://www.nawl.ca/ns/en/documents/Pub_Report_Trans03_en.doc.

Derrida, J. 1988. *Limited Inc.* Trans. S. Weber. Evanston, IL: Northwestern University Press.

Deveaux, M. 2000a. "Conflicting Equalities? Cultural Group Rights and Sex Equality." *Political Studies* 48, 3: 522-39.

–. 2000b. *Cultural Pluralism and Dilemmas of Justice.* Ithaca and London: Cornell University Press.

–. 2006. *Gender and Justice in Multicultural Liberal States.* Oxford: Oxford University Press.

Dhaliwal, A.K. 1994. "Reading Diaspora." *Socialist Review* 4, 24: 13-43.

Dhamoon, R. 2006. "Shifting from Culture to Cultural: Critical Theorizing of Identity/

Difference Politics." *Constellations: An International Journal of Critical and Democratic Theory* 13, 3: 354-73.

–. 2007. "The Politics of Cultural Contestation." In *Sexual Justice/Cultural Justice: Critical Perspectives in Political Theory and Practice*, ed. B. Arneil, M. Deveaux, R. Dhamoon, and A. Eisenberg, 30-49. London and New York: Routledge.

Dua, E. 2000. "'The Hindu Woman's Question': Canadian Nation Building and the Social Construction of Gender for South Asian-Canadian Women." In *Anti-racist Feminism: Critical Race and Gender Studies*, ed. G.J.S. Dei, 55-72. Halifax: Fernwood.

Durham, L. 1839. *The Report on the Affairs of British North America*. http://faculty. marianopolis.edu/c.belanger/quebechistory/docs/durham/index.htm.

Dyer, O. 1996. "Canadian Women Compensated for Sterilization." *Student British Medical Journal* 312, 7027: 330-31.

Eisenberg, A. 2002. "Context, Cultural Difference, Sex and Social Justice." *Canadian Journal of Political Science* 35, 3: 613-28.

–. 2006. "Reasoning about Identity: Canada's Distinctive Culture Test." In *Diversity and Equality: The Changing Framework of Freedom in Canada*, ed. A. Eisenberg, 34-53. Vancouver: UBC Press.

–. 2007. "Identity, Multiculturalism and Religious Arbitration: The Debate over Shari'a Law in Canada." In *Sexual Justice/Cultural Justice: Critical Perspectives in Political Theory and Practice*, ed. B. Arneil, M. Deveaux, R. Dhamoon, and A. Eisenberg, 211-30. London and New York: Routledge.

Eisenberg, A., and J. Spinner-Halev, eds. 2005. *Minorities within Minorities: Equality, Rights and Diversity*. Cambridge: Cambridge University Press.

Entwisle, S. 2000. "HIV and Men." AIDS Calgary. http://www.aidscalgary.org/pdf/33_Men.pdf.

Fellows, M.L., and S. Razack. 1994. "Seeking Relations: Law and Feminism Roundtables." *Signs: A Journal for Women in Culture and Society* 19, 4: 1048-83.

–. 1998. "The Race to Innocence: Confronting Hierarchical Relations among Women." *Journal of Gender, Race and Justice* 1, 2: 335-52.

Ferguson, M.L. 2007. "Sharing without Knowing: Collective Identity in Feminist and Democratic Theory." *Hypatia* 22, 4: 30-45.

Findlay, B. 1999. "An Introduction to Transgendered Women: An Equality Analysis." Paper presented at the Justice and Equality Summit, Vancouver, British Columbia, June.

–. 2003. "Real Women: Kimberley Nixon v. Vancouver Rape Relief." *UBC Law Review* 36, 1: 1-31.

Finkelstein, V. 1991. "'We' Are Not Disabled, 'You' Are." In *Constructing Deafness*, ed. S. Gregory and G.M. Hartley, 265-71. London: Pinter.

Fischgrund, J.E., and C.T. Akamatsu. 1993. "Rethinking the Education of Ethnic/Multicultural Deaf People: Stretching the Boundaries." In *Multicultural Issues in Deafness*, ed. K.M. Christensen and G.L. Delgado, 169-78. New York: Longman.

Fisher, J., R. Jurgens, A. Vassal, and R. Hughes. 1998. *Gay and Lesbian Issues and HIV/AIDS: Final Report*. Canadian HIV/AIDS Legal Network and Canadian AIDS Society, Montreal. http://www.aidslaw.ca/publications/interfaces/downloadFile.php?ref=220.

Fleras, A. 2004. "Racialising Culture/Culturalising Race: Multicultural Racism in a Multi-cultural Canada." In *Racism, Eh? A Critical Inter-disciplinary Anthology of Race and Racism in Canada*, ed. C.A. Nelson and C.A. Nelson, 429-41. Concord, ON: Captus Press.

Fogg-Davis, H.G. 2006. "Theorizing Black Lesbians within Black Feminism: A Critique of Same-Race Street Harassment." *Politics and Gender* 2: 57-76.

Folson, R.B. 2004. "Representation of the Immigrant." In *Calculated Kindness: Global Restructuring, Immigration and Settlement in Canada*, ed. R.B. Folson, 21-32. Halifax: Fernwood.

Foster, S., and W. Kinuthia. 2003. "Deaf Persons of Asian American, Hispanic American and African American Backgrounds: A Study of Intraindividual Diversity and Identity." *Journal of Deaf Studies and Deaf Education* 8, 3: 271-90.

Foucault, M. 1980. *Power/Knowledge: Selected Interviews and Other Writings, 1972-1977 Michel Foucault*. Trans. C. Gordon, L. Marshall, J. Mepham, and K. Soper. New York: Pantheon Books.

–. 1984. *The Foucault Reader*. Ed. Paul Rabinow. New York: Pantheon.

–. 1988. *The History of Sexuality: An Introduction*. Vol. 1. Trans. R. Hurley. New York: Vintage Books.

–. 1995. *Discipline and Punish: The Birth of the Prison*. Trans. A. Sheridan. New York: Vintage Books. (Orig. pub. 1977.)

Friedman, S.S. 1995. "Beyond White and Other: Relationality and Narratives of Race in Feminist Discourse." *Signs* 21, 1: 1-49.

Fuss, D. 1991. "Inside/Outside." In *Inside/Out: Lesbian Theories, Gay Theories*, ed. D. Fuss, 1-11. New York and London: Routledge.

Gannon, J. 1981. *Deaf History: A Narrative History of Deaf America*. Silver Spring, MD: National Association of the Deaf.

Gaon, S. 2004. "Judging Justice: The Strange Responsibility of Deconstruction." *Philosophy and Social Criticism* 30, 1: 97-114.

Garber, M. 1992. *Vested Interests: Cross-Dressing and Cultural Anxiety*. New York: Harper-Perennial.

Garland-Thomson, R. 2002. "Integrating Disability, Transforming Feminist Theory." *NWSA Journal* 14, 3: 1-32.

Geertz, C. 1973. *The Interpretation of Cultures: Selected Essays*. New York: Basic Books.

Goldberg, D.T. 1993. *Racist Culture: Philosophy and the Politics of Meaning*. Oxford and Cambridge, MA: Blackwell.

Grace, S., and G. Helm. 1998. "Documenting Racism: Sharon Pollock's *The Komagata Maru Incident*." In *Painting the Maple: Essays on Race, Gender, and the Construction of*

Canada, ed. V. Strong-Boag, S. Grace, A. Eisenberg, and J. Anderson, 85-99. Vancouver: UBC Press.

Green, J. 2000. "The Difference Debate: Reducing Rights to Cultural Flavours." *Canadian Journal of Political Science* 33, 1: 133-44.

Gunew, S. 2004. *Haunted Nations: The Colonial Dimensions of Multiculturalisms.* London and New York: Routledge.

Hancock, A.M. 2007a. "Intersectionality as a Normative and Empirical Paradigm." *Politics and Gender* 3, 2: 248-54.

–. 2007b. "When Multiplication Doesn't Equal Quick Addition: Examining Intersectionality as a Research Paradigm." *Perspectives on Politics* 5, 1: 63-79.

Harper, P.B., A. McClintock, J.E. Muñoz, and T. Rosen. 1997. "Queer Transexions of Race, Nation and Gender: An Introduction." *Social Text* 52-53: 1-4.

Hawley, J.C., ed. 2001. *Post Colonial, Queer: Theoretical Intersections.* New York: State University of New York Press.

Honig, B. 1996. "Democracy, Dilemmas and the Politics of Home." In *Democracy and Difference: Contesting the Boundaries of the Political,* ed. S. Benhabib, 257-77. Princeton: Princeton University Press.

–. 2001. *Democracy and the Foreigner.* Princeton: Princeton University Press.

hooks, b. 1989. *Talking Back: Thinking Feminist, Thinking Black.* Boston: South End Press.

–. 1994. *Teaching to Transgress: Education as the Practice of Freedom.* New York and London: Routledge.

Hoy, D.C. 2005. *Critical Resistance: From Poststructuralism to Post-critique.* Cambridge, MA, and London: MIT Press.

Ivison, D. 2002. *Postcolonial Liberalism.* Cambridge: Cambridge University Press.

Jakubowicz, A., and H. Meekosha. 2003. "Can Multiculturalism Encompass Disability?" In *Disability, Culture and Identity,* ed. N. Watson, 180-99. Harlow, Essex, UK: Pearson Education.

Jamieson, K. 1978. *Indian Women and the Law in Canada: Citizens Minus.* Ottawa: Minister of Supply and Services.

Jhappan, R. 2006. "Postmodern Race and Gender Essentialism or a Post-mortem of Scholarship." In *Identity and Belonging: Rethinking Race and Ethnicity in Canadian Society,* ed. S.P. Hier and B.S. Bolaria, 57-71. Toronto: Canadian Scholars' Press.

Jiwani, Y. 2005a. "The Great White North Encounters September 11: Race, Gender, and Nation in Canada's National Daily, *The Globe and Mail.*" *Social Justice* 32, 4: 50-68.

–. 2005b. "Orientalizing 'War Talk': Representations of the Gendered Muslim Body Post 9/11 in *The Montreal Gazette.*" In *Situating "Race" and Racisms in Space, Time, and Theory,* ed. J.-A. Lee and J. Lutz, 178-204. Montreal and Kingston: McGill-Queen's University Press.

Johnson, J. 2000. "Why Respect Culture?" *American Journal of Political Science* 44, 3: 405-18.

Josephson, J. 2008. "Sexual Citizenship, Sexual Regulation, and Identity Politics." Paper presented at the Western Political Science Association annual meeting, San Diego, CA, 21 March.

Kernerman, G. 2005. *Multicultural Nationalism: Civilizing Difference, Constituting Difference.* Vancouver: UBC Press.

Kessler, S. 1990. *Lessons from the Intersexed.* Piscataway, NJ: Rutgers University Press.

Khan, S. 1993. "Canadian Muslim Women and Shari'a Law: A Feminist Response to 'Oh Canada!'" *Canadian Journal of Women and the Law* 6, 1: 52-65.

–. 2002. *Aversion and Desire: Negotiating Muslim Female Identity in the Diaspora.* Toronto: Women's Press.

King, D.K. 1988. "Multiple Jeopardy, Multiple Consciousness: The Context of a Black Feminist Ideology." *Signs* 14, 1: 42-72.

Kirkness, V. 1987-88. "Emerging Native Women." *Canadian Journal of Women and the Law* 2, 2: 408-15.

Klein, A. 2001. *HIV/AIDS and Immigration Report.* Canadian HIV/AIDS Legal Network. http://www.aidslaw.ca/publications/interfaces/downloadFile.php?ref=853.

Kliewer, C., and L.M. Fitzgerald. 2001. "Disability, Schooling and the Artifacts of Colonialism." *Teachers College Record* 103, 3: 450-70.

Kompridis, N. 2005. "Normativizing Hybridity/Neutralizing Culture." *Political Theory* 33, 3: 318-43.

–. 2006. "The Unsettled and Unsettling Claims of Culture." *Political Theory* 34, 3: 389-96.

Kros, C. 2005. "Secularity in a World 'Torn by Difference': A Consideration of the French Headscarf Affair from South Africa." *Politikon: South African Journal of Political Studies* 32, 1: 1-16.

Kukathas, C. 1988. "Liberalism and Multiculturalism: The Politics of Indifference." *Political Theory* 26, 5: 686-99.

–. 1992. "Are There Any Cultural Rights?" *Political Theory* 20, 1: 105-39.

–. 2003. *The Liberal Archipelago: A Theory of Diversity and Freedom.* Oxford: Oxford University Press.

Kuzio, T. 2005. "Western Multicultural Theory and Practice and Its Applicability to the Post-Soviet States." *Journal of Contemporary European Studies* 13, 2: 221-37.

Kymlicka, W. 1989. *Liberalism, Community and Culture.* Oxford: Oxford University Press.

–. 1992. "The Rights of Minority Cultures: Reply to Kukathas." *Political Theory* 20, 1: 140-45.

–. 1994. "Individual and Group Rights." In *Group Rights,* ed. J. Baker, 17-33. Toronto: University of Toronto Press.

–. 1995a. *Multicultural Citizenship.* Oxford: Clarendon Press.

–. 1995b. *The Rights of Minority Cultures.* Oxford: Oxford University Press.

–. 1996. "Social Unity in a Liberal State." *Social Philosophy and Policy* 13, 1: 105-36.

–. 1998. *Finding Our Way: Rethinking Ethnocultural Relations in Canada.* Don Mills, ON: Oxford University Press.

–. 2001. *Politics in the Vernacular: Nationalism, Multiculturalism, and Citizenship.* New York: Oxford University Press.

–. 2002. *Contemporary Political Philosophy: An Introduction.* Oxford and New York: Oxford University Press.

–. 2003. "Being Canadian." *Government and Opposition* 38, 3: 357-85.

–. 2005a. "Liberal Multiculturalism: Western Models, Global Trends, and Asian Debates." In *Multiculturalism in Asia,* ed. W. Kymlicka and B. He, 22-55. Oxford: Oxford University Press.

–. 2005b. "The Uncertain Futures of Multiculturalism." *Canadian Diversity* 4, 1: 82-85.

–. 2007a. *Multicultural Odysseys: Navigating the New International Politics of Diversity.* Oxford: Oxford University Press.

–. 2007b. "The New Debate on Minority Rights (and Postscript)." In *Multiculturalism and Political Theory,* ed. A.S. Laden and D. Owen, 25-59. Cambridge: Cambridge University Press.

Kymlicka, W., and B. He, eds. 2005. *Multiculturalism in Asia.* Oxford: Oxford University Press.

Kymlicka, W., and M. Opalski, eds. 2001. *Can Liberal Pluralism Be Exported? Western Political Theory and Ethnic Relations in Eastern Europe.* Oxford: Oxford University Press.

Ladd, P. 2003. *Understanding Deaf Culture: In Search of Deafhood.* Buffalo, Toronto, and Sydney: Multilingual Matters.

Lahey, K. 1999. *Are We 'Persons' Yet? Law and Sexuality in Canada.* Toronto: University of Toronto Press.

Lane, H. 1984. *When the Mind Hears: A History of the Deaf.* New York: Random House.

–. 1997. "Constructions of Deafness." In *The Disability Studies Reader,* ed. L.J. Davis, 153-71. New York: Routledge.

Lawrence, B., and E. Dua. 2005. "Decolonizing Antiracism." *Social Justice* 32, 4: 120-43.

Lecours, A. 2000. "Historical Institutionalism as a Challenge to the Culturalists." *Canadian Journal of Political Science* 33, 3: 499-522.

Lee, T.M.L. 2006. "Multicultural Citizenship: The Case of the Disabled." In *Critical Disability Theory: Essays in Philosophy, Politics, Policy, and Law,* ed. D. Pothier and R. Devlin, 87-105. Vancouver: UBC Press.

LEGIT (Lesbian and Gay Immigration Taskforce of Canada). 2003. "The Canadian Immigration System: An Overview." http://www.legit.ca/imm.html.

Levi, J.L., and B.H. Klein. 2006. "Pursuing Protection for Transgender People through Disability Laws." In *Transgender Rights,* ed. P. Currah, R.M. Juang, and S.P. Minter, 74-92. Minneapolis: University of Minnesota Press.

Li, P.S. 2004. "The Place of Immigrants: Politics of Difference in Territorial and Social Space." *Canadian Diversity* 3, 2: 23-28.

Lowe, L. 1996. *Immigrant Acts: On Asian American Cultural Politics.* Durham: Duke University Press.

Mahtani, M. 1994. "Polarity versus Plurality: Confessions of an Ambivalent Woman of Colour." *Canadian Woman Studies* 14, 2: 14-18.

–. 2006. "Interrogating the Hyphen-Nation: Canadian Multicultural Policy and 'Mixed Race' Identities." In *Identity and Belonging: Rethinking Race and Ethnicity in Canadian Society,* ed S.P. Hier and B.S. Bolaria, 163-77. Toronto: Canadian Scholars' Press.

Mamdani, M. 2004. *Good Muslim, Bad Muslim: America, the Cold War, and the Roots of Terror.* New York: Three Leaves Press, Doubleday.

Mansbridge, J. 1996. "Using Power/Fighting Power: The Polity." In *Democracy and Difference: Contesting the Boundaries of the Political,* ed. S. Benhabib, 46-66. Princeton: Princeton University Press.

Markell, P. 2003. *Bound by Recognition.* Princeton: Princeton University Press.

Martinez, E. 1993. "Beyond Black/White: The Racisms of Our Time." *Social Justice* 20, 1-2: 22-34.

Matsuda, M.J. 1992. "When the First Quail Calls: Multiple Consciousness as Jurisprudential Method." *Women's Rights Law Reporter* 14: 297-300.

McElroy, W. 2002. "Victims from Birth: Engineering Defects in Helpless Children Crosses the Line." Fox News.com, 9 April. http://www.foxnews.com/story/0,2933,49849,00.html.

McIvor, S.D. 1995. "Aboriginal Women's Rights as 'Existing Rights.'" *Canadian Woman Studies/Les Cahiers de la Femme* 15, 4: 34-38.

McPherson, D.H. 2006. "Indian on the Lawn: How Are Research Partnerships with Aboriginal Peoples Possible?" *American Philosophy Association Newsletter* 5, 2: 1-12.

McRanor, S. 2006. "The Imperative of 'Culture' in a Colonial and *de facto* Polity." In *Diversity and Equality: The Changing Framework of Freedom in Canada,* ed. A. Eisenberg, 54-77. Vancouver: UBC Press.

Mills, C.W. 1997. *The Racial Contract.* Ithaca: Cornell University Press.

–. 2007. "Multiculturalism as/and/or Anti-racism?" In *Multiculturalism and Political Theory,* ed. A.S. Laden and D. Owen, 89-114. Cambridge: Cambridge University Press.

Modood, T. 2007. *Multiculturalism: A Civic Idea.* Cambridge: Polity Press.

Mohanty, C.T. 2003. *Feminism without Borders: Decolonizing Theory, Practicing Solidarity.* Durham and London: Duke University Press.

Monture, P.A. 2007. "Racing and Erasing: Law and Gender in White Settler Societies." In *Race and Racism in 21st Century Canada: Continuity, Complexity, and Change,* ed. S.P. Hier and B.S. Bolaria, 197-216. Peterborough, ON: Broadview Press.

Monture-Angus, P.A. 1995. *Thunder in My Soul: A Mohawk Woman Speaks.* Halifax: Fernwood.

–. 1999. "Standing against Canadian Law: Naming Omissions of Race, Culture and Gender." In *Locating Law: Race/Class/Gender Connections,* ed. E. Cormack, 76-97. Halifax: Fernwood.

Mosoff, J. 1999. "Excessive Demand on the Canadian Conscience: Disability, Family and Immigration." *Manitoba Law Journal* 26, 1: 149-79.

Mundy, L. "A World of Their Own." 2002. *Washington Post Magazine,* 31 March.

Najmabadi, A. 2006. "Gender and Secularism of Modernity: How Can a Muslim Woman Be French?" *Feminist Studies* 32, 2: 239-55.

Namaste, V. 2005. *Sex Change, Social Change: Reflections on Identity, Institutions, and Imperialism.* Toronto: Women's Press.

Napolean, V. 2001. "Extinction by Number: Colonialism Made Easy." *Canadian Journal of Law and Society* 16, 1: 113-45.

Narayan, U. 1997. "Contesting Culture: 'Westernization,' Respect for Cultures and Third World Feminists." In *The Second Wave: A Reader in Feminist Theory,* ed. L. Nicholson, 396-414. New York: Routledge.

–. 2000. "Essence of Culture and a Sense of History: A Feminist Critique of Cultural Essentialism." In *Decentering the Center: Philosophy for a Multicultural, Postcolonial, and Feminist World,* ed. U. Narayan and S. Harding, 80-100. Bloomington and Indianapolis: Indiana University Press.

Nicholson, L. 1996. "To Be or Not To Be: Taylor and the Politics of Recognition." *Constellations: An International Journal of Critical and Democratic Theory* 3, 1: 10-16.

Noble, J.B. 2006. *Sons of the Movement: FtMs Risking Incoherence on a Post-queer Cultural Landscape.* Toronto: Women's Press.

OHRC (Ontario Human Rights Commission). 2000. "Policy on Discrimination and Harassment Because of Gender Identity." http://www.ohrc.on.ca/en/resources/Policies/PolicyGenderIdent.pdf.

Okin, S.M. 1994. "Gender Inequality and Cultural Differences." *Political Theory* 22, 1: 5-24.

–. 1998. "Feminism and Multiculturalism: Some Tensions." *Ethics* 108: 661-84.

–. 1999. "Is Multiculturalism Bad for Women?" In *Is Multiculturalism Bad for Women?* ed. J. Cohen, M. Howard, and M.C. Nussbaum, 9-24. Princeton: Princeton University Press.

Owens, A.M. 2001. "Father's Sex Change Does Not Alter Custody, Court Says." *National Post,* 2 February. http://fact.on.ca/news/news0102/np010202.htm.

Parekh, B. 1995. "Liberalism and Colonialism: A Critique of Locke and Mill." In *The Decolonization of the Imagination: Culture, Knowledge and Power,* ed. B. Parekh and J.N. Pieterse, 1-19. Atlantic Highlands, NJ: Zed Books.

–. 1997. "Dilemmas of a Multicultural Theory of Citizenship." *Constellations: An International Journal of Critical and Democratic Theory* 4, 1: 54-62.

–. 2000. *Rethinking Multiculturalism.* Basingstoke, UK: Macmillan Press.

Peritz, D. 2004. "Toward a Deliberative and Democratic Response to Multicultural Politics: Post-Rawlsian Reflections on Benhabib's *The Claims of Culture*." *Constellations: An International Journal of Critical and Democratic Theory* 11, 2: 266-90.

Phelan, S. 1994. *Getting Specific: Postmodern Lesbian Politics*. Minneapolis: University of Minnesota Press.

Phillips, A. 2003. "When Culture Means Gender: Issues of Cultural Defence in the English Courts." *Modern Law Review* 66: 510-31.

–. 2007. *Multiculturalism without Culture*. Princeton: Princeton University Press.

Phoenix, A., and P. Pattynama. 2006. "Editorial." *European Journal of Women's Studies* 13, 3: 187-92.

Povinelli, E. 2002. *The Cunning of Recognition: Indigenous Alterities and the Making of Australian Multiculturalism (Politics, History, and Culture)*. Durham: Duke University Press.

Puar, J.K., and A. Rai. 2004. "The Remaking of a Model Minority: Perverse Projectiles under the Specter of (Counter) Terrorism." *Social Text* 22, 3: 75-104.

Pyeatt, M. 2002. "Deaf Lesbians Criticized for Efforts to Create Deaf Child." CNSNews. com. http://sci.rutgers.edu/forum/showthread.php?t=29323.

Razack, S.H. 1998. *Looking White People in the Eye: Gender, Race, and Culture in Courtrooms and Classrooms*. Toronto: University of Toronto Press.

–. 2002. "Gendered Racial Violence and Spatialized Justice: The Murder of Pamela George." In *Race, Space and the Law: Unmapping a White Settler Society*, ed. S. Razack, 121-56. Toronto: Between the Lines.

–. 2005. "Geopolitics, Culture Clash, and Gender after September 11." *Social Justice* 32, 4: 11-31.

–. 2007. "'Your Client Has a Profile': Race and National Security in Canada after 9/11." *Studies in Law, Politics and Society* 40: 3-40.

–. 2008. *Casting Out: The Eviction of Muslims from Western Law and Politics*. Toronto: University of Toronto Press.

Roediger, D.R. 2002. "Whiteness and Ethnicity in the History of 'White Ethnics' in the United States." In *Race Critical Theories: Text and Context*, ed. D.T. Goldberg, 325-43. Malden, MA, and Oxford: Blackwell.

Roots, J. 2003. "Deaf Education and Advocacy: A Short History of the Canadian Association of the Deaf." In *Making Equality: History of Advocacy and Persons with Disabilities in Canada*, ed. W.C. Watters, 73-86. Concord, ON: Captus Press.

Rupp, S. 2005. "Duelling Rights." Straight.com, 3 February. http:www.straight.com/article/duelling-rights.

Said, E. 1978. *Orientalism*. London: Routledge and Kegan Paul.

Satzewich, V. 2000. "White Limited: Racialization and the Social Construction of 'Peripheral Europeans.'" *Histoire sociale/Social History* 33, 6: 271-89.

–. 2007. "Whiteness Studies: Race, Diversity and the New Essentialism." In *Race and Racism in 21st Century Canada: Continuity, Complexity, and Change*, ed. S.P. Hier and B.S. Bolaria, 67-84. Peterborough, ON: Broadview Press.

Scott, D. 2003. "Culture in Political Theory." *Political Theory* 31, 1: 92-115.

Shachar, A. 2000. "Should Church and State Be Joined at the Altar? Women's Rights and the Multicultural Dilemma." In *Citizenship in Diverse Societies*, ed. W. Kymlicka and W. Norman, 199-223. New York: Oxford University Press.

–. 2001. *Multicultural Jurisdictions: Cultural Differences and Women's Rights.* Cambridge: Cambridge University Press.

–. 2005. "Religion, State, and the Problem of Gender: New Modes of Citizenship and Governance in Diverse Societies." *McGill Law Journal* 50: 49-88.

Sharpe, A.N. 1998. "Institutionalizing Heterosexuality: The Legal Exclusion of 'Impossible' (Trans)sexualities." In *Legal Queeries: Lesbian, Gay and Transgender Legal Studies*, ed. S. Beresford, 26-41. London and New York: Cassell.

Shirazi, F. 2001. *The Veil Unveiled: The Hijab in Modern Culture.* Gainsville: University of Florida Press.

Shuttleworth, R.P. 2001. "Symbolic Contexts, Embodied Sensitivities, and the Lived Experience of Sexually Relevant Interpersonal Encounters for a Man with Cerebral Palsy." In *Semiotics and Disability*, ed. B.B. Swadener, 75-96. Albany: State University of New York Press.

Singh, J. 2007. "Fuelling Fear in Canada." *Rabble News*, 26 February. http://www.rabble.ca/everyones_a_critic.shtml?sh_itm=0a243a0a6eb62b305808bd724d238aa2&rXn=1&.

Smith, A. 1999. "Sexual Violence and American Indian Genocide." In *Remembering Conquest: Feminist/Womanist Perspectives on Religion, Colonization, and Sexual Violence*, ed. N.B. Lewis and M.M. Fortune, 31-52. Binghamton, NY: Haworth Press.

Smith, A., and L. Ross. 2004. "Introduction: Native Women and State Violence." *Social Justice* 31, 4: 1-7.

Smith, L.T. 1999. *Decolonising Methodologies: Research and Indigenous Peoples.* London: Zed Books.

Spivak, G.C. 1987. *In Other Worlds: Essays in Cultural Politics.* New York and London: Methuen.

–. 1988. "Can the Subaltern Speak?" In *Marxism and the Interpretation of Culture*, ed. C. Nelson and L. Grossberg, 271-315. Urbana: University of Illinois Press.

–. 1997. "'In a Word': Interview with Ellen Rooney." In *The Second Wave: A Reader in Feminist Theory*, ed. L. Nicholson, 356-78. New York: Routledge.

–. 1999. *A Critique of Postcolonial Reason: Toward a History of the Vanishing Present.* Cambridge, MA, and London: Harvard University Press.

Spriggs, M. 2002. "Lesbian Couple Create a Child Who Is Deaf Like Them." *Journal of Medical Ethics Online* 28: 283. http://jme.bmjjournals.com/cgi/content/full/28/5/283.

Srivastava, S. 2005. "You're Calling Me a Racist? The Moral and Emotional Regulation of Antiracism and Feminism." *Signs: Journal of Women in Culture and Society* 31, 1: 29-61.

–. 2007. "Troubles with 'Anti-racist Multiculturalism': The Challenges of Anti-racist and Feminist Activism." In *Race and Racism in 21st Century Canada: Continuity,*

Complexity, and Change, ed. S.P. Hier and B.S. Bolaria, 291-311. Peterborough, ON: Broadview Press.

Statistics Canada. 2001. "Immigration Population by Place of Birth and Period of Immigration (2001 Census)." Government of Canada. http://www40.statcan.ca/l01/cst01/demo24a.htm?sdi=countries%20immigration.

Stoler, A.L. 2000. "Sexual Affronts and Racial Frontiers." In *Theories of Race and Racism: A Reader,* ed. J. Solomos, 324-53. London and New York: Routledge.

Suzack, C. 2007. "Notes towards Establishing a Property Interest in Aboriginal Culture." In *Race and Racism in 21st Century Canada: Continuity, Complexity, and Change,* ed. S.P. Hier and B.S. Bolaria, 217-34. Peterborough, ON: Broadview Press.

SWC (Status of Women Canada). 1998. "Gender-Based Analysis: A Guide for Policy-Makers (Revised Edition)." Government of Canada. http://www.swc-cfc.gc.ca/pubs/gbaguide/index_e.html.

–. 2000. "Aboriginal Women's Roundtable on Gender Equality: Roundtable Report." http://www.swc-cfc.gc.ca/pubs/abwomenroundtable/010914_e.pdf.

–. 2001. "Canadian Experience in Gender Mainstreaming." http://www.swc-cfc.gc.ca/pubs/0662667352/index_e.html.

–. 2003. "Gender-Based Analysis (GBA): Performance Measurement of Its Application." http://www.swc-cfc.gc.ca/pubs/gbaperformance/index_e.html.

–. 2004. "An Integrated Approach to Gender-Based Analysis." http://www.swc-cfc.gc.ca/pubs/gbainfokit/index_e.html.

Syed, I. 2006. "The Great Canadian 'Shariah' Debate or How to Police the National Imaginary in 3 Easy Steps." Master's thesis, Women's Studies, University of British Columbia.

Taylor, C. 1985. *Philosophy and the Human Sciences: Philosophical Papers 2.* Cambridge: Cambridge University Press.

–. 1991. *The Malaise of Modernity.* Toronto: House of Anansi Press.

–. 1993. *Reconciling the Solitudes: Essays on Canadian Federalism and Nationalism.* Montreal and Kingston: McGill-Queen's University Press.

–. 1994a. "Can Liberalism Be Communitarian?" *Critical Review* 8, 2: 257-84.

–. 1994b. "The Politics of Recognition." In *Multiculturalism: Examining the Politics of Recognition,* ed. A. Gutmann, 25-74. Princeton: Princeton University Press.

–. 1996. "Book Review of *Multicultural Citizenship* by Will Kymlicka." *American Political Science Review* 92, 2: 408.

–. 1998. "Living with Difference." In *Debating Democracy's Discontent,* ed. M.C. Regan, 212-27. Oxford: Oxford University Press.

Thobani, S. 2007. *Exalted Subjects: Studies in the Making of Race and Nation in Canada.* Toronto: University of Toronto Press.

Torr, C.W.D. 2004. "Diversity in a Multicultural and Poly-ethnic World: Challenges and Responses." *Religion and Theology* 11, 3-4: 239-55.

Tully, J. 1995. *Strange Multiplicity: Constitutionalism in an Age of Diversity.* Cambridge: Cambridge University Press.

Turner, T. 1994. "Anthropology and Multiculturalism: What Is Anthropology That Multiculturalists Should Be Mindful of It?" In *Multiculturalism: A Critical Reader*, ed. D.T. Goldberg, 406-25. Boston: Blackwell.

Upadhya, C. 2002. "Culture Wars: The Anthropological Debate on Multiculturalism." In *Mapping Multiculturalism*, ed. K. Deb, 172-87. Jaipur and New Delhi: Rawat.

Uprety, S.K. 1997. "Disability and Postcoloniality in Salman Rushdie's *Midnight's Children* and Third-World Novels." In *The Disability Studies Reader*, ed. L. Davis, 366-81. New York and London: Routledge.

Vallance, N. 2006. "The Misuse of 'Culture' by the Supreme Court of Canada." In *Diversity and Equality: The Changing Framework of Freedom in Canada*, ed. A. Eisenberg, 97-113. Vancouver: UBC Press.

Vernon, A. 1999. "The Dialectics of Multiple Identities and the Disabled People's Movement." *Disability and Society* 14, 3: 385-98.

Wallerstein, I. 1976. *The Modern World-System: Capitalist Agriculture and the Origins of the European World-Economy in the Sixteenth Century*. New York: Academic Press.

Wedeen, L. 2002. "Conceptualizing Culture: Possibilities for Political Science." *American Political Science Review* 96, 4: 713-28.

Wing, A.K. 1997. "Brief Reflections towards a Multiplicative Theory and Praxis of Being." In *Critical Race Feminism: A Reader*, ed. A.K. Wing, 27-34. New York: New York University Press.

Young, I.M. 1997. "A Multicultural Continuum: A Critique of Will Kymlicka's Ethnic-Nation Dichotomy." *Constellations: An International Journal of Critical and Democratic Theory* 4, 1: 48-53.

–. 2000. *Inclusion and Democracy*. New York: Oxford University Press.

–. 2005. *On Female Body Experience: "Throwing Like a Girl" and Other Essays*. Oxford and New York: Oxford University Press.

Young, R.J.C. 1995. *Colonial Desire: Hybridity in Theory, Culture and Race*. London and New York: Routledge.

Yúdice, G. 2003. *The Expediency of Culture: Uses of Culture in the Global Era*. Durham and London: Duke University Press.

Yuval-Davis, N. 2006. "Intersectionality and Feminist Politics." *European Journal of Women's Studies* 13, 3: 193-209.

Zine, J. 2006. "Unveiled Sentiments: Gendered Islamophobia and Experiences of Veiling among Muslim Girls in a Canadian Islamic School." *Equity and Excellence in Education* 39, 3: 239-52.

JURISPRUDENCE

C.D.P. (M.L.) c. Maison des jeunes (T.D.P.Q. Montreal, No. 500-53-000078-970).

Egan v. Canada, [1995] 2 S.C.R. 513.

Eldridge v. British Columbia (Attorney General), [1997] 3 S.C.R. 624.

Kavanagh v. Attorney General of Canada (2001), T.D. 11/01 (C.H.R.T.).

Mamela v. Vancouver Lesbian Connection, [1999] B.C.H.R.T.D. No. 51.

Nixon v. Vancouver Rape Relief Society, [1995] R.S.B.C. c. 210 (British Columbia Human Rights Tribunal).

R. v. Powley, 2003 SCC 43 (CanLII).

Sherwood Atkinson (Sheri de Cartier), [1972] 5 Imm. A.C. (2d) 185 (Immigration Appeal Board).

Tchernilevski v. Canada (Minister of Citizenship and Immigration) (1995), 30 Imm. L.R. (2d) 67 (F.C.T.D.).

Thangarajan v. Canada, Minister of Citizenship and Immigration, [1999] 4 F.C. 167.

Vancouver Rape Relief v. Nixon et al., [2003] B.C.S.C. 1936 (CanLII)

LEGISLATION

Americans with Disabilities Act, 42 U.S.C., c. 126 (1990).

Chinese Immigration Act, R.S.C. 1906, c. 95, s. 7.

Gender Recognition Act 2004 (U.K.), (Commencement) Order 2005 No. 54.

Indian Act, R.S.C. 1985, c. I-5.

Immigration Act, 1906, R.S.C. 1906, c. 93.

Immigration Act, 1952, S.C. 1952, c. 42.

Immigration Act, 1976, S.C. 1976-77, c. 52.

Immigration and Refugee Protection Act, S.C. 2001, c. 27.

Sexual Sterilization Act [of Alberta], S.A. 1928, c. 37.

Vital Statistics Act, R.S.B.C. 1996, c. 476.

Index

Printed and bound in Canada by Friesens

Set in Giovanni and Scala Sans by Artegraphica Design Co. Ltd.

Copy editor: Deborah Kerr

Proofreader: Jillian Shoichet

Indexer: Patricia Buchanan

Marquis Book Printing Inc.

Québec, Canada
2009